What in the World
Is Going On?

What in the World Is Going On?

10 Prophetic Clues You Cannot Afford to Ignore

Dr. David Jeremiah

THOMAS NELSON
Since 1798

NASHVILLE   DALLAS   MEXICO CITY   RIO DE JANEIRO

Published in Nashville, Tennessee, by Thomas Nelson. Thomas Nelson is a registered trademark of Thomas Nelson, Inc.

Published in association with Yates & Yates, LLP, www.yates2.com.

Thomas Nelson, Inc. titles may be purchased in bulk for educational, business, fund-raising, or sales promotional use. For information, please e-mail SpecialMarkets@ThomasNelson.com.

"Battle of Armageddon" © 1944 Sony/ATV Music Publishing LLC. All rights administered by Sony/ATV Music Publishing LLC, 8 Music Square West, Nashville, TN 37203. All rights reserved. Used by permission.

Unless otherwise noted, Scripture quotations are taken from the New King James Version®. © 1982 by Thomas Nelson, Inc. Used by permission. All rights reserved.

Scripture quotations marked ASV are from the American Standard Version.

Scripture quotations marked KJV are from the King James Version.

Scripture quotations marked NASB are from the New American Standard Bible®, © The Lockman Foundation 1960, 1962, 1963, 1968, 1971, 1972, 1973, 1975, 1977, 1995. Used by permission.

Scripture quotations marked NIV are from the Holy Bible: New International Version®. © 1973, 1978, 1984 by International Bible Society. Used by permission of Zondervan Publishing House. All rights reserved.

Scripture quotations marked NLT are from the Holy Bible, New Living Translation. © 1996. Used by permission of Tyndale House Publishers, Inc., Wheaton, Illinois 60189. All rights reserved.

ISBN 978-0-8499-2147-6 (SE)
ISBN 978-0-7852-3117-2 (trade paper)

Library of Congress Cataloging-in-Publication Data
Jeremiah, David.
    What in the world is going on? : 10 prophetic clues you cannot afford to ignore / David Jeremiah.
      p. cm.
    ISBN 978-0-7852-2887-5 (hardcover)
      1. Bible—Prophecies. 2. World politics—21st century—Forecasting. 3. International relations—Forecasting. 4. Civilization, Modern—21st century—Forecasting. 5. World politics—21st century. 6. International relations—21st century. 7. Civilization, Modern—21st century. I. Title.
BS647.3.J47 2008
236'.9—dc22
          2008029176

Printed in the United States of America

10 11 12 13 14 RRD 5 4 3 2 1

"Blessing and honor and glory and power

Be to Him who sits on the throne,

And to the Lamb, forever and ever!" (Revelation 5:13*b*)

Contents

Acknowledgments

LAST FALL, WHEN I BEGAN TO TEACH THE TRUTHS OF THIS BOOK TO the church I pastor in Southern California, I was taken aback by the number of people who came to me each week and said, "You are going to put this information in a book, aren't you?" Here's my answer! Thanks for your encouragement!

Barbara Boucher is my administrative assistant at Shadow Mountain Community Church. Her servant-hearted willingness to serve where she is needed reflects the spirit of this church family.

I owe a great deal to the team of people who surround me at Turning Point Ministries. Diane Sutherland understands the pressures that descend upon our office when a book is in the making. During those days especially, she guards my time and organizes my life. I dare not think of the chaos of my existence without her dedicated ministry.

Since this book seeks to shine the light of the Scriptures on twenty-first-century world events, the burden of research has been huge. Cathy Lord excels at this task. She never rests until she has found the exact quote, statistic, or source we are looking for. Cathy, your commitment to detail amazes me. Thank you for your hard work!

Paul Joiner is the creative services director at Turning Point. He is an integral part of all that we do around the world through radio, television, and print media. Paul, your creativity is infectious, and your fingerprints are all over this project.

Rob Morgan and William Kruidenier read each chapter and added their suggestions. Rob and William, thank you for your thoughtful contributions. Thanks also to my friend Chuck Emert for his valuable input.

Thomas Nelson editor Joey Paul has been encouraging me to write another book on prophecy for several years. When I sent him the preliminary notes for this book, he called back immediately and said, "David, this is it!" Joey, your friendship is a blessing in my life.

This was my first opportunity to work with writer and editor Tom Williams. He has been a gracious addition to our publication team. Tom, I hope we get to work together again soon.

On the first pages of all my books, you will see the name of Yates and Yates, the literary agency founded by Sealy Yates. Thank you, Sealy, for believing in this book and for coordinating the efforts between the Turning Point team and the Thomas Nelson team.

I want to express my gratitude to my son David, whose leadership at Turning Point makes it possible for me to invest my time in studying and writing.

Finally, I give thanks to Almighty God for my wife, Donna. When I first started talking about *What in the World Is Going On?*, I told her that my plans were to teach this material in our Sunday night services. She looked at me and said, "David, that needs to be taught in the morning services so everyone can hear it." I always do what she tells me to do!

Most of all, I want to express my hope that God will be glorified as we tell the story of His plans for our future!

Knowing the Signs

WHAT IN THE WORLD IS GOING ON? NEVER BEFORE IN MY lifetime have I read such jarring headlines, distressing news analyses, or dire predictions for America and the world. Things are getting so chaotic that many pundits are using the term *perfect storm* to explain the confluence of wide-ranging food shortages, record-high fuel prices, and natural disasters.

In a recent twenty-four-hour period, major newswires carried the following disturbing reports: A cyclone in Myanmar caused upwards of eighty-four thousand deaths, along with the loss of primary rice fields in a time of severe global rice shortages. A powerful volcano that had been considered dormant for nine thousand years erupted in Chile. A virulent new virus infected tens of thousands of China's children, causing mounting fears of a widespread epidemic. Longtime antagonists China and Japan announced a pledge of "peace, friendship and cooperation as neighbors," including a joint venture in oil refining. In resurgent Russia, newly installed president Dmitri Medvedev promptly named Vladimir Putin as prime minister, calling it "the most important position in the executive power."[1]

Within that same time frame, housing defaults and foreclosures continued to fuel America's economic tailspin. As if that weren't enough bad news, oil soared to its highest closing price on the New York Mercantile Exchange since oil trading began twenty-five years ago, and the dollar continued to sputter against most foreign currencies. When stories like these pile one on top of the other, we can't help but wonder . . . what in the world is going on?

As we look out at the world of the early twenty-first century, food shortages are producing widespread hunger in places that have previously known plenty. Outright starvation is replacing hunger in regions that have known want. Among the poorest, it has become a struggle just to survive. In Thailand, the world's leading rice exporter, prices doubled in the first quarter of this year. Food prices have fueled riots in Haiti, Cameroon, Egypt, Mexico, Philippines, Indonesia, Ivory Coast, and several other African nations. Desperation is so high in Thailand, Philippines, and Pakistan that armed personnel have been called in to protect food harvesters, supervise grain sales, and guard warehouses. A UN observer warned, "A hungry man is an angry man, and as food gets more and more difficult to access . . . we can expect to see more incidents of civil unrest."[2]

While natural disasters cannot be prevented, the wise remain alert to signs of their approach so they can take protective measures. This was done when the volcano erupted in Chile. Despite being perceived as benign or even extinct, the Chaitén volcano gave off dozens of warning signs, in the form of earthquakes. Surprised by the first eruption, wise government officials recognized the continuing danger. They ordered mandatory evacuations as the volcano again turned violent and spewed deadly ash and lava into the air. As a result, not one death was directly attributed to the eruption.[3] When signs are recognized and appropriate warnings are issued, disaster can often be avoided.

On the other hand, the disaster in Myanmar shows what happens when the signs are ignored. As early as six days before Cyclone Nargis made landfall, Myanmar officials were notified of the potential for a large-scale storm. Throughout the next several days, as the storm intensified and took direct aim at the country's heavily populated delta, the ruling military junta received regular weather updates and warnings. Even with the increasing urgency of these warnings and the obvious signs in the intensely churning sky, the government issued no warnings and ordered no evacuations. Their failure left the people at the mercy of the 160-mile-per-hour winds and twelve-foot storm surges. The result? Several weeks later, with the number of dead and missing already totaling more than 78,000, and with more than 2.5 million left homeless, global relief teams remained poised to deliver food and supplies but, for political reasons, were denied entry into the country.

Within days, before the world could absorb the events in Myanmar, a 7.9 earthquake decimated southern China. Seven thousand school-children and their teachers were buried beneath the rubble of their schools. Upwards of 70,000 died, and 5 million were left homeless. Scores of powerful aftershocks continued to threaten further destruction and hampered rescue efforts. China tested her new friendship agreement with Japan by requesting that they send their crack rescue teams to supplement the 130,000 military personnel already mobilized by China. One aftershock that no one anticipated was China's request for aid from Taiwan, long considered a renegade, if not an enemy. China also accepted help from Russia and North Korea.

Are we seeing signs today that should warn us of anything? What in the world is going on when enemies of Israel bestow posthumous honors to the headmaster of a UN school in Gaza for his work as chief engineer of the Islamic Jihad's bomb squad?[4] What about that parade of tankers, fighter jets, and missiles in Moscow on May Day, reminiscent of the Cold War era? What about the doubling of millions of dollars of investments in Iraqi stocks, currently traded by scribbles on a dry-erase board? Or what about the largest US embassy complex ever built now ready for occupancy in Baghdad, formerly the infamous ancient Babylon, the city that throughout the Bible stands as the antithesis of everything good? What about the planned restoration of Babylon to its fabled glory? What about the increased use of biometrics, those scans of fingerprints, irises, and faces used for personal identification in Iraq and other "places of global conflict"? Currently such forms of ID are used to bar people from markets or certain neighborhoods, and they are ready to be implemented worldwide in the name of security. When you hear these reports, do you find yourself thinking, *What in the world is going on?*

The events unfolding in today's world are ominously threatening to unsettle institutions, reorder national political alignments, change the balance of world power, and destabilize the equitable distribution of resources. People everywhere are beginning to live in a state of fear and anxiety. Serious people are asking, "If these things are happening today, what will the future be like for my children and grandchildren? Do current headlines give us any signs about what is coming next?"

There is one reliable source of information about the future—one that has an astounding record of accuracy. The Bible! But, strangely, many who purport to preach God's Word shy away from teaching prophecy. A preacher friend tells of "a pastor who once boasted that he didn't preach about prophecy because, in his words, 'Prophecy only distracts people from the present.' An astute colleague deftly retorted, 'Well, then, there's certainly a lot of distraction in the Scripture!' Fulfilling prophecy is one of God's calling cards."[5]

Indeed, one of the most convincing evidences of biblical inspiration is the staggering number of prophecies that have been fulfilled with pinpoint accuracy. Perhaps the most familiar examples are the fulfillments of more than three hundred prophecies relating to Christ's first coming to earth. In his book *The Rapture*, Dr. Tim LaHaye remarked, "No scholar of academic substance denies that Jesus lived almost 2,000 years ago. And we find three times as many prophecies in the Bible relating to His second coming as to His first. Thus, the second advent of our Lord is three times as certain as His first coming, which can be verified as historical fact."[6]

The Bible has proven to be absolutely dependable. Therefore we can trust it as the one source of reliable information about the meaning of the events of our day and what those events tell us about our hope for the future as we look toward the return of Christ. The Lord Jesus Himself spoke of the wisdom of discerning the signs of the times and of taking appropriate action as we wait for His return (Matthew 24, Mark 16). The Bible gives us clues conveying crucial information for interpreting the signs as the days of man's rule on earth wind toward their end. In each of the ten chapters of this book, we will apply these clues and point out these signs, viewing current events from the perspective of God's wonderful Word. We will be warned and challenged, but we will also be encouraged and comforted. Our purpose is not to make you fearful, but to make you aware so you can be prepared.

Popular radio personality Clifton Fadiman was a certifiable book-worm. Not only was he the book editor for a national magazine and a published author, but his love of books and his sense of what made a book good landed him the position of an editor for the Book of the Month Club, a post he held for fifty years. He once explained how he went about deciding what kind of book the reading public wanted: "What do our members, in the depths of their being, hanker for? They want books that explain our terrifying age honestly ... Our age is so scary and fractionated that we need this kind of help more than people did in the [last] century. We thirst for books that put together pieces of the jigsaw puzzle."[7]

I am sure there have never been any times more "scary and fraction-ated" than these early days of the twenty-first century. In this book, I want to help you find the truth about what is going on. I want to show you that while our age is certainly "fractionated," it need not be scary—not for Christians who trust the Lord and know how to read the signs and understand coming events. As you read this book, I trust you will begin to put together the pieces of the puzzle, that you will recognize the clues that God has given us to find peace in "our terrifying age," and that you will come to an understanding of what in the world is going on. But mostly, I hope this book will help to "Let not your heart be troubled, neither let it be afraid" (John 14:27).

—David Jeremiah
San Diego, California
July 2008

ONE

The Israel Connection

MAY 14, 1948, WAS A PIVOTAL DAY IN HUMAN HISTORY. ON THAT afternoon, a car carrying prominent Jewish leader David Ben-Gurion rushed down Rothschild Boulevard in Tel Aviv and stopped in front of the Tel Aviv Art Museum. Four o'clock was only minutes away, and inside, more than four hundred people—Jewish religious and political leaders and press representatives from all over the world—were assembled in an auditorium, anxiously awaiting his arrival. Ben-Gurion quickly bounded up the steps. Precisely at four o'clock, local time, he stepped to the podium, called the meeting to order, and read these historic words[1]

> This right is the natural right of the Jewish people to be masters of
> their own fate, like all other nations, in their own sovereign State.
> Accordingly, we . . . are here assembled . . . and by virtue of our natural
> and historic right, and on the strength of the resolution of the General
> Assembly of the United Nations, hereby declare the establishment of
> the Jewish State in Eretz-Israel, to be known as the State of Israel.[2]

Six thousand miles away, President Truman sat in the Oval Office, reading a forty-word statement about to be released to the press. He penciled in a few added words, then signed his approval and noted the time. It was 6:10 p.m. One minute later, the White House press secretary read the release to the world. The United States had officially recognized the birth of the modern nation of Israel.

Isaiah's prophecy, written 740 years before the birth of Jesus, declared: "Who has heard such a thing? Who has seen such things? Shall the earth be made to give birth in one day? Or shall a nation be born at once?" (Isaiah 66:8). Secular Israel was born that day.

As I write this chapter, Israel is about to celebrate her sixtieth anniversary as a nation. What amazes many people is that in those six decades, this tiny nation with a population of slightly more than 7 million has become the geopolitical center of the world. Why is this so? Why is a fledgling country with a total land space smaller than New Jersey mentioned in the nightly news more than any other nation except the United States?

To answer these questions, we must understand what happened on that day in 1948, what is happening today in Israel, and how these events affect the entire world. For answers, we must turn not to the evening news or the front page of the newspaper, but to the Bible. As Rabbi Binyamin Elon, a member of the Israeli Knesset, wrote:

> I believe that if you do not know how to read the Bible, you cannot understand the daily newspaper. If you do not know the biblical story of Abraham, Isaac, and Jacob, you cannot possibly understand the miracle of the modern state of Israel.[3]

The story of Israel begins at the very beginning of the Bible, in the book of Genesis. The very proportion of the coverage tells us something about the importance of Israel. Only two chapters are given to the whole story of creation. One chapter records the fall of man. Eight chapters cover the thousands of years from creation to the time of Abram. Then we find that fully thirty-eight chapters deal with the life stories of Abraham, Isaac, and Jacob—the progenitors of the Jewish race. Apparently God finds Abraham and his descendants to be of enormous importance.

The Abrahamic Covenant

The Almighty God of heaven and earth made a binding covenant with Abraham, who was to be the father of the Jewish nation. The provisions of that covenant are recorded in Genesis 12:1–3:

> Now the LORD had said to Abram:
> "Get out of your country,
> From your family
> And from your father's house,
> To a land that I will show you.
> I will make you a great nation;
> I will bless you
> And make your name great;
> And you shall be a blessing.
> I will bless those who bless you,
> And I will curse him who curses you;
> And in you all the families of the earth shall be blessed."

Notice that God's covenant with Abraham consists of four unconditional promises. First, God promised to bless Abraham. That promise has been lavishly kept; Abraham has been blessed in many ways. For thousands of years, the very name of Abraham has been revered by Jews, Christians, and Muslims alike—a significant portion of the world's population. Abraham has also been blessed through the gifts God gave to his descendants, the Jews. Mark Twain once wrote:

Jews constitute but one percent of the human race. It suggests a nebulous dim puff of star dust in the blaze of the Milky Way. Properly the Jew ought hardly to be heard of; but he is heard of. He is as prominent on this planet as any other people. His commercial importance is extravagantly out of proportion to the smallness of his bulk. His contributions to the world's list of great names in literature, science, art, music, finance, medicine, and abstruse learning are also altogether out of proportion to the weakness of his numbers. He has made a marvelous fight in the world in all ages and he has done it with his hands tied behind him.[4]

One astounding fact that dramatically illustrates Twain's point is the disproportionate number of Nobel Prizes awarded to Jews. From 1901 to 2007, a total of 777 Nobel Prizes have been given to individuals in recognition of significant contributions to mankind. Of that total, 176 have been awarded to Jews. Of the 6 billion inhabitants of the world, only slightly more than 13 million are Jewish—less than two-thirds of 1 percent of the total world population. That miniscule percentage of the population has won 22.6 percent of all the Nobel Prizes awarded to date.[5]

Second, God promised to bring out of Abraham a great nation. Currently, nearly 5.4 million Jews live in Israel alone. Another 5 million live in the United States, and a significant Jewish population remains scattered throughout the world.[6] Add to these present figures all the descendants of Abraham who have lived throughout history and you truly have a population as uncountable as the nighttime stars (see appendix A for a chart of Jewish population statistics).

Third, God promised to make Abraham a blessing to many. That promise has been spectacularly kept. Just think what the world would be missing had it not been for the Jews. Without the Jews, we would have no Bible. Without the Jews, there would have been no Jesus. Without the Jewish Jesus, there would be no Christianity. Without the Jews, there would be no Ten Commandments, the Law that has largely been the basis of jurisprudence and statutory proceedings among most of the civilized nations of the world.

Fourth, God promised to bless those who blessed Israel and curse those who cursed her. He has kept that promise faithfully. No nation has blessed Israel like the United States of America, and no nation has been as blessed as the United States. In one of my previous books, I elaborated on this fact:

> I believe one of the reasons America has been blessed as a nation is that she has become a homeland for the Jewish people. Here the Jews can retain their religion. Here they have economic, social, and educational opportunities. Today the Christian church in America stands firmly between the Jew and the repetition of any further anti-Semitism.[7]

Throughout history, the judgments of God have fallen heavily upon Israel's oppressors—Egypt, Assyria, Babylon, Rome, and in more modern times, Spain, Germany, and Russia. Today, as forces less friendly to Israel gain influence in the United States, there are many who believe that America is dangerously close to being added to this hit list. Hal Lindsey wrote:

Although America continues to be Israel's principal protector, and continues to enjoy the concomitant blessings that come with it, America's good fortunes began to wane about the time the White House forced Israel into the Oslo Agreement. The "land for peace" formula called for Israel to give up some of the land of Promise in exchange for peace. In other words, it was a form of blackmail whose terms were drawn up in Washington and forced upon Israel for the express purpose of undoing what God had already done, including dividing Jerusalem and taking part of it from the Jews.[8]

God has certainly kept his promise to Abraham. He has blessed him and the nation that has come from him; He has multiplied his seed as the sands of the earth and stars of the sky; He has made him a blessing to the whole world; those who have blessed him have been blessed, and those who have cursed him have been cursed.

Of all God's covenant promises to Abraham, I believe the most amazing is His promise concerning the land. God told Abraham to leave his country, his family, and his father's house and go "to a land that I will show you" (Genesis 12:1). God then led Abraham to the land that would belong to his descendants forever. You can feel the awe and sense the meaning this promise has to Jews in this passage from Rabbi Binyamin Elon's book, *God's Covenant with Israel*:

I travel to my home in Beth El from Jerusalem on the same route that Abraham and others traveled in Biblical times, from Shechem to Hebron and places in between. Today we pass many other beautiful flourishing Jewish communities along the way . . . When I reach the Givat Assaf intersection, I am always inspired by the large sign posted there, sponsored by our local grocer: "Here, in Beth El, 3800 years ago, the Creator of the World promised the Land of Israel to the people of Israel. It is by virtue of this promise that we dwell today in Haifa, Tel Aviv, Shilo, and Hebron."[9]

The Record of Israel's Land

To this very day, the issue of who controls the Promised Land is the most volatile in international politics. But we need not worry; the right to the Promised Land has already been determined by the only One who has the authority to determine it. The land is called holy because it belongs to God. The Bible tells us that the earth is the Lord's to do with as He wills (Psalm 24:1; Exodus 19:5). In His covenant with Abraham, God designated who would control this land: He gave it to Abraham and his descendants, the people of Israel.

We read of God's choice of the Jews in Deuteronomy 7:6, where He declared the people of Israel holy, chosen to be "a people for Himself, a special treasure above all the peoples on the face of the earth." When I first began studying prophecy, I remember reading an offbeat little rhyme about Israel by British journalist William Norman Ewer: "How odd of God to choose the Jews." And when you think about it, this poetic quip expresses a valid observation. Doesn't it seem a little odd that of all the people on earth, God selected these particular people to be His chosen nation? Why would God choose the Jews?

The Bible tells us that His choice of Israel had nothing to do with merit. It was not because she was more numerous than other people in the world; she was the least (Deuteronomy 7:7). It was not because Israel was more sensitive to God than other nations. Although God called her by name, Israel did not know Him (Isaiah 45:4). It was not because Israel was more righteous than other nations. When God later confirmed His promise of land to the Jews, He reminded them that they were a rebellious, stiff-necked people (Deuteronomy 9:6–7).

If God chose to bless the nation of Israel not because she was more populous or spiritually responsive or righteous than other nations, just why did He choose the Jews? The answer: because *it was His sovereign purpose to do so.* His sovereign purpose means He cares what happens to His people and their land. He is not merely a passive observer to all that is taking place in Israel. As He told the people through Moses, theirs was "a land for which the LORD your God cares; the eyes of the LORD your God are always on it, from the beginning of the year to the very end of the year" (Deuteronomy 11:12).

God's Covenant and the Land of Israel

The people of Israel today are the beneficiaries of God's covenant with Abraham. And to those who are sensitive to the historical nature of the covenant, their possession of the land God promised to Abraham thousands of years ago has great meaning. The deep feeling Jews have for their land is powerfully expressed in this passage by Rabbi Binyamin Elon:

> I walk the streets of the Promised Land where Abram walked. I drive through the roads and plains where Isaac tended his flocks. I hike to the hilltops from where Jacob peered expectantly in all directions . . . I see these things and remember clearly the biblical truth. God gave the Promised Land, all of it, to our Patriarchs: Abraham, Isaac, and Jacob.[10]

Another rabbi, Abraham Joshua Heschel, attributes the Jews' strong connection with their land to the power of God's covenant with

...vish people together thr...

...ove for the land:

...ve of this land was due to an imperative, not an insti...

a sentiment. There is a covenant, an engagement of the people

land. We live by covenants. We could not betray our pledge or disc...

the promise. When Israel was driven into exile, the pledge became a

prayer; the prayer a dream; the dream a passion, a duty, a dedication

. . . It is a commitment we must not betray . . . To abandon the land

would make a mockery of all our longings, prayers, and commit-

ments. To abandon the land would be to repudiate the Bible.[11]

An Exact Covenant

Some have suggested that the promise of land to Abraham's descendants is not to be taken literally. They say it is merely a symbol that
indicates a general blessing, or perhaps the promise of heaven. But the
Bible is too specific to let us get by with such ephemeral vagueness. It
describes the land in definite terms and outlines it with clear geographical boundaries. Dr. John Walvoord stressed this point when he wrote:

The term *land* . . . used in the Bible, means exactly what it says. It is not
talking about heaven. It is talking about a piece of real estate in the
Middle East. After all, if all God was promising Abraham was heaven,
he could have stayed in Ur of the Chaldees. Why go on the long journey? Why be a pilgrim and a wanderer? No, God meant *land*.[12]

The land promised to Abraham takes in much more area than
what the present nation of Israel occupies. Genesis 15:18 tells us that
it stretches all the way from the Mediterranean Sea on the west to the

...he east. Ezekiel fixes the northern bounda

...n, one hundred miles north of Damascus (Ez...

...southern boundary at Kadesh, about one hund...

...of Jerusalem (Ezekiel 48:28).

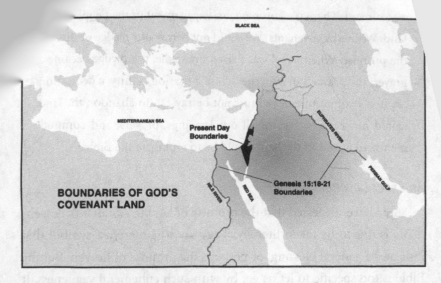

BOUNDARIES OF GOD'S COVENANT LAND

An Everlasting Covenant

And I will establish My covenant between Me and you and your descendants after you . . . Also I give to you and your descendants after you the land in which you are a stranger, all the land of Canaan, as an everlasting possession; and I will be their God. (Genesis 17:7–8)

In this remarkable prophecy God promised Abraham and his descendants the land of Canaan as their possession in perpetuity. When you look at a map and locate that tiny strip of land Israel now claims as hers, you can see that she does not now, nor has she ever fully occupied the land that was described to Abraham in God's covenant promise. If Israel were currently occupying all the land promised to her, she would control all the holdings of present day Israel, Lebanon, the West Bank of Jordan, and substantial portions of Syria, Iraq, and Saudi Arabia. Not until the Millennium will Israel occupy all the land the Lord gave her in His promise to Abraham.

The Relocation of the People of Israel

The Scattering of the Jews

Just as the people of Israel were about to enter the land of promise, Moses told them that a time was coming when their idolatry would cause them to be driven from the land: "And the LORD will scatter you among the peoples, and you will be left few in number among the nations where the LORD will drive you" (Deuteronomy 4:27). God reiterated this prophecy through Ezekiel and Hosea (Ezekiel 12:15; Hosea 9:17). Israel had no excuse. Her people had been warned again and again that God was a jealous God and would not tolerate His people worshipping false gods (Exodus 34:14).

Centuries before the Roman emperor Titus destroyed Jerusalem in AD 70, Jews had been scattered into the world by the Assyrians and Babylonians. Describing the prevalence of Jews throughout the known world, the historian and philosopher Strabo wrote:

> This people has already made its way into every city, and it is not easy to find any place in the habitable world which has not received this nation and in which it has not made its power felt.[13]

After the fall of Jerusalem to the Romans, this dispersion intensified, and Jews were scattered like chaff in the wind to the four corners of the earth.

The Suffering of the Exiled Jews

No doubt you remember the poor Jewish milkman Tevye in the classic movie *Fiddler on the Roof*. Burdened with poverty and trying to maintain traditions while coping with oppression from the Jew-hating Russians, he cries out to God, "I know, I know, we are Your chosen people. But, once in a while, can't You choose someone else?"[14] Tevye is a picture of the quintessential displaced Jew. What he experienced was exactly what Moses prophesied:

> And among those nations you shall find no rest, nor shall the sole of your foot have a resting place; but there the LORD will give you a trembling heart, failing eyes, and anguish of soul. (Deuteronomy 28:65)

Tevye illustrated this prophecy by providing a vivid picture of what scattered Jews have endured throughout the centuries since their dispersions from their promised land. Like Tevye, Jews in many lands have faced persecution in the form of pogroms, discrimination, exclusion from certain occupations, isolation in ghettos, and forced evacuation when the space they occupied was wanted for other purposes.

To appreciate the broad scope and magnitude of Jewish dispersion and persecution, consider the following historical facts:

> Before and during World War II, Jews throughout Europe were the target of merciless state-sponsored persecution. In 1933, nine million Jews lived in twenty-one European countries. By 1945, two out of three European Jews had been murdered. When the smoke finally cleared, the terrible truth came out. The Holocaust brought about the extermination of one-third of the worldwide Jewish population

at the time. Following the German invasion of the Soviet Union in 1941, mobile killing units following the German army began shooting massive numbers of Jews on the outskirts of conquered cities and towns. Seeking more efficient means to accomplish their obsession, the Nazis created a private and organized method of killing huge numbers of Jewish civilians. Extermination centers were established in Poland. Millions died in the ghettos and concentration camps through starvation, execution, brutality and disease. Of the six million Jews murdered during the Second World War, more than half were exterminated in the Nazi death camps. And the names Treblinka, Auschwitz, and Dachau became synonymous with the horrors of the Holocaust.[15]

Yes, God chose the Jews. He singled them out to be the recipients of His great and unique covenant blessings. But the greater the blessing, the greater the burden they bore for failing God. So the question is, was it worth it? How should Tevye's question be answered—would the Jews have been better off if God had chosen someone else? Rabbi Leo Baeck (1873–1956) weighed the sufferings of the Jewish people against their covenant blessings and drew a helpful conclusion:

> No people is heir to such a revelation as the Jew possesses; no people has had such a weight of divine commandment laid upon it; and for this reason no people has been so exposed to difficult and exacting times. The inheritance has not always been realized, but it is one that will endure, awaiting its hour.[16]

Baeck tells us that the story of the Jews is not over yet. It may seem that their sufferings outstrip their blessings, but that's because the fullness of their inheritance is yet to come. It is *awaiting its hour*. In other words, if you think the Jews have not yet been sufficiently blessed, just wait; you ain't seen nothing yet. God's promise in its fullness is yet to be kept.

The Rebirth of the Nation of Israel

Do we have reason to believe that God's promise to Israel will be kept? Will the Jews ever realize the fulfillment of the covenant to possess that particular tract of land with clear geographic boundaries promised as an everlasting possession? The prophet Isaiah asserted that it would happen in the Millennium. He prophesied that the Lord would "set His hand again the second time to recover the remnant of His people who are left" (Isaiah 11:11). God also addressed the issue through Ezekiel when He said, "I will take you from among the nations, gather you out of all countries, and bring you into your own land" (Ezekiel 36:24).

The fulfillment of those prophecies was set in motion on that day in 1948 when the United States recognized the new state of Israel. On the evening of that announcement, popular radio commentator Lowell Thomas said in his evening broadcast that Americans in every part of the country would be turning to their Bibles for historical background, enabling them to understand "this day in history."[17] And indeed, as the prophecies found in Isaiah, Ezekiel, Matthew, and Revelation show, both the Old Testament and the New Testament pointed to this day when the Jews would return to the land promised them and initiate fulfillment of the ancient prophecies.

To comprehend what an incredible act of God it is to preserve the beleaguered Jews throughout history and then return them to their land, consider this observation by Gary Frazier:

You cannot find the ancient neighbors of the Jews anywhere. Hav you ever met a Moabite? Do you know any Hittites? Are there any tours to visit the Ammonites? Can you find the postal code of a single Edomite? No! These ancient peoples disappeared from history and from the face of the earth. Yet the Jews, just as God promised, returned to their land.[18]

While the complete fulfillment is yet to come, the return of the Jews to Israel in 1948 was an astounding event unprecedented in world history. Never had a decimated ancient people managed to retain their individual identity through almost twenty centuries and reestablish their nation in their original homeland. The event was specifically prophesied, and it happened exactly as foretold. It was clearly a miraculous act of God.

Many events had to dovetail perfectly to bring about the fulfillment of God's promise to Israel, but I want to point out two events in particular that serve to illustrate the miraculous nature of the rebirth of the nation of Israel. You will be amazed at the mysterious workings of God's providence.

The single most influential event that triggered the return of the scattered Jews to their homeland began with Chaim Weizmann. Weizmann was a Russian Jew, a brilliant chemist and a leader in the Zionist movement, who immigrated to England in 1904. During World War I, English armies used gunpowder made of cordite, which produced little smoke and thus did not blind gunners to their targets or reveal their positions. But since the manufacture of cordite required acetone made from a compound imported from their enemy, Germany, the English government was desperate to find another source. Prime Minister Lloyd George and Winston Churchill turned to Weizmann and set up in a gin distillery, where he quickly developed a biochemical process for producing synthetic acetone.

The success of his ingenious process for creating acetone contributed to the ultimate Allied victory. The minimal salary and token reward that Weizmann received from the government earned him significant leverage when he pressed his persistent petitions for a Jewish homeland in Israel.[19]

As it happened, by the war's end, England gained possession of the land of Palestine—the very land promised in God's covenant with Abraham—from the defeated Ottoman Empire. As an act of a grateful nation and through Weizmann's influence within the government, England officially issued the Balfour Declaration of 1917, which declared:

> His Majesty's Government views with favor the establishment in Palestine of a national home for the Jewish people, and will use their best endeavors to facilitate the achievement of this object . . .[20]

The second influential event that brought the scattered Jews back to Palestine was the liberation of Jewish prisoners from Auschwitz, Dachau, and other Nazi concentration camps. When Germany collapsed at the end of World War II, the liberation of these Jewish prisoners caused worldwide shock at the grossly inhumane treatment inflicted by the Nazis. This generated sympathy that drew Jewish wealth from around the world and enabled the relocation of more than a million displaced Jews to Palestine.

That brings us all the way back to May 14, 1948. On this day, the United Nations officially recognized the State of Israel, with US president Harry Truman determining the deciding vote. The Israeli government established the State of Israel, thus fulfilling the twenty-five-hundred-year-old prophecy recorded in the Bible. Great Britain ended its mandate in Palestine and removed its troops, leaving more than 650,000 Jews to govern themselves in their own land.

The Return to the God of Israel

I am often asked if Israel's presence in her own land today is the final fulfillment of God's promise to regather His people. Many assume that it is, but I have to tell them that the answer is no! What is happening in Israel today is primarily the result of a secular Zionist movement, whereas Ezekiel wrote about a spiritual return of God's people to Him when he said:

> For I will take you from the nations, gather you from all the lands and bring you into your own land . . . Moreover, I will give you a new heart and put a new spirit within you . . . I will put My Spirit within you and cause you to walk in My statutes, and you will be careful to observe My ordinances. You will live in the land that I gave to your forefathers; so you will be My people, and I will be your God. (Ezekiel 36:24–28 NASB)

The return of Jews to the refounded nation of Israel is the first stage of that regathering, but it certainly does not fulfill the requirements of a spiritual return to the Lord. Secularist Israeli Yossi Beilin makes this point abundantly clear. Beilin is an agnostic and proponent of "secular conversion to Judaism," who has served in many roles in Israel's government. He speaks for many Israelis when he says that "secular Jews are not a marginal group in Jewish life. We are the mainstream. We are people in the government, we are people in the Parliament."[21] To him,

Judaism is "a people, a culture, an existence" as well as a religion; therefore, the Jewishness of its atheists and agnostics goes unquestioned.[22]

From the moment of God's promise to Abraham to this present hour, the prophecies concerning Israel's total possession and blessing in the land remain unfulfilled. The most dramatic events lie ahead of us. Israel today is an island of a few million immigrants surrounded by a sea of three hundred million enemies, many of them militant and eager to wipe the tiny nation off the map. From a purely human point of view, it would seem inevitable that, sooner or later, Israel will be destroyed.

Indeed, Israel has been attacked over and over since its founding, sometimes in all-out wars and incessantly by terrorists. The Jewish people have survived by remaining vigilant, but they long for peace. According to the Bible, a future leader will fulfill this longing by brokering a seven-year peace deal with Israel's enemies. But Scripture also tells us that this peace plan will be broken, and Israel will be attacked once again, this time as never before. Countless armies will amass against the boxed-in nation, leaving it with no human hope of victory. Only Christ's return, His judgment, and His reign will finally bring true peace to Israel.

It is then that God's covenant with Abraham will reach its ultimate fulfillment. The Jews will return to the Lord, and as Ezekiel and Jeremiah prophesied, they will be His people, and He will be their God. The borders of the land will expand to the dimensions described in Genesis 15 and Ezekiel 48. Christ's return will also fulfill the prophecy of Jeremiah that God would gather the Jews. "Behold, I will gather them out of all countries where I have driven them . . . I will bring them back to this place, and I will cause them to dwell safely. They shall be My people, and I will be their God" (Jeremiah 32:37–38).

Ezekiel makes it clear that this gathering means He will return every single living Jew back to the land. For he wrote that the Lord said He would gather them again to their own land "and . . . none of them [will be] captive any longer" (Ezekiel 39:28).

Today we see this prophecy being fulfilled right before our eyes. In 2006, for the first time in nineteen hundred years, Israel became home to the largest Jewish community in the world, surpassing the Jewish population in the United States. From the 650,000 who returned when the Jewish state was founded in 1948, the population of Israel has swelled to approximately 5.4 million, and it is expected to exceed 6 million by 2020.[23]

The significance of Israel's reemergence in her ancient homeland is that this had to occur in order to set the stage for the final fulfillment of biblical prophecies. Israel had to be a nation in her own land before the predictions previously noted could come about. The return of the Jews to their homeland is also significant in another way: it pinpoints where we are on history's timeline. As author Milton B. Lindberg pointed out:

> Without the existence of the nation of Israel, we would not be able to say with certainty that we are in the last days. That single event, more than any other, is the most prominent sign that we are living in the final moments before the coming of Jesus! The Hebrew People have been called God's timepiece of the ages.[24]

God's Providence in Action: The Story Behind the Story

Clark Clifford (1906–1998), an influential Washington lawyer, became a political advisor to President Harry Truman. He also became one of Truman's most trusted personal counselors and friends. Clifford opened his memoirs, *Counsel to the President,* by describing a meeting in the president's office on a Wednesday afternoon in the spring of 1948.

"Of all the meetings I ever had with the Presidents," wrote Clifford, "this one remains the most vivid." President Truman was meeting with Secretary of State General George C. Marshall, whom Truman regarded as "the greatest living American," about whether or not to recognize the state of Israel. British control of Palestine would run out in two days, and when it did, the Jewish Agency intended to announce the creation of a new state, still unnamed at that time. Most observers thought it would be named Judea.[25]

Marshall, mastermind of America's victory in World War II and author of the Marshall Plan, inspired a respect bordering on awe. He was adamantly opposed to recognizing Israel and not at all hesitant to express his opinion forcefully. His view was shared by almost every member of Truman's White House—except Clifford—and by virtually everyone in the State Department and Defense Department.

Several months before that meeting, James Forrestal, Truman's secretary of defense, had bluntly told Clifford, "You fellows over at the White House are just not facing up to the realities in the Middle East. There are thirty million Arabs on one side and about six hundred thousand Jews on the other. It is clear that in any contest, the Arabs are going to overwhelm the Jews. Why don't you face up to the realities? Just look at the numbers!"[26]

Clifford, however, knew that Truman had strong reasons for wanting to help the Jews, reasons that would not register on the scale of values at the departments of State or Defense. Truman detested intolerance and discrimination and had been deeply moved by the plight of the Jews during World War II. More to the point, Clifford wrote, Truman was "a student and believer in the Bible from his youth. From his reading of the Old Testament he felt the Jews derived a legitimate historical right to Palestine, and he sometimes cited such biblical lines as Deuteronomy 1:8, 'Behold, I have given up the land before you; go in and take possession of the land which the Lord hath sworn unto your fathers, to Abraham, to Isaac, and to Jacob.'"[27]

So at 4:00 p.m. on that Wednesday, May 12, the president met with his advisors in the Oval Office. Truman sat at his desk facing his famous plaque that read, *The Buck Stops Here*. Around the desk sat General Marshall and his deputy, officials from the State Department, and a handful of Truman's counselors, including Clark Clifford. They were exactly fifty hours away from the birth of the new, unnamed nation.

One by one, the president's advisors gave reasons for deferring any decision on the recognition of Israel. Finally it was Clifford's turn. Bucking the overwhelming consensus in the room, he boldly presented reasons for recognizing the new state. He barely finished before General Marshall erupted in a torrent of anger, and the officials from the State Department backed his opposition unanimously and vigorously. After the heated discussion, Marshall glared icily at the president and said, "If you follow Clifford's advice and if I were to vote in the election, I would vote against you!"[28]

Everyone in the room was stunned. The meeting came to an abrupt end with the question unresolved. Truman himself was greatly shaken by the fierceness of the general's opposition. The president, running for reelection, was on thin ice politically, and he could not afford to lose the support of such a towering figure as Marshall. Clifford left the meeting thinking the case was lost.

But over the next two days, Clifford, Truman, and a handful of others worked toward reaching a compromise within the administration. They succeeded when General Marshall finally said bitterly that while he could not support the president's position, he would not oppose it. So at 6:11 p.m. on May 14, 1948, Truman's press secretary, Charlie Ross, stepped out to meet an awaiting press and read these words:

> The government has been informed that a Jewish state has been pro-claimed in Palestine . . . The United States recognizes the provisional government as de facto authority of the new State of Israel.[29]

Another biographer wrote that "he [Truman] felt great satisfaction in what he had been able to do for the Jewish people, and was deeply moved by their expressions of gratitude, then and for years to come. When the Chief Rabbi of Israel, Isaac Halevi Herzog, called at the White House, he told Truman, 'God put you in your mother's womb so that you would be the instrument to bring about the rebirth of Israel after two thousand years.'" Another witness to the scene, Truman's administrative assistant David Niles, reported the president's reaction to Herzog's generous assertion: "I thought he was overdoing things," remembered Niles, "but when I looked over at the President, tears were running down his cheeks."[30]

What Does All this Mean to Me?

Let's return to the questions we posed at the beginning of this chapter. Why has this tiny nation with a population of less than six million become the geopolitical center of the world? Why is a fledgling country with a total land space hardly larger than New Jersey mentioned in the nightly news more than any other nation except the United States? Or, to sum it up, why is Israel so important? I hope this chapter has helped you answer that question. Israel is important because the fulfillment of

God's covenant with its founder, Abraham, greatly affects every one of us. We have shown why it's important for our nation to continue to support and protect Israel. Nations who befriend Israel will be blessed; those that do not will be cursed.

We have shown how the playing out of prophetic events concerning Israel places us in the last days of history's timeline. We have shown how the miraculous survival of God's covenant people, the Jews, demonstrates God's providence and His ability to accomplish His purpose in the face of what seems to human minds impossible odds. The existence of Israel today is exhibit A in the lineup of convincing evidences that the Bible's prophecies concerning the future ahead of us will be fulfilled. This means the future not only of Israel, but also of our world, our nation, as well as your future and mine. This, perhaps, is the most important blessing we can receive from the astounding history of the Jews. It reveals the reality of God—His overwhelming power, the authenticity of His promises, the certainty of His existence, the urgency of His call to us, and His claim on our very being.

When we consider all this, perhaps we can see that it's not so odd of God to choose the Jews.

TWO

The Crude Awakening

WHO DOESN'T KNOW THE WORDS TO THE THEME SONG OF *The Beverly Hillbillies* by heart? If you're not old enough to have heard this ditty in the original episodes of the popular sixties sitcom, you've no doubt seen reruns. The series features a dirt-poor hillbilly family that strikes it rich in oil and moves to the upscale Hollywood neighborhood of Beverly Hills. The sitcom plays on the fact that discovering oil on one's property means becoming instantly wealthy, a phenomenon that occurs because oil has become vital to running our highly industrialized society.

America's quest for oil began forty years before Spindletop ever spouted its first Texas oil, when "the most important oil well ever drilled was [bored] in the middle of quiet farm country in northwestern Pennsylvania in 1859." Oil had actually been found and used on our continent much earlier: centuries before, Native Americans had noticed oil seeping out of the rocks and had used it for medicine and in trade with neighboring tribes. Almost thirty years before the signing of the American Declaration of Independence, a map had already been printed showing known oil springs in Pennsylvania.[1]

But on August 27, 1859, Edwin Drake launched the modern petroleum industry by drilling a 69.5-foot well near Titusville, Pennsylvania. It was the first well purposely drilled to find oil, and thus began a search for petroleum that quickly became international and changed the way we live . . . *forever!*

Now, fast-forward to the twenty-first century and observe what has happened in the decades since the drilling of Edwin Drake's little well:

- Mankind's thirst for oil has passed 86 million barrels per day and is expected to rise to 98.5 million barrels a day in 2015.[2]

- The psychological barrier of one hundred dollars a barrel was finally breached in early 2008.

- Oil prices have quintupled in the past six years.[3]

- As I write this, surplus oil production has doubled over recent years, and demand is somewhat reduced,[4] but new, unsettling record highs have been registered so far this year in all gasoline products: home heating fuels, automobile fuel, and, especially, diesel fuel.[5]

Oil is the new gold in the world economy, and more than any factor other than the nation of Israel, oil holds the key to the prophetic events of the future. Oil explains why the Bible focuses its end-time attention on the Middle East. The demand for oil in America has outstripped its capacity to produce the black gold, and the same holds true for much of the rest of the world. Therefore, since the discovery of huge supplies of oil in the Middle Eastern countries, world attention has focused on that area. In an article entitled "The Power of Oil," Dilip Hiro wrote:

> The overarching fact is that political leaders all over the world are committed to raising living standards through economic growth, heavily dependent on energy in the form of gas and oil. That includes the United States. Ever since 1932, when American oil companies acquired a stake in the oil resources of Saudi Arabia, Washington's policies have been geared to securing Middle East oil at the expense of all else.[6]

Few would question the fact that oil has become the new basis for our world economy. It is now the stuff of life, the resource most highly valued by the industrialized and emerging nations of the world, the blood that flows through their economic veins and gives life to prosperity in today's global economy. The greatest source of that lifeblood is now in the Middle East, so that is where the eyes of the world are focused.

What does this tell us about coming events? In Luke's gospel, Jesus contrasts our ability to discern weather signs with our inability to understand the more important signs of the time: "You can discern the face of the sky and of the earth, but how is it you do not discern this time?" (Luke 12:56). Surely the world's fascination with oil—a hot commodity with a source in lands hostile or borderline hostile to Israel and to us—qualifies as a "sign."

The Control of the World's Oil Supply

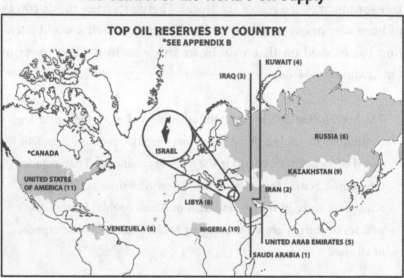

TOP OIL RESERVES BY COUNTRY
*SEE APPENDIX B

To get a clear picture of the primary sources for oil, here is a 2007 list of the world's greatest conventional oil reserves by country:[7]

Rank	Country	Billions of Barrels
1	Saudi Arabia	264.3
2	Iran	137.5
3	Iraq	115.0
4	Kuwait	101.5
5	United Arab Emirates	97.8
6	Venezuela	80.0
6	Russia	79.5
8	Libya	41.5

The United States is ranked eleventh with a mere 29.9 billion barrels! The five top countries with the greatest known oil reserves are Arab nations, and the reserves in those countries total almost *716 billion barrels*. The Middle East/Persian Gulf area has about 60 percent of the world's known oil reserves lying beneath its desert sands. The sophisticated handling and processing facilities developed in those countries by the major Western oil companies have been nationalized. They are now controlled by a few Arab leaders.

Furthermore, Arab control of oil goes beyond the realities of supply and demand. Historically, all of the world's oil has been traded in US dollars, which has assured stability for the dollar and the US economy. The dollar had always been backed by the gold standard until President Nixon took it off in 1971. But then in 1973, oil prices rose sharply, threatening to throw the dollar into free fall around the world. In order to stabilize the dollar, the US government entered into a relationship with Saudi Arabia, the world's largest oil supplier. According to the agreement, the United States would back the Saudi government as an ally if the Saudis would demand that all purchases of its oil be in US dollars. This would ensure the primacy of the dollar in the world economy. The net effect of this agreement was that the US dollar was, in effect, backed by oil instead of gold. Then on February 17, 2008, Iran opened its own trading exchange in which oil is brokered in euros instead of dollars, further threatening the stability of the US dollar.

The Middle Eastern countries are not the only ones giving the United States trouble in the global oil market. You probably noticed that Venezuela, tied for number six on the oil reserve list, is another primary source of America's oil. But Hugo Chavez, the president of Venezuela, is no friend of America. During the 2006 United Nations sessions in New York City, Chavez verbally assaulted the American government and called our president a devil. Chavez has met several times with Iranian president Mahmoud Ahmadinejad and has vowed to "unite the Persian Gulf and the Caribbean, giving Iran entrée into Latin America."[8] This could bring even more insecurity to United States oil sources, giving powerful influence over South American oil to a Middle Eastern country. So as you can see, control of the lion's share of the world's oil is centralized in the Middle East.

No doubt you've heard preachers assert that civilization as we know it will face a gargantuan, final showdown in the Middle East. In the not-too-distant past you may have wondered, *Why the Middle East? Why would this handful of relatively small countries become so important to world powers?* Perhaps you figured the showdown would more likely be brought on by the population masses in China, the wealth and global power of the United States, the ingenuity of Japan, or the rising up of poverty-oppressed multitudes in India. Why, of all places, would things come to a head in the Middle East? Today, after considering the source of the world's oil and all the global hands reaching out to grasp it, we don't ask that question nearly as often!

Here's an interesting sidelight about world oil reserves. My friend Robert Morgan flew into New Orleans several years ago, and the man who met him at the airport was a geophysicist for a major oil company. Driving to the hotel, he explained to Robert that oil deposits result from the decomposition of plant and animal life now buried by eons of time. Oil is found all over the world, he said, even under the ice of the Arctic and Antarctic. That means forests and abundant vegetation once covered the world until destroyed in a vast global cataclysm (such as a worldwide flood).

The geophysicist went on to say that the earth's richest, deepest, and largest deposits of petroleum lie under the sands of countries just to the east of Israel, in the location pinpointed in the Bible as the garden of Eden. Eden was a teeming expanse of forests, foliage, and gardens with rich fertility unparalleled in human history.[9]

Barren sand and blazing desert now exist where once grew a garden flourishing with dense, lush flora, the likes of which the world has not seen since. It was destroyed in some disastrous upheaval and has decayed into the largest deposits of oil in the world. I had never before imagined that the gasoline I pump into my car might be the ruined remains of the rich, vast foliage of the garden of Eden.

It's ironic to think that Satan may finance the Battle of Armageddon at the end of human history with revenues generated from the garden he spoiled at the beginning of human history.

The Consumers of the World's Oil Supply

The vast majority of the world's oil is consumed by four entities. Russia ranks fourth with 2.92 million barrels used per day. Japan is third, consuming 5.16 million barrels per day. China, the world's largest country in terms of population, is now number two in oil consumption at 7.27 million barrels per day. At a rate of 20.7 million barrels per day, the United States ranks first in oil consumption.[10]

China continues to increase her thirst for oil. In 2005, China had a total of twenty million cars on the road.[11] One well-known investment firm now estimates that China will have 1.1 billion cars on the road by 2050.

The European Union, once the number-two consumer of oil, now burns 1.83 million barrels per day and has fallen to thirteenth place

among the top oil-consuming nations, an overall usage reduction
despite growth in the number of member nations.[12] Last year when we
visited London, our hosts told us how Brits had handled the oil situation in their country. Responding to the energy crisis in 1973, they
reduced consumption and imposed taxes on gasoline to raise significant revenue to import high-priced oil. By 2007, conservation had
become a way of life in England, even as the price per gallon of gas
more than doubled its cost in the United States. I later discovered that
the same thing had happened all over Europe.

It probably comes as no surprise to anyone that the world's number-
one consumer of oil is America, guzzling almost 21 million barrels of
crude oil per day, or 25 percent of all the oil produced in the world. If
present trends continue, US consumption will rise to 27 million barrels a day by 2020, and demand will expand to 34 percent by 2030.
Added to this is the fact that the United States consumes 43 percent of
the world's motor gasoline, and no new gasoline refinery has been
built in the United States since 1976. Stop for a moment and ponder
the meaning of all this: the United States is number eleven in oil reserves
and number one in oil consumption, with the demand growing by
leaps and bounds. It doesn't take a rocket scientist to see that a crisis is
looming in our future.

Many forward-looking statesmen worldwide, aware of the coming crisis, have mandated the development and use of alternative
energy sources such as solar and wind power and alternative fuels
for motor vehicles. However, recent studies have shown that despite
such mandates for biofuels use, the "law of unintended consequences"
is at work. Rather than saving the planet from oil dependence and global
warming, biofuels are raising food prices, endangering the hungry, and
only slightly reducing the need for oil. Even if all the corn and soybean

crops produced in the United States were converted for fuel, it would only be enough to meet 20 percent of consumption demands.[13]

At this point in time, no alternative energy source shows promise of solving the problem. And until that solution surfaces, the United States will continue to be heavily dependent on foreign sources to maintain its vital influx of oil.

The Conflicts over the World's Oil Supply

In 1973 a group of Arab nations launched an attack on Israel, initiating the Yom Kippur War. One result of this war was the uniting of Arab nations in a common cause as never before. This new show of unity was manifest partly in the military conflict and partly in a less obvious way. On October 17, 1973, the Arab nations conspired to reduce their oil production below the previous norm and attempted to embargo nations that favored Israel, principally the United States and the Netherlands. This hostile act made it increasingly evident that the Arab world would use their control of major oil reserves to leverage their bid for world power.

Some US citizens will remember the effect of that Arab embargo. The price of oil quadrupled to twelve dollars a barrel. Cars formed long, winding lines at gas stations. Conservation measures were put into effect, including a national highway speed limit of 55 mph. We were being attacked in a new kind of war—an economic war with ominous implications. The price of oil did not go down after the Arab oil blackmail of 1973–74, and that crisis precipitated the fastest transfer of money in history, sucking dollars out of the United States and stashing them in swelling Arab treasuries. The ultimate price of the war, however, would not be exacted in money alone, but in the political and economic reshaping of the world. For the first time in centuries, the Middle East became a major consideration in every international event.

The first acknowledgment of this new political reality came from President Jimmy Carter in his State of the Union address on January 23, 1980. In that address Carter announced an important policy change concerning the Middle East:

> Let our position be absolutely clear: An attempt by any outside force to gain control of the Persian Gulf region will be regarded as an assault on the vital interests of the United States of America, and such an assault will be repelled by any means necessary including military force.[14]

This became known as the Carter Doctrine: the determination to protect the Persian Gulf even at the expense of our own troops. This paradigm shift in foreign policy would soon be tested.

In August 1990, Iraqi dictator Saddam Hussein sent troops into Kuwait to take over that nation's oil fields. President George H. W. Bush and his defense secretary, Dick Cheney, put the Carter Doctrine into action, sending US troops to Kuwait to repel the Iraqi invasion. President Bush defended his action to the nation, saying, "Our country now imports nearly half the oil it consumes and could face a major threat to its economic independence . . . The sovereign independence of Saudi Arabia is of vital interest to the United States."[15]

While other justifications for the war were given, experts agree that the Gulf War in 1990–91 was the first in world history fought almost entirely over oil. And make no mistake: while the war in Iraq is about terrorism, it is also about oil—oil that is sold to finance the Muslim terrorist regime and oil that is necessary for the West to function economically.

The Concerns About the World's Oil Supply

Are We Running Out of Oil?

It was Saturday morning, and I was on my way to my office to put the final touches on the message for the weekend. I was scheduled to preach on the importance of oil in the prophetic program of the end times. When I stopped to get a cup of coffee, I spotted the weekend edition of the *Wall Street Journal*. The headline read, "Where Has All The Oil Gone?" The article, written by Ann Davis, was about the huge oil tanks in Cushing, Oklahoma, where many of our reserves are stored. According to the article, a run on oil futures has depleted the tanks to their lowest level ever.[16]

So where *has* all the oil gone? Do these near-empty tanks mean we are running out of it? This is a difficult question to answer. According to the CEO and president of the Saudi Aramco, we have tapped "only 18 percent of [global] conventional and non-conventional producible potential." In his words, "we are looking at more than 4.5 trillion barrels of potentially recoverable oil"—enough to power the globe at current levels of consumption for "more than 140 years."[17] On the other hand, we do not have access to all of that oil, nor do we have the present-day capacity to harvest it all if we knew where it was.

The rate of oil discovery has been falling ever since the 1960s when 47 billion barrels a year were discovered, mostly in the Middle East. In the '70s the rate dropped to about 35 billion barrels while the industry concentrated on the North Sea. In the '80s it was Russia's turn, and the discovery rate dropped to 24 billion. It dropped even further in the '90s as the industry concentrated on West Africa but only found some 14 billion barrels.[18]

To say that we are running out of oil might be untrue but to say that we are consuming at the level of our current ability to produce oil is true. The oil shortage is real and will continue to have an enormous effect upon our culture. According to the official energy statistics posted by the U.S. government, last updated in July of 2007, the total world oil supply in 2006 was exceeded by the total world petroleum consumption in 2005.[19]

Did you catch the sobering point in this quote? Let me repeat it: in 2005 the world used more oil than was even produced in the following year. And there is one energy rule that even I can understand: energy use cannot exceed available supply.

Can We Protect Our Sources of Oil?

Our dependence on foreign oil has become a major concern—especially since the oil lies under the control of nations with which we have tenuous or hostile relationships. Paul Roberts addressed this concern in his book, *The End of Oil: On the Edge of a Perilous New World.* Perhaps the greatest casualty of the Iraq war may be the very idea of energy security:

> But with the continuing fiasco in Iraq, it is now clear that even the most powerful military entity in world history cannot stabilize a country at will or "make it" produce oil simply by sending in soldiers and tanks. In other words, since the Iraqi invasion, the oil market now understands that the United States cannot guarantee the security of oil supplies—for itself or for anyone else. That new and chilling knowledge, as much as anything else, explains the high price of oil.[20]

According to Roberts, our ability to protect our foreign oil inflow is limited at best. Even if we commit to using brute military force, as the Carter Doctrine says we are ready to do, we cannot ensure an endless supply of oil from hostile countries.

Is There Any Oil in Israel?

It would help, of course, if we could depend on oil from our one staunch Middle Eastern ally, Israel. But as former prime minister Golda Meir ruefully quipped, "Let me tell you something we Israelis have against Moses. He took us forty years into the desert in order to bring us to the one place in the Middle East that has no oil."[21]

While little oil has ever been discovered in Israel, today there is a growing belief that there may be significant oil deposits under its surface. Two major oil companies have been formed to explore oblique references to oil found in the Bible. Ezekiel speaks of a time when God would do better for Israel than at her beginnings (36:11). How could Israel ever be more prosperous than she was in the days of King Solomon? During his reign the wealth of Israel was the wonder and envy of the known world. Yet here is God telling Israel that at some time in the future she will be wealthier still.

In his book *The Coming Peace in the Middle East*, Dr. Tim LaHaye suggests one way that this coming wealth could be explained:

Suppose that a pool of oil, greater than anything in Arabia . . . were discovered by the Jews . . . This would change the course of history. Before long, Israel would be able independently to solve its economic woes, finance the resettlement of the Palestinians, and supply housing for Jews and Arabs in the West Bank, East Bank, or anywhere else they might choose to live.[22]

In an article written for WorldNet Daily, Aaron Klein asked this question: "Is Israel sitting on an enormous oil reserve mapped out in the Old Testament that when found will immediately change the geopolitical structure of the Middle East and confirm the validity of the Bible to people around the world?"[23] John Brown, an evangelical Christian and founder and chairman of Zion Oil and Gas, believes that there is indeed oil in Israel. He is certain that several biblical passages indicate where rich deposits might be found. As examples, he cites two passages: "Let Asher be blessed . . . and let him dip his foot in oil" (Deuteronomy 33:24 KJV). "Joseph is . . . a fruitful bough by a well . . . Blessings of heaven above, blessings of the deep that lies beneath . . . shall be on the head of Joseph, and on the crown of the head." (Genesis 49:22–26 NKJV).

Brown's explanation of why these passages indicate the presence of oil is fascinating. He says that maps of the territory allotted to the twelve tribes when they entered Palestine show that the shape of Asher's area resembles a giant foot. That foot is "dipped" into the top, or "crown" area belonging to the land given to the tribe of Joseph's son Manasseh. "The oil is there," Brown asserts, "where Joseph's head is met by Asher's foot."[24] And Brown is willing to put his money where his mouth is. In 2007, his company was granted two extended licenses for approximately 162,100 acres that include the Joseph and Asher-Menashe areas, which Brown believes contain oil.[25]

The discovery of oil on Israeli soil would greatly reduce the threat against Israel from her hostile allies, taking the oil weapon out of their hands. "Finding oil will give Israel a huge strategic advantage" over its Arab enemies, Brown said. "It will change the political and economic structure of the region overnight."[26]

But in spite of the tantalizing possibilities of oil in Israel, it has not yet been found. This means we must continue to deal with the reality of a world in which oil remains in the control of countries essentially hostile to us or at best only tenuously allied.

How Does the Oil Situation Affect Our Future?

The Emergence of Prophetic Alliances

Ezekiel foretold a time when Russia would attack Israel. In detailing how the military aggression would take place, the prophet listed a coalition of some of the nations that would join with Russia in the attack. "I will turn you around, put hooks into your jaws, and lead you out, with all your army, horses, and horsemen, all splendidly clothed, a great company with bucklers and shields, all of them handling swords. Persia, Ethiopia, and Libya are with them, all of them with shield and helmet" (38: 4–5).

Until March 21, 1935, Persia was the official name of the country we now call Iran. Not once in the past twenty-five hundred years has Russia formed a military connection with Persia/Iran, until now.[27] But now these two nations have formed a military alliance that continues to be strengthened by the political situation in our world. Russia recently signed a billion-dollar deal to sell missiles and other weaponry to Iran. And the connection is even broader, as Joel C. Rosenberg, former aid to Israeli prime minister Benjamin Netanyahu, points out: "Over 1000 Iranian nuclear scientists have been trained in Russia by senior Russian scientists."[28] Here is an end-time alliance that was prophesied twenty-five hundred years ago, and in the last five years it has become a reality. Obviously, the stage is being set!

The Emergence of Petroleum Alliances

Omer Selah, with Israel's Fuel Authority, was recently quoted in the *Jerusalem Post*:

The issue of oil becomes more and more critical with each passing year, for Western democracies in general, and for Israel in particular. What we are seeing is a confluence of several negative factors and processes in this region . . . A huge percentage of the world's oil reserves . . . is found in the possession of powers not friendly to the West or to Israel.[29]

And the wealth of these few oil-producing nations is growing at such an exponential rate that they are struggling to find ways to invest their exploding resources. The magnitude of their investment "problem" was reported in a *New York Times* article. Between 2000 and 2007, oil revenues for the OPEC nations went from $243 billion to $688 billion, not including the price spikes that occurred in November and December of 2007. It's estimated that these countries have $4 trillion invested around the world from the money earned in oil exports.[30]

Our enemies consider this kind of wealth to be a gigantic weapon with the blessing of Allah. As author Don Richardson puts it: "Muslim strategists ask their followers, *Why do we find in these modern times that Allah has entrusted most of the world's oil wealth primarily to Muslim nations?* Their answer: Allah foresaw Islam's need for funds to finance a final politico-religious victory over what Islam perceives as its ultimate enemy: Christianized Euro-American civilization."[31]

Another *New York Times* article headlined in the spring of 2002, "Iranian Urges Muslims to Use Oil as a Weapon." In this article, Ayatollah Ali Khamenei is quoted as having said:

The oil belongs to the people and can be used as a weapon against the West and those who support the savage regime of Israel . . . If Islamic and Arab countries . . . for only one month suspend the export of oil to Israel and its supporter, the world would be shaken.[32]

It should be clear to us that America's ride on the crest of wealth and power faces unprecedented threats from newly rich, newly united Middle Eastern countries that have no love for us. Indeed, many of them would love to see us reduced to the ashes of history. And it should be just as clear that they are feeling the newfound power that control of most of the world's oil has given them. These factors do not bode well for the United States, Israel, and their Western allies.

What Are We to Do?

So far this chapter has given you very little good news and little reason to be optimistic—that is, if your outlook is entirely earthly. As we look back on where we have been as a nation and where we find ourselves today, we could easily become discouraged. The secret, however, is to look beyond both the past and the present and focus on the future. We are, in fact, unusually blessed. We are being given the opportunity to be firsthand observers to the staging of events that will precede the ultimate coming of Christ to this earth. Events written about centuries ago are now unfolding right before our eyes and are telling us that our patient anticipation will soon be rewarded. In the meantime, we must . . .

Keep on Waiting

Jesus told His disciples that just as you can tell that summer is near when the fig tree puts forth leaves, you can also tell that the Son of Man is returning by recognizing the signs given by the prophets

(Matthew 24:32). As we see these signs appearing, our question is, what shall we do?

First of all, we wait. There is nothing we can do to hasten His coming, so we have been called to be patient. "Therefore be patient, brethren, until the coming of the Lord. The farmer waits for the precious produce of the soil, being patient about it, until it gets the early and late rains. You too be patient; strengthen your hearts, for the coming of the Lord is near" (James 5:7–8 NASB). No man knows exactly when the Lord will return (Matthew 24:36), but by the signs we can discern the season of His coming. And I am not alone in believing we are in that season. We do not, however, know exactly how long that season will be, so our duty as faithful servants is to wait patiently.

Keep on Working

Some modern believers seem to have concluded that the coming of Christ is a call to passivity. Their attitude seems to be, *Well, since He's coming soon, there's no point in making any big plans or working to fulfill them. It's all about to come to an end anyway.* Over the years we've seen extreme examples of passive waiting. People who believed they had pinpointed the time of His coming to the day got rid of their earthly goods, gathered on a mountaintop or in a compound, and simply waited passively. That is emphatically not what is meant by waiting. The Lord Himself set the example while He was on this earth. He said, "I must work the works of Him who sent Me while it is day; the night is coming when no one can work" (John 9:4 NKJV). In one of His parables, He also said, "Blessed is that servant whom his master, when he comes, will find so doing [serving]" (Matthew 24:46 NKJV).

That is the key to pleasing the Lord in these last days—continue to work diligently at what God has called you to do. Believing in the imminent return of Jesus involves more than simply waiting, as important as that may be. It is rather a matter of *working* while we wait. Working hard. Working faithfully. Working in the power and joy and filling of the Holy Spirit.

Someone once asked me what I would like to be doing when the Lord comes back. That's easy. I would like to be standing behind my pulpit before my flock, declaring and explaining and applying the Word of God. For me there is nothing better. There is no greater joy.

What would you like to be doing when He returns? Where would you like to be when the trumpet sounds, when the archangel shouts, and when, in the twinkling of an eye, we are changed and rise into the clouds to meet Him?

Keep on Watching

On numerous occasions Jesus told His followers to watch. He exhorted them to be full of anticipation, to look up and lift their heads up and realize that their redemption was drawing near (Luke 21:28). The apostle Paul continued the theme of watchfulness, telling the Roman believers to awake out of their sleep, for their salvation was nearer than when they first believed (Romans 13:11).

Wait, work, and watch: these are the three things Christians are exhorted to do when they see the signs of Christ's imminent coming. What does this look like for Christians today? How can we gear up our wills and our emotions to keep on going in this era of church history when the future looks so ominous?

C. S. Lewis answered that question almost seventy years ago in another time when extreme danger loomed on the horizon. In an address to

Oxford University students shortly after the English declared war with Germany, Lewis stated well the attitude Christians should have in times like his and ours:

> This impending war has taught us some important things. Life is short. The world is fragile. All of us are vulnerable, but we are here because this is our calling. Our lives are rooted not only in time, but also in eternity, and the life of learning, humbly offered to God, is its own reward.[33]

In his speech, Lewis asserted that an impending crisis makes no difference to the nature of our duty and our calling. The truth is that danger is always part of our environment in this fallen world; the presence of an obvious and immediate danger merely intensifies our awareness of this reality that we tend to ignore. Any one of us could meet death at any moment through an accident, an invisible blood clot, or by an act of a deranged gunman. An impending war such as that which Lewis and his students faced, or an impending battle that may be in our own future changes nothing. Our task as faithful stewards to God's calling is to keep to our duty—to be patient and watch, but also to keep on working.

We need not despair. As children of the living God, we live with continual hope. We work, we love, and we laugh and find joy because we always know that an end is coming. Whether the battle does or doesn't come in our lifetime changes nothing about the way we should live. Our own "end time" will come, and it could arrive at any moment. So our task is to keep on plugging along, faithfully fitting into the place where God put us as productive members of society.

I am convinced that God puts each one of us exactly where He wants us and gives each of us a task that advances His eternal plan in a particular way. Remember the words of Queen Esther's guardian Mordecai when she was afraid to face the deadly danger of appearing uninvited before the king to plead for her people: ". . . If you remain silent at this time, relief and deliverance will arise for the Jews from another place . . . And who knows whether you have not attained royalty for such a time as this?" (Esther 4:14 NASB). God raised up Esther at a particular time for a particular purpose. Today is the time God has ordained for you and me to be alive, and we are placed in our time and place with no less purpose than Esther. Your task may not be as grandiose as hers; you may not be called on to save your nation. But as Lewis said elsewhere in his speech to the Oxford undergraduates, "The work of a Beethoven and the work of a char-woman become spiritual on precisely the same condition, that of being offered to God, of being done humbly 'as to the Lord.'"[34]

You may wonder, *What's the point in keeping on doing my little insignificant job when such doom hangs over the world?* The point is that you are filling your role as an agent of God in this particular time, and your work may have a greater effect than you imagine. Few of us see the ultimate result of our actions. But by the power of the ripple effect, what you do either as a CEO or a salesclerk may join the current of God's intent and bring about His will in enormous ways you would never dream of. So it is vital that each of us takes our God-given tasks seriously. We must stick to our work, remain watch-ful, and patiently wait on the timing of the Lord.

Southern evangelist Vance Havner gives us the real key to keeping to our task and finding joy in the face of impending doom: "We are not just looking for something to happen, we are looking for Someone to come! And when these things begin to come to pass, we are not to drop our heads in discouragement, or shake our heads in despair, but we are to lift our heads in delight."[35]

THREE

Modern Europe . . . Ancient Rome

THE RED, STAMPED WORDS *TOP SECRET* GLARED OMINOUSLY from the manila envelope on the president's desk. The top government officials had been ordered to the Oval Office promptly at 8:00 a.m. Security was at its highest level; word must not leak out that the president of the United States, the vice president, the joint chiefs of staff, the National Security Council, congressional leaders, and selected members of the cabinet had been called for this executive briefing.

The president had never looked more serious. As the high officials and advisors assembled—men entrusted with decisions that could affect millions of lives—the president's face was ashen and grim. With his fingers pressed together under his chin, he looked as if he were praying. Considering the news he was about to share, his attitude was perfectly appropriate. When the group was assembled, he signaled to an armed guard, who opened a door to allow one more man to enter.

The man hesitated for a moment until the president pointed to a chair directly in front of the polished executive desk. The man took his seat before the leadership advisers of the most powerful nation on earth and awaited the president's signal.

"Gentlemen," the president said soberly, "prepare yourself to hear stunning news that will profoundly affect our nation and the future of the world as we know it. Listen carefully, for your very lives are at stake."[1]

This scene has not occurred exactly as described, yet it is not altogether fiction. It did occur at a different time in a different place with different players. And it may easily occur again in the near future. Let's begin by examining the time when it did occur—when one man, divinely moved to write the inspired words, accurately prophesied the rise and fall of empires and their rulers.

The Vision of the King

More than two thousand years ago, God gave His servant Daniel a vision of the future that we recognize as the most comprehensive prophetic insight ever given to man. While it was not uncommon for God to communicate to His own people through dreams and visions, it is astounding to realize that He gave this greatest vision of all time not only to Daniel, but also to a Babylonian king named Nebuchadnezzar, one of history's most wicked Gentile rulers.

Here is how that message came about. It was the second year of Nebuchadnezzar's rule over Babylon. Although the king was secure on his throne with all of his enemies subdued or in captivity, he nevertheless found himself in great anxiety about the future. His anxiety stemmed from a recurring dream sent to him by Almighty God—a vivid, nightmarish dream, and one he could not understand, though he sensed ominous implications within it. So the king called in his counselors. But since he had forgotten important details of the dream, he demanded that his brain trust not only interpret the nightmare, but that they also give him a vivid description of it.

The king's demand was unprecedented and, as you can imagine, his counselors thought it a bit unfair. When they could not meet his demand, Nebuchadnezzar, in a fit of pique, ordered the execution of all the wise men of Babylon (Daniel 2:12–13).

When the Jewish captive Daniel heard of the king's edict, he and his friends prayed to God for a vision of Nebuchadnezzar's dream and its interpretation. Then he went to the executioner and said, "Do not destroy the wise men of Babylon; take me before the king, and I will tell the king the interpretation" (v. 24).

Daniel soon found himself standing before Nebuchadnezzar, who asked him if he could reveal the meaning of his dream. Daniel explained that he could not, but he had connections with Someone who could: "The secret which the king has demanded, the wise men, the astrologers, the magicians, and the soothsayers cannot declare to the king. But there is a God in heaven who reveals secrets, and He has made known to King Nebuchadnezzar what will be in the latter days. Your dream, and the visions of your head upon your bed were these" (vv. 27–28).

As Daniel explained, just as God had sent the dream to Nebuchadnezzar, God had also revealed the dream and its interpretation to Daniel (v. 19). Then came the scene in Nebuchadnezzar's "oval office" as the Jewish prophet stood before the king and unfolded for him the future of his nation.

First Daniel described the king's vision:

"As for you, O king, thoughts came to your mind while on your bed, about what would come to pass after this; and He who reveals secrets has made known to you what will be . . . You, O king, were watching; and behold, a great image! This great image, whose splendor was excellent, stood before you; and its form was awesome. This image's head was of fine gold, its chest and arms of silver, its belly and thighs of bronze, its legs of iron, its feet partly of iron and partly of clay." (Daniel 2:29, 31–33)

The overarching purpose of this image was to teach Nebuchadnezzar, Daniel, and everyone else on the planet what happens when man puts himself in control. This vision gives us the history of human civilization, written not by Will Durant or Edward Gibbon, but by God Himself.

While the events Daniel unfolded may seem to come about by the power of kings and armies, he understood that the collapse and rise of empires is all God's doing: "*He* changes the times and the seasons; *He* removes kings and raises up kings; *He* gives wisdom to the wise and knowledge to those who have understanding" (Daniel 2:21, *emphasis added*).

Daniel then began to explain to Nebuchadnezzar that his dream was about the kingdoms of this world—his own kingdom and those that would succeed it. He told the king that the colossal metallic image represents four successive gentile world powers that would rule over Israel in the days ahead. The word *kingdom* is used ten times in these verses (vv. 36–45). Exactly what is a kingdom? It is the dominion that a king rules, or a "*king-dom*inion." It designates the people and territory under the rule of a single government. As Daniel was about to explain, the varied components of this statue represent the worldwide dominions that would follow and replace one another in the future.

The Four World Empires

Through Daniel, God gave King Nebuchadnezzar a composite history of the remaining days of the world. We know this because he spoke specifically of "days to come" and "things to come" (Daniel 2:28, 29 NIV).

He began to reveal the meaning of the dream of the statue in five sections: the head of gold, the breast and arms of silver, the belly and thighs of copper and brass, the legs of iron, and the feet . . . part iron, part clay.

The first world empire, represented by the statue's head of gold, was Nebuchadnezzar's own kingdom of Babylon. Daniel's words to the king are clear. "You, O king, are a king of kings. For the God of heaven has given you a kingdom, power, strength, and glory; and wherever the children of men dwell, or the beasts of the field and the birds of the heaven, He has given them into your hand, and has made you ruler over them all—you are this head of gold" (Daniel 2:37–38 NKJV).

Nebuchadnezzar would not have doubted that the head of gold referred to his kingdom since the chief deity of Babylon was Marduk, known as "the god of gold." The historian Herodotus described the image of Marduk as a dazzling sight—a golden statue seated upon a golden throne before a golden table and a golden altar. Pliny tells us that the robes of Marduk's priests were interlaced with gold.[2]

The second world empire revealed in the king's dream is represented by the image's chest of silver, from which two silver arms emerge (Daniel 2:32). This is the Medo-Persian Empire that conquered Babylon in 539 BC and remained in power for approximately two hundred years. We need feel no uncertainty about that interpretation because later, when Daniel reported the events surrounding the end of the Babylonian empire, he stated clearly that it would be the dual monarchy of the Medes and the Persians that would take control of Nebuchadnezzar's empire (Daniel 5:28). The two nations are again confirmed as Babylon's successor in Daniel 8:20.

The third world empire revealed within the image is represented by its belly and thighs of bronze. Daniel told the king it will be a "kingdom of bronze, which shall rule over all the earth" (Daniel 2:39). This is the empire of Greece, the kingdom of Phillip of Macedon and his famous son, Alexander the Great. Not only does history confirm Greece as the empire that succeeded the Medo-Persians, but Daniel himself affirmed it by naming Greece specifically in Daniel 8:21. Under Alexander, the Greek empire was unified and encompassed more territory than either of the previous empires. Alexander had such a lust for conquest that after subduing virtually all of the known world, he sat down and wept, fearing there were no more territories left to conquer. It is appropriate that this third kingdom is characterized by the bronze midsection of the massive image. Alexander's soldiers armored themselves in bronze and brass helmets and breastplates, and carried bronze and brass shields and swords.

The fourth empire displayed in the image is symbolized by its legs of iron. Daniel describes this empire as "strong as iron, inasmuch as iron breaks in pieces and shatters everything; and like iron that crushes, that kingdom will break in pieces and crush all the others" (2:40). History shows us clearly that Rome is the fourth kingdom. Not only was Rome the successor to the Greek empire, but the iron legs of the image provide a powerful symbol that characterizes the nature of the Romans. The word *iron* is used fourteen times in the text describing Rome in Daniel 2. Historians often use *iron* as an adjective when characterizing the Roman Empire: Rome's *iron hand*. Rome's *iron grip.* Rome's *iron rule.* Rome's *iron fist.* Rome's *iron heel.* Rome's *iron legions.*

History confirms the progression of Daniel's explanation of Nebuchadnezzar's dream. The Babylonians were overthrown by the Medo-Persians; the Medo-Persians were conquered by the Greeks; and when the Grecian empire was conquered by Rome, all of the lands and peoples of the previous kingdoms were assimilated into one kingdom known as the Roman Empire. This empire came into existence fifty years before Jesus was born, and it continued in power throughout the Lord's earthly ministry and beyond. It was Roman rule that put Jesus on the cross. It was the imperialistic Romans who ruled ruthlessly throughout the world during the early days of the church.

The fact that Rome is represented in the statue by its two iron legs is also significant, as the following quote explains:

By A.D. 395 the Roman Empire had split into two political areas of rule: the [Latin-speaking] West with its capital in Rome, and the [Greek-speaking] East with its capital in Constantinople (modern Istanbul, Turkey), which included the land of Israel. This division of the empire is depicted in the statue's two legs.

But this splitting of the mighty Roman Empire into two political units was not to be the last division that kingdom would suffer as Daniel explained to Nebuchadnezzar when he turned his attention to the statue's feet and toes. He noted that in the king's dream, the feet and toes were composed of a mixture of iron and clay. Though positioned at the bottom of the image, these extremities are apparently highly important, for Daniel said as much about the feet and toes as he had said about all the other parts of the image combined.

Here are Daniel's words as he explained to the king the meaning of
the material composing the image's feet:

"Whereas you saw the feet and toes, partly of potter's clay and partly
of iron, the kingdom shall be divided; yet the strength of iron shall be
in it, just as you saw the iron mixed with ceramic clay. And as the toes
of the feet were partly of iron and partly of clay, so the kingdom shall
be partly strong and partly fragile. As you saw iron mixed with
ceramic clay, they will mingle with the seed of men; but they will not
adhere to one another, just as iron does not mix with clay." (Daniel
2:41–43)

According to Daniel, there is to be yet another division in the
Roman Empire. Not a division of two, as indicated by the image's two
legs, but of ten, as symbolized by its ten toes. Daniel foretells a time
when the Roman Empire will consist of ten kingdoms or leaders. Since
the downward movement from one section of the statue to the next
represents the passage of time, the "feet and toes" stage must follow
the "legs" stage. But when we look back at the history that followed
Daniel's prediction, we find nothing in history that even remotely cor-
responds to a tenfold Roman coalition. That shows us that this fifth
and final feet-and-toes-stage kingdom is yet to come and is yet to perform its prescribed role in human history.

Daniel gives us one other piece of information that enables us to
understand the timing of the events conveyed in Nebuchadnezzar's
dream. He tells us that this final form of the Roman Empire will be
on the earth when God sets up His earthly kingdom. "And in the days
of these kings [the rulers of the ten segments of the Roman king-
dom], the God of heaven will set up a kingdom which shall never be

destroyed; and the kingdom shall not be left to other people; it shall break in pieces and consume all these kingdoms, and it shall stand forever" (Daniel 2:44).

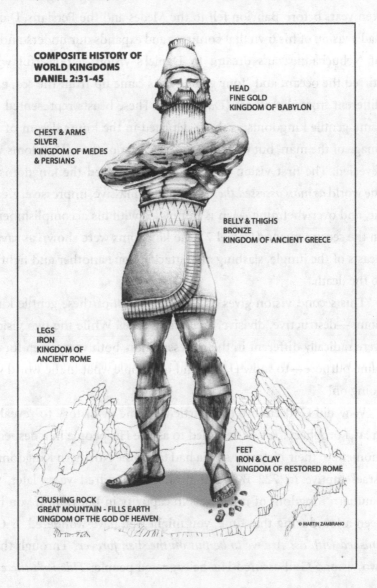

COMPOSITE HISTORY OF
WORLD KINGDOMS
DANIEL 2:31-45

HEAD
FINE GOLD
KINGDOM OF BABYLON

CHEST & ARMS
SILVER
KINGDOM OF MEDES
& PERSIANS

BELLY & THIGHS
BRONZE
KINGDOM OF ANCIENT GREECE

LEGS
IRON
KINGDOM OF
ANCIENT ROME

FEET
IRON & CLAY
KINGDOM OF RESTORED ROME

CRUSHING ROCK
GREAT MOUNTAIN - FILLS EARTH
KINGDOM OF THE GOD OF HEAVEN

© MARTIN ZAMBRANO

Daniel's Corroborating Dream

Years after Nebuchadnezzar's dream of the towering image and four-teen years before Babylon fell to the Medes and the Persians, Daniel had a vision of his own that confirms and expands our understanding of Nebuchadnezzar's dream. In Daniel's vision, a powerful wind stirred the ocean, and "four great beasts came up from the sea, each different from the other" (Daniel 7:3). These beasts represented the same gentile kingdoms as those depicted in the king's dream of the image of the man, but this time the character of those kingdoms was revealed. The first vision (Daniel 2) characterized the kingdoms of the world *as man assessed them*—majestic, massive, impressive, gigan-tic, and overwhelming. Man is impressed with his accomplishments. In the second vision (Daniel 7), the kingdoms were shown as savage beasts of the jungle, slashing and attacking one another and fighting to the death.

This second vision gives us *God's appraisal* of these gentile king-doms—destructive, divisive, angry, and cruel. While the two visions were radically different in their presentation, both were given for the same purpose—to show Daniel and his people what in the world was going on!

Why did God choose this particular time in history to reveal so great a prophecy? It was designed to assure His people in a desperate moment of their history. Assyria had taken the Northern Kingdom of Israel captive in 722 BC, and now, two hundred years later, the Southern Kingdom of Judah was in captivity in Babylon. If you had been a Jew during that time, you might well have wondered, *Is God finished with us? Are we to be put on the shelf forever?* Through these two visions, God assured His beleaguered people: *This isn't the end.*

There is a time in the future when I will once again be involved with you as a nation. But I want you to know what is going to happen between now and then.

Much of what was revealed to Daniel in these dreams has already happened. But not all of it. The three prophesied kingdoms have come and gone, and the fourth kingdom has also made its appearance in history. But Daniel's later vision included additional information about the future of the fourth kingdom not given to the Babylonian monarch—information about events that are yet in the future. Let's look at how Daniel describes it: "After this I saw in the night visions, and behold, a fourth beast, dreadful and terrible, exceedingly strong. It had huge iron teeth; it was devouring, breaking in pieces, and trampling the residue with its feet. It was different from all the beasts that were before it, and it had ten horns" (Daniel 7:7). Daniel is careful to explain that the ten horns are ten kings who shall arise from this kingdom (v. 24).

We know that this ten-kingdom prophecy of Daniel's remains in the future because not only has the ten-leader form of the Roman Empire never existed in history, but neither has such a kingdom been suddenly crushed as prophecy indicates it will be. According to Daniel 2, the Roman Empire in its final form will experience sudden destruction. The Roman Empire of Jesus' day did not end suddenly. It gradually deteriorated and declined over many centuries until the western part, the Holy Roman Empire, fell in AD 476, and the eastern part, the Byzantine Empire, fell in AD 1453. You can hardly imagine a more gradual slide from glory to oblivion! We must conclude, then, that some form of the Roman Empire must emerge in the end times, and according to Daniel, it will be in place prior to the coming of Christ to rule and reign over the earth.

The Rebirth of the Roman Empire

The future manifestation of the Roman Empire that Daniel prophesied twenty-five hundred years ago will take the form of a coalition or confederation of ten world leaders and will encompass the same territory as the historic Roman Empire. And today we can see that coalition taking shape right before our eyes! It began as early as 1930, when the French statesman Aristide Briand attempted to enlist twenty-six nations in what he first called "the United States of Europe" and modified to "the European Union." In his proposal he said, "The nations of Europe today must unite in order to live and prosper." The European press gave Briand's novel idea little attention, and nothing came of it.[4]

That is, nothing came of it *at that time*. But Briand's call for European unity was merely one world war ahead of the curve. Fewer than twenty years later, one of the world's most respected leaders issued the same call:

> In 1946, following the devastation of Europe during the Second World War, Winston Churchill forcefully asserted that "the tragedy of Europe" could only be solved if the issues of ancient nationalism and sovereignty could give way to a sense of European "national grouping." He said that the path to European peace and prosperity on the world stage was clear: "We must build a United States of Europe."[5]

Churchill's call initiated a series of steps toward unification; some were faltering, but others gained traction. The Benelux Conference of 1948, held in Brussels, Belgium, would lay the foundation for a new organization "to unite European countries economically and politically to secure a lasting peace."[6] Only three tiny nations attended the meeting—the Netherlands, Luxembourg, and Belgium. These nations came together because they saw unity as their only hope of survival in the postwar world.

Another step was taken in April 1951, when these three nations signed the Treaty of Paris with three additional nations, Germany, France, and Italy, forming a common market for coal and steel in an environment of peace and equality.

March 25, 1957, saw a major step toward European unification when the Treaty of Rome was signed on Capitoline Hill, one of the famous Seven Hills of Rome. On this occasion, Italy, France, and Germany joined the Netherlands, Luxembourg, and Belgium, creating the European Economic Community—the Common Market.

In 1973, the United Kingdom, Ireland, and Denmark joined the EEC, and Greece was added in 1981, making it a ten-nation confederation. On January 1, 1986, Spain and Portugal came into the union, and the agenda expanded beyond economics when the EEC officially adopted the goal of a politically unified Europe. In 1987 the Single European Act was implemented. With the fall of the Berlin Wall in 1989, Germany was reunified, and East Germany was integrated into the membership. In December 1992, the economic borders between the nations of the European community were removed, and a common passport was issued to travelers. Study in universities within the nations was also permitted without any restrictions. Austria, Finland, and Sweden joined the Union in 1995.

In 2002, eighty billion coins were produced for use in the twelve participating nations of the Eurozone, thus introducing the new monetary unit, the euro. Despite expected fluctuations, the rise in euro value has been steady and observable. The dollar is declining against the euro, and many experts believe that within five years the euro may actually replace the US dollar as the standard world currency. As we learned in the previous chapter, the Iranians have recently refused to accept the American dollar as payment for oil, requiring payment to be made in euro.

The march toward European unification continued on May 1, 2004, when Cyprus, the Czech Republic, Estonia, Hungary, Latvia, Lithuania, Malta, Poland, Slovakia, and Slovenia were added, bringing the total to twenty-five nations. These nations brought 75 million people into the European Union, expanding its population to 450 million people and surpassing North America as the world's biggest economic zone. In January 2007, Romania and Bulgaria were admitted to the EU, bringing the total number of nations to twenty-seven.[7]

While Israel was part of the original Roman Empire, it is not currently a part of the European Union. The EU considers Israel ineligible for membership due to human rights violations, based on its occupation of the West Bank, Gaza Strip, Golan Heights, and East Jerusalem. It has been proposed, however, that if Israel would sign a peace treaty with its hostile neighbors, it would be offered membership in the EU.[8]

Gradually yet steadily, the nations of Europe have come together, creating a modern replica of the ancient Roman Empire. Europe is more integrated today than at any time since the days of ancient Rome. The United States of Europe is considered by many to be the second most powerful political force in our world.

ROMAN EMPIRE
THEN & NOW

Old Roman Empire Outlined in Black
European Union Nations in Gray

FINLAND

SWEDEN

ESTONIA

DENMARK

LATVIA

LITHUANIA

IRELAND

ENGLAND

NETHERLANDS
LUXEMBOURG
BELGIUM

POLAND

GERMANY

CZECH

SLOVAKIA

AUSTRIA HUNGARY

SLOVENIA

FRANCE ITALY

ROMANIA

BULGARIA

SPAIN

PORTUGAL

GREECE

NORTHERN AFRICA

MALTA

CYPRUS

LIBYA

EGYPT

Consolidation of the European Government

Currently the EU government is organized into three bodies: a Parliament, the Council of European Union, and the European Commission. The Parliament is considered "the Voice of the People" because citizens of the EU directly elect its 785 members. The Parliament passes European laws in conjunction with the Council. Its president is elected to serve a five-year term.

The Council, "the Voice of the Member States," consists of twenty-seven members who are also the heads of their national governments. This body participates with Parliament in the passing of laws and also establishes common foreign policy and security policies. As I write this book, a Reform Treaty is currently in the ratification process. This treaty contains proposals for two major changes to the structure of the Council. First, it will reduce the membership of the Council from twenty-seven to seventeen and elect a full-time president for a two and a half-year extendable term, replacing the current rotating presidency, which changes every six months. These steps toward power consolidation may have very serious implications for the future.

The third body of EU government, the European Commission, consists of twenty-seven commissioners whose tasks are to draft new laws and implement policies and funding. Its president is nominated by the Council of European Union for a five-year term.[9]

Other EU governmental entities include: the Court of Justice, the Court of Auditors, the European Central Bank, and the European Investment Bank.[10]

Former British prime minister Tony Blair is rumored to be the likely candidate for Europe's first president of the Council. These rumors circulated as far back as 2002 and gained momentum in 2007 after Blair stepped down from his position as prime minister of Great Britain. French president Nicolas Sarkozy was the first leader to propose Blair for Europe's first president. In a speech given in January 2008, Sarkozy said this about Tony Blair:

> He is intelligent, he is brave and he is a friend. We need him in Europe. How can we govern a continent of 450 million people if the President changes every six months and has to run his own country at the same time? I want a President chosen from the top—not a compromise candidate—who will serve for two-and-a-half years.[11]

As we track these developments toward ever-increasing unity and more centralized power among the European nations, we can see a new empire in the making—an empire that occupies the same territory as the ancient Roman Empire. Turning back to Daniel for further insight into the nature of this rising coalition, we are intrigued by his description of it as a mixture of two noncohering materials. We already know that iron represented the strength of the old Roman Empire. In the newly constituted empire, however, the prophecy tells us that iron will be mixed with ceramic clay. Clay is nothing like the other materials that composed the image of Nebuchadnezzar's dream. Clay speaks of weakness and instability.

The best interpretation of this unstable mix is that the combination of clay and iron represents the diverse racial, religious, and political elements that will comprise this final form of the Roman Empire. That is, in fact, what we see today in the early manifestation of the European coalition. While the EU has great economic and political clout, the cultures and languages of its various countries are so incredibly diverse that it cannot hold together any more than iron and clay unless unity is imposed and enforced by an extremely powerful leader. As the EU prepares to elect a strong president for a longer term, we can see how an uneasy unity could come about.

The Need for Renewed Vigilance

From this brief study of modern Europe and ancient Rome, we can begin to understand the meaning of what is going on in the world today. Three things in particular emerge from our study that should increase our vigilance.

The Consolidation of World Power

Since the time of the Roman Empire, there has been no nation or empire with the power to govern or dominate the known world. But it is coming. In the future there will be a short period of time when the world will be unified under one dominant leader.

We saw in Daniel's second vision that the fourth beast had ten horns growing from its head. We need not wonder at the meaning of the beast and the ten horns, for the meaning of Daniel's dream was given directly to him: "The fourth beast shall be a fourth kingdom on earth, which shall . . . devour the whole earth, trample it and break it in pieces. The ten horns are ten kings who shall arise from this kingdom" (Daniel 7:23–24). The fourth beast represents the fourth successive kingdom after Babylon, which history identifies as the Roman Empire. But since Rome was never ruled simultaneously by ten kings, we know that those kings are yet to arrive on the stage of world history to rule a newly formed empire that overlays the territory of the ancient Roman Empire. Today the concentration of power in the European Union signals the beginning of this new world order.

The Coming of One World Leader

According to Daniel's prophecy, a supreme leader will rise from among the ten-leader confederacy in Europe. "And another shall rise after them; he shall be different from the first ones, and shall subdue three kings. He shall speak pompous words against the Most High, shall persecute the saints of the Most High, and shall intend to change times and law. Then the saints shall be given into his hand for a time and times and half a time" (Daniel 7:24–25). This leader will emerge from the group of ten to take control of the new European Union. He will become the final world dictator. We know him as the Antichrist, and we will have more to say about him in chapter 7. But the point we must not miss now is this: the new European Union is one of the conditional preludes to the coming of the Antichrist. As Arno Froese, executive director of Midnight Call Ministries, wrote:

> The new European power structure will fulfill the prophetic predictions which tell us that a one world system will be implemented. When established, it will fall into the hands of the Antichrist.[12]

And we can have little doubt that such a thing could easily happen when we see how glibly statesmen and politicians can gravitate to power. Paul-Henri Spaak, the first president of the UN General Assembly, first president of the European Parliament, and onetime secretary general of NATO, is credited with making this stunning statement:

> We do not need another committee. We have too many already. What we want is a man of sufficient stature to hold the allegiance of all people, and to lift us out of the economic morass into which we are sinking. Send us such a man and be he god or devil, we will receive him.[13]

Statements such as this should chill us to the bone. It shows that the world as a whole in its ignorance will actually embrace the power that will seek to enslave it. The European Union is the kindling awaiting the spark of the Antichrist to inflame the world with unprecedented evil. It is certainly a time to be vigilant.

The Condition for the Treaty with Israel

In the ninth chapter of Daniel's prophecy, he tells us of a treaty that will be signed between his people and the world leader who will head the realigned Roman Empire: "Then he shall confirm a covenant with many for one week; but in the middle of the week he shall bring an end to sacrifice and offering" (Daniel 9:27). Daniel tells us here that Israel will sign a treaty with the Antichrist, and that this treaty will be forged to last for a "week," literally in prophetic language, a "week of years," or seven years. This treaty will be an attempt to settle the Arab-Israeli controversy that today focuses the world's attention on the Middle East. After three and one-half years, that treaty will be broken, and the countdown to Armageddon will begin.

Heeding the Warning

The stage is now set in Europe for these events to occur. Israel is back in her land, oil is concentrating world focus on the Middle East, and the nations of the ancient Roman Empire are reunifying. Prophecies of events long predicted are coming to pass. I think any honest person must admit that something big is going on in the world. The prophecies of Daniel show us what it is: the hands on the prophetic clock are moving toward midnight. The warning has been sounded, and we will do well to heed it.

I live in San Diego, and these days the people of my area get a bit edgy as the end of October approaches. While most of the country is gathering frost on pumpkins, we are experiencing extreme heat, low humidity, and powerful winds—perfect conditions for devastating wildfires that devour everything in their path.

In 2003 we lived through the firestorm that consumed more than 390,000 acres of land, destroyed 2,430 homes, and inflicted $2.2 billion in property damage.[14] In October 2007, the National Weather Service issued a Red Flag Warning, indicating that conditions were ripe for another major wildfire. On Sunday, October 21, while we were worshipping in our first morning service, ominous billows of smoke began to rise from the backcountry, thirty-three miles away. When I walked out of church that morning, I could see the smoke, and the frightening images of 2003 returned to my mind.

The San Diego Fire Department, using a sophisticated new warning system called Reverse 9-1-1, sent phone messages to homes that were in harm's way. The messages were short and to the point: "This area, get out! This area, get out!" Thousands of San Diegans evacuated their homes, but as is always the case, some refused to leave.

In an attempt to protect their home, one father and his fifteen-year-old son chose to remain behind when the rest of their family evacuated. Two and a half hours into the fire, Capt. Ray Rapue of Cal Fire ordered them to evacuate the area immediately. The father got into his pickup truck, his son got on an ATV, and they started to leave their property. But for reasons unknown, when Fire Engine 3387 drove onto their property, both the father and his son turned around and went back to the house.

The captain again warned them to evacuate because of the dense smoke. The father jumped on the ATV with his son, but lack of oxygen caused the ATV to stall out. Then they both climbed into the fire engine and were warned to stay in the cab while the firefighters continued their work. Soon, depleted oxygen, intense heat, and choking smoke drove the firefighters to attempt their own escape. But the now-overloaded fire engine also stalled.

What happened next is called a *burnover*. Before the firefighters could deploy their tentlike emergency shelters inside the cab, the windows exploded from the heat of the fire advancing from the double-wide home. Fireman Brooke Linman was trying to comfort the panicked young man when voracious flames leapt into the cab. The boy let out a terrible scream as nearly half his body was severely burned. "He kept asking me if we were going to die," reported the fireman later. "I said, 'No, we're not going to die.'" The captain ordered the firefighters and the young man out of the burning cab, and they sought refuge behind large rocks on the property.

Overhead in a command airplane, CAL FIRE chief Ray Chaney reported hearing over his radio a primal scream from the ground below. "Ahhhh! Ahhhh! Ahhhh!" came the wrenching sound in plaintive, agonized spurts. Chief Chaney was able to guide a helicopter through the dense smoke to within a few feet of the trapped group. Two minutes later the helicopter lifted off with its cargo of the injured and quickly returned for the two others. All the rescued were then transported to a trauma center. The father died in that blaze. The son and four heroic fire personnel were severely burned. As I write this chapter five months later, the young man remains hospitalized.[15]

The Importance of Warnings

We will never know why this man and his son chose to disregard the repeated warnings, but the point came when all warnings were futile.

There was no longer any time to run. Living in the fire zone of Southern California has made me aware of the importance of warnings.

As I look at world events through the lens of God's prophetic Word, I have become acutely aware of the warning signs. But warnings are useful only if we heed them. As the prophetic clock moves toward its final strike, we must not wait until it's too late to move out of harm's way. The admonition of Paul to the Roman believers should spur us to action: "Knowing the time, that now it is high time to awake out of sleep: for now our salvation is nearer than when we first believed" (Romans 13:11).

Knowing the meaning behind the events we see in the daily news helps us to understand what is going on in the world. Today's headlines show the wisdom of Paul's warning—it is high time for us to awake out of sleep and realize that things will not continue to go on indefinitely as they are now. Indeed, as the signs from Daniel's prophecies show us, things are coming to a head. Events are moving us toward the moment when warnings will be too late, and we will be caught in the firestorm of a great evil that will trouble the world before Christ finally returns to set things right.

The question for you is, are you heeding the warnings? Are you prepared to stand before God? Have you accepted His offer of salvation? He is telling us by the events that surround us that the window of opportunity will soon be gone. Please do not wait until it is too late!

FOUR

Islamic Terrorism

GEORGES SADA WAS AN AIR FORCE GENERAL UNDER SADDAM Hussein. Though ethnically an Iraqi, he was not a Muslim but an Assyrian Christian. He refused to join the Baathist Party under Saddam, which blocked his ascent into the ranks of power. But he was a military hero, Iraq's top air force pilot, and the man Saddam called on to hear the truth about military matters because Saddam knew his yes-men would tell him only whatever he wanted to hear.

In his book, *Saddam's Secrets: How an Iraqi General Defied and Survived Saddam Hussein*, Sada speaks about the spreading impact of Islam around the world:

I'm often asked about militant Islam and the threat of global terrorism. More than once I've been asked about the meaning of the Arabic words *Fatah* and *Jihad*. What I normally tell them is that to followers of the militant brand of Islam, these doctrines express the belief that Allah has commanded them to conquer the nations of the world both by cultural invasion and by the sword. In some cases this means moving thousands

71

of Muslim families into a foreign land—by building mosques and
changing the culture from the inside out, and by refusing to assimilate
or adopt the beliefs or values of that nation—to conquer the land for
Islam. This is an invidious doctrine, but it's . . . being carried out in
some places today by followers of this type of Islam.[1]

Sada went on to warn Americans not to think that the Islamic
revolution is a Middle Eastern or European problem. Their ultimate
goal is conquest of the West and America:

[They] won't be stopped by appeasement. They are not interested in
political solutions. They don't want welfare—their animosity is not
caused by hunger or poverty or anything of the sort. They understand
only one thing: total and complete conquest of the West and of anyone who does not bow to them and their dangerous and out-of-date
ideology of hate and revenge.[2]

Americans do not seem to take the threat of Islam seriously. In
fact, the Pew Research Center tells us that US citizens are essentially
oblivious to the potential danger of radical Muslims. "According to
poll results issued recently, 58 percent of Americans indicated that
they knew either 'not very much' or 'nothing' about the Muslim religion, Islam . . . the fastest growing religion in America."[3]

According to Sada, Americans are particularly vulnerable to the
spread of militant Islam because our enemies take advantage of traits
that we consider socially positive:

What I want to say next is not easy for me to say but I think I must
say it anyway. One of the nicest things about the American people is

that you are generous and friendly people, and because of this you are sometimes naïve and overly trusting. You want to be friendly, so you open up to people and then you're surprised when they stab you in the back. Many brave young soldiers have died in Iraq for this reason, but I think this is also a big part of the problem with the State Department and others in government who fail to understand the true nature of this enemy.[4]

General Sada's book addresses a major phenomenon that is going on in our world today, and one that we all should want to know more about. The rise of radical Islam has changed the lives of everyone, especially since 9-11. We experience it every time we wait in an airport security line, every time we hear news reports of another terrorist bombing, and indeed, every time we turn on the news and hear reporters and commentators speak of how Islamic culture is growing in our own land. Most of us don't know how to respond. We hear on the one hand that Islam is a major threat to our world, and on the other that Muslims are greatly misunderstood and want nothing more than to be at peace with us. In this chapter I hope to show you what is going on in the world behind the headlines and give you information on how to understand and deal with the new rise of Islam.

Is Islam Militant or Peaceful?

Last year Fox News aired a special called "Radical Islam: Terror in Its Own Words," which revealed "the evil aims of radical Islam." The documentary included shocking clips from Islamic television, showing clerics and political leaders openly advocating attacks on the United States and Israel. The documentary also included programs shown on

Islamic TV in which young children sing of their desire to participate in violent *jihad* or to become suicide bombers. The program went on to show never-before-aired footage from a radical Islamic rally in California where the audience was told, "One day you will see the flag of Islam over the White House."[5]

More recently, al-Aqsa, the Hamas-owned television station in Gaza, aired a children's program in which a boy puppet sneaks into the White House, kills President George W. Bush with "the sword of Islam," and vows "the White House would be turned into a mosque."[6]

In the face of such reports as these, one of the most baffling and unsettling puzzles about Islam is the constant contention on the part of some Muslim leaders that they are a peace-loving people. Yet even as they make the claim, Islamic terrorists continue to brutally murder any person or group with whom they find fault. In his foreword to Don Richardson's book *The Secrets of the Koran*, former radical Shi'ite Muslim Reza F. Safa asked:

If Islam is a peaceful religion, then why did Mohammed engage in 47 battles? Why, in every campaign the Muslim armies have fought throughout history, have they slaughtered men, women and children who did not bow their knees to the lordship of Islam? The reign of terror of men such as Saddam, Khomeini, Ghadafi, Idi Amin and many other Muslim dictators are modern examples. If Islam is so peaceful, why are there so many verses in the Koran about killing the infidels and those who resist Islam? If Islam is peaceful, why isn't there even one Muslim country that will allow freedom of religion and speech? Not one! If Islam is peaceful, who is imparting this awful violence to hundreds of Islamic groups throughout the world who kill innocent people in the name of Allah?

But since the statehood of Israel . . . men such as Ghadafi and Osama bin Laden have been blowing the dust off the sword of a forceful world-invading religion.[7]

To get a handle on these two contradictory sides of Islam, it will help us to delve briefly into the history of how the religion came to be and what beliefs it holds today.

The History of Islam

In his book *The Age of Faith*, Will Durant wrote:

In the year 565 Justinian died, master of a great empire. Five years later Mohammed was born into a poor family in a country three quarters desert, sparsely peopled by nomad tribes whose total wealth could hardly have furnished the sanctuary of St. Sophia. No one in those years would have dreamed that within a century these nomads would conquer half of Byzantine Asia, all of Persia and Egypt, most of North Africa, and be on their way to Spain. The explosion of the Arabian peninsula into the conquest and conversion of half the Mediterranean world is the most extraordinary phenomenon of medieval history.[8]

The name *Islam* literally means *submission*. A Muslim is "one who submits to God." According to conservative estimates, there are about 1.5 billion Muslims in our world today. Approximately 1.4 million live in the United States, which is about 6 percent of the US adult population. While we usually associate Islam with the Middle East, the largest Muslim populations are actually in Asia.[9]

According to Islamic tradition, the founder of Islam, Mohammad, was born in Mecca (in present-day Saudi Arabia) in AD 570. Mecca was a thriving center of religious pilgrimage, filled with numerous temples and statues dedicated to the many gods the Arabian people worshipped at the time.

Mohammad's father died before the prophet was born, and his mother died when he was six years old. He was raised by his paternal grandfather, grew up to become a camel driver and then a merchant, and at the age of twenty-six, married a wealthy caravan owner named Khadija. Khadija was forty years old and had been divorced four times. In spite of her age, she and Mohammad had six children together.

Durant further noted, "Mohammad's son-in-law, Ali, described his father-in-law as being "of middle stature, neither tall nor short. His complexion was rosy white; his eyes black; his hair, thick, brilliant, and beautiful, fell to his shoulders. His profuse beard fell to his breast . . . There was such sweetness in his visage that no one, once in his presence, could leave him. If I hungered, a single look at the Prophet's face dispelled the hunger. Before him, all forgot their griefs and pains."[10]

Mohammad worked in professions that brought him into contact with a number of Christians and Jews who caused him to question the religion of his own people. He was forty years old and meditating in a cave outside Mecca when he received his first revelation. From that moment on, according to his testimony, God occasionally revealed messages to him, which he declared to the people. These messages, which Muhammad received throughout his life, form the verses of the Qu'ran, which Muslims regard as the divine word of God.

In the seventh-century Arabian world of Mohammad, the people worshipped more than 360 different gods, one for each day of the lunar year. One of these was the moon god, the male counterpart to the female sun god. The moon god was called by various names, one of which was Allah, and it was the favorite god of Mohammad's family. As Dr. Robert Morey explains, "The literal Arabic name of Muhammad's father was Abd-Allah. His uncle's name was literally Obied-Allah. These names . . . reveal the personal devotion that Muhammed's pagan family had to the worship of Allah, the moon god."[11]

As Mohammad began to promote his new religion, it was only natural that he would choose to elevate the moon god, Allah, and declare him to be the one true God. His devotion to Allah was single-minded and fierce, and in establishing and spreading his religion of Islam, Mohammad slaughtered thousands of people who resisted conversion. As his instructions to his followers show, there was no subtlety in his evangelistic technique. Abd El Schafi, an expert on ancient Muslim scholarship, informs us: "One of Muhammad's popular claims is that God commanded him to fight people until they became Muslims . . . All Muslim scholars without exception agree on this."[12]

Opposition in Mecca forced Mohammad and his followers to flee to Medina in AD 620, where he became the head of the first Muslim community. In AD 631 he returned to Mecca, where he died the following year. At his death, the Islamic community became bitterly divided over the question of who would be Mohammad's successor. Even today that division survives in the two Islamic sects, now known as Shi'ite and Sunni. Conflict between these sects is one of the major stress points in Iraq and throughout the Islamic world.

At the death of Mohammad, the group we know as the Sunni followed the leadership of Abu Bakr, Mohammad's personally chosen successor. The Sunni now comprise about 90 percent of the Islamic world. They believe that Muhammad's spiritual gifts died with him and that their only authority today is the Qu'ran. The Baath party of Saddam Hussein was part of the Sunni sect.

The Shi'ites maintained that Mohammad passed on a legacy of personal authority in addition to the Qu'ran, called the Hadith, as author Winfried Corduan explains:

> The Shi'ites, on the other hand, identified with Muhammad's son-in-law Ali, whom they saw as possessing a spiritual endowment directly from the prophet. The Shi'ites believe that their leaders, the imams, have authority on par with the Qu'ran. It is the Shi'ites that believe that the Twelfth Imam went into concealment hundreds of years ago and continues to live there until he returns as the Mahdi . . . the Muslim Messiah![13]

When Abu Bakr succeeded Mohammad, he and his successors launched *jihads* (or holy wars) that spread the religion of Islam from northern Spain to India and threatened Christian Europe. Christians resisted the threat, and a series of wars followed that drove the Islamic invaders back into the Middle Eastern countries, where they still dominate. Their zeal to have their religion dominate the world has not diminished, however, and it remains a threat to all who do not maintain vigilance.

The Habits of Islam

Sunni Muslims mandate five acts of worship, which are frequently referred to as the five pillars of Islam. Shi'ite Muslim worship comprises eight ritual practices, but these overlap and encompass the same five pillars of Islam as practiced by the Sunni. The five pillars are as follows:[14]

1. *To recite the* Shahadah: The *Shahadah* is the Islamic creed, "There is no god but Allah, and Muhammad is his messenger." Its recitation is the duty of every Muslim.

2. *To pray* (*salat*): Muslims pray while bowing toward Mecca five times each day: in the early morning, in the early and late afternoon, at sunset, and an hour after sunset.

3. *To fast* (*sawm*): Muslims refrain from food during the daylight hours throughout the lunar month of Ramadan. This month is to be given over to meditation and reflection, and it ends with a joyous celebration.

4. *To give alms* (*zakat*): Muslims are required to give 2.5 percent (one-fortieth) of their income to the poor and those in need. They may give more as a means of gaining further divine reward, but the 2.5 percent is an obligatory minimum. The percentage is based on the amount of accumulated wealth or income held for a lunar year above a minimum of three ounces of gold.

5. *To make the pilgrimage* (*hajj*): Those physically and financially able must visit Mecca at least once during their lifetime. The journey usually takes at least a week and includes many stops at other holy sites along the way.

The Hatred of Islam

No doubt the most frightening word associated with Islam is *jihad*. Sometimes called the "sixth pillar" of Islam, *jihad* actually means "struggle." The "Greater Jihad" is the inner struggle of each Muslim to submit to Allah. The "Lesser Jihad" is the outward struggle to defend the Islamic community. This is the jihad that strikes fear in the hearts of any who reject radical Islam. These Muslims take jihad to mean violent defense of Islam; to them it authorizes the expansion of the Islamic religion even by means of deadly aggression.

The overt hatred for the West expressed in jihad has already spawned many mortal attacks, and the fanaticism that produced them has not diminished. In her book, completed days before her assassination, former prime minister of Pakistan Benazir Bhutto wrote that one of the primary aims of the militants is:

> . . . to provoke a clash of civilizations between the West and . . . Islam. The great hope of the militants is a collision, an explosion between the values of the West and what the extremists claim to be the values of Islam . . . The attacks on September 11, 2001, heralded the . . . dream of bloody confrontation . . . if the fanatics and extremists prevail . . . then a great *fitna* (disorder through schism or division) would sweep the world. Here lies their ultimate goal: chaos.[15]

The hatred that the Muslims have for the Jews needs no documentation. But the settlement of Israel into her homeland in 1948 took this hatred to a level of murderous fury. The militants and radicals refer to Israel as "little Satan," and the United States as "big Satan," and they are determined to wipe both countries off the map.

While the majority of the world's 1.5 billion Muslims want no part of this deadly violence and attempt to live in peace with their neighbors, the number of radicals who preach violence and terror is mushrooming around the world. Experts say that 15 to 20 percent of Muslims are radical enough to strap a bomb on their bodies in order to kill Christians and Jews. If this number is accurate, it means about three hundred million Muslims are willing to die in order to take you and me down.

To get a picture of how bitterly Islam hates Jews and Christians, one has only to listen to the speeches of their clerics and leaders. Recently, Sheikh Ibrahim Mdaires delivered a sermon at a mosque in the Gaza Strip that was broadcast live to the Arab world. The text of that sermon has circulated around the globe. It represents the alarming doctrines and attitudes being taught and preached in many mosques and Islamic schools.

With the establishment of the state of Israel, the entire Islamic nation was lost, because Israel is a cancer . . . The Jews are a virus resembling AIDS, from which the entire world suffers. You will find that the Jews were behind all the civil strife in this world. The Jews are behind the suffering of the nations . . . We [the Muslims] have ruled the world before, and by Allah, the day will come when we will rule the entire world again. The day will come when we will rule America. The day will come when we will rule Britain and the entire world—except the Jews. The Jews will not enjoy a life of tranquility under our rule, because they are treacherous by nature, as they have been throughout history. The day will come when everything will be relieved of the Jews . . . Listen to the Prophet Muhammad, who tells you about the evil that awaits the Jews. The stones and trees will want the Muslims to finish off every Jew.[16]

If this diatribe does not give you reason enough to believe that Islam is the enemy of America and Christianity, consider that today, as I write these words, there is not a single one of the fifty-five predominately Muslim nations on earth today where Christians are not persecuted. As General Sada warned, we cannot afford to relax our vigilance in the name of naïve tolerance and multiculturalism.

The Hopes of Islam

Speeches like that of Mdaires show us that radical Islam has a vision of its future that does not bode well for those who stand in the way. To get a better understanding of this vision, we will now look briefly at some of the goals the Islamic world hopes to achieve.

Islam Hopes to Rule the World

In his book *Secrets of the Koran,* Don Richardson tells the chilling story of Islam's plan to gain political and religious control of the entire world:

> The world needs to be warned. At least 40 million Muslim youth in the Muslim world's religious schools, called madrasas, are avidly memorizing the entire Koran plus a generally extremist body of related traditions—the hadiths . . . These schools are breeding grounds for potential terrorists . . . Hatred for Jews and Christians (largely synonymous with Israel and America) and general disdain for all non-Muslims . . . are deeply instilled . . . Simply put, 40 million trainees in Muslim madrasas are a societal nuclear bomb.
>
> Consider this from professor Mochtar Buchori, a member of the Indonesian Parliament: If we add all the universities, colleges, high schools, junior high schools, and elementary schools in the United States, we find that the total is about 24,000 institutions. Yet Buchori counts 37,362 Muslim madrassas in Indonesia, alone! Of these only 8 percent have any input from Indonesia's government. In 92 percent, the teaching agenda is controlled by Muslim clerics.[17]

Traditionally in the United States, Arabic language courses have been taught only at universities, mosques, and Islamic schools. But that has recently changed. In September 2006, Carver Elementary School, a publicly financed K–8 school in San Diego, absorbed into its enrollment about one hundred students from a defunct charter school serving mostly Somali Muslims. To accommodate the special religious customs of the Muslim children, the administration formed, in effect, an Islamic school within an American school. Accommodations included adding courses in the Arabic language, modifying the cafeteria menu in accordance with Islamic dietary restrictions, providing gender-separated classes, and establishing an afternoon recess allowing for the Islamic prayer specified for that time of the day—all at an additional cost to the school district of $450,000!

Just when Carver was becoming comfortable with this arrangement, a substitute teacher observed that the afternoon Muslim prayer was being led by an employee of the school district. The sub reported the apparent "indoctrination" of students to Islam at a public session of the school board. Investigations began into the accommodations and the apparent double standard that bans Christianity from public institutions and yet accommodates "an organized attempt to push public conformance with Islamic law."[18]

Here we see General Sada's warning played out in tangible form. We Americans want to be nice. We want to accommodate. We want to believe that if we are tolerant of others, they will reciprocate. We tend to forget the general's warning that militant Muslims don't think that way, and each inch we give in the name of accommodation, they will take in the name of conquest.

It is one thing to read about Muslim determination to take over the world; it is quite another to watch it happening right before our eyes, as it is in Europe. The most startling and underreported social migration of our age is the Islamification of Europe, which has great bearing on the territories of the old Roman Empire that we discussed in the previous chapter. Tony Blankley of the *Washington Times* devoted his book, *The West's Last Chance*, to sounding an alarm about this Islamic infiltration. This is how he sees this threat to Western culture:

> In much of the West, and particularly in Europe, there is blind denial that radical Islam is transforming the world. Most Europe elites and far too many American politicians and journalists believe that our challenges are business and politics as usual. They are sheep who cannot sense the wolf pack in the woods . . . The threat of the radical Islamists taking over Europe is every bit as great to the United States as was the threat of the Nazis taking over Europe in the 1940s. We cannot afford to lose Europe. We cannot afford to see Europe transformed into a launching pad for Islamist jihad . . .
>
> The moral threat we face comes not merely from Osama bin Laden and a few thousand terrorists. Rather, we are confronted with the Islamic world—a fifth of mankind—in turmoil, and insurgent as it has not been in at least five hundred years, if not fifteen hundred years. The magnitude of this cultural upheaval cannot yet be measured . . . To point out the obvious, the resurgence of a militant Islam drove America to fight two wars in Muslim countries in two years, disrupted America's alliance with Europe, caused the largest reorganization of the American government in half a century (with the creation of the Department of Homeland Security), changed election results in Europe, and threatened the stability of most of the governments in the Middle East.[19]

We can easily see and resist the effects of jihad in militant terrorism, but we have trouble seeing and resisting the more subtle strategy that the Muslims call *fatah*. *Fatah* is infiltration, moving into a country in numbers large enough to affect the culture. It means taking advantage of tolerant laws and accommodative policies to insert the influence of Islam. In places where a military invasion will not succeed, the slow, systematic, and unrelenting methods of *fatah* are conquering whole nations. Two illustrations are instructive, the first concerning France:

What we're seeing in many places is a "demographic revolution." Some experts are projecting that by the year 2040, 80 percent of the population of France will be Muslim. At that point the Muslim majority will control commerce, industry, education, and religion in that country. They will also, of course, control the government, as well, and occupy all the key positions in the French Parliament. And a Muslim will be president.[20]

Islamification is also happening in England, but the Muslims there are not waiting for further population growth to institute *fatah*. They are advancing their goal of dominance by taking advantage of the British policy of pluralistic tolerance. An example occurred in September 2006 when the British home secretary, John Reid, gave a speech to Muslim parents in east London, encouraging them to protect their children from pressure to become suicide bombers. A robed and turbaned fundamentalist Muslim leader who had lavishly praised the suicide bombers of the horrific attack on London's transportation system was in the audience. He got up and shouted the speaker down. He ranted at the home secretary for five minutes, shouting, "How dare you come to a Muslim area? . . . I am furious. I am absolutely furious—John Reid should not come to a Muslim area." Muslims are not only immigrating massively to western countries but also claiming entitlement to keep their settlements off-limits to native citizens. The "ghettoization" of London into "non-Muslim no-go zones" is an ongoing controversy in the British press.[21]

Earlier this year in the city of Oxford—where Hugh Latimer, Nicholas Ridley, and Thomas Cranmer were martyred for their Christian faith and the famous Oxford Movement began—the seven hundred members of a mosque, which is valued at two million British pounds, petitioned "for their right as British citizens to practice their faith." What right did they demand? The right to broadcast a two-minute *adhan*—the Muslim call to prayer—from the mosque minaret three times a day. The amplified call would be heard a mile or more away, meaning the volume would disrupt the lives of countless non-Muslims. One Oxford University professor summed up the controversy in this way: "It's not a matter of people's right to religious freedom, it's about making Islam the religion of public space."[22]

In early 2008, England's archbishop of Canterbury, Rowan Williams, gave the world a stunning example of General Sada's claim of Western naiveté concerning Islamic intentions. Williams told a BBC correspondent that the growing Islamic population in Britain made it expedient to be accommodative. He said "the UK had to face up to the fact" that it "seems unavoidable" that Islam's legal system, *sharia* law, will be "incorporated into British law." His term for this blending of laws was "constructive accommodation."[23] *Sharia* law, derived from the Qu'ran and teachings of Muhammad, is the legal system by which Muslims are to live. In the West, the law is fairly benign and deals mainly with family and business. But in Muslim countries it can include such things as "honor killings" in cases of suspected immorality.

Some foresee the incorporation of *sharia* into English law as a fatal blow to the historic Christianity of England. A recent Church of England General Synod survey reported that "63 percent fear that the Church will be disestablished within a generation, breaking a bond that has existed between the Church and State since the Reformation."[24] The controversy is not merely about allowing religious freedom, but rather about how intrusive a tolerant nation should allow an immigrant religion to be.

You may hear other terms used to describe the Islamic goal of world domination. For example, "biological jihad" or "demographic jihad" describes the nonviolent strategy of Muslims moving into Europe and the West and having more babies than their hosts. Within several generations they hope to repopulate traditionally Christian cultures with their own people, and they are certainly on track to reach that goal. According to a Vatican report issued recently, the Roman Catholic Church understands this: "For the first time in history, we are no longer at the top: Muslims have overtaken us."[25]

Islam Hopes to Return Its Messiah

This Islamic hope surfaced in a speech by Iranian president Mahmoud Ahmadinejad, a disciple of Ayatollah Khomeini, the cleric who launched the successful 1979 revolution that turned Iran into a strict Islamic state. In 2005, Ahmadinejad was called before the United Nations Security Council to explain his continued determination to develop nuclear weapons. He began his speech by declaring: "In the Name of the God of Mercy, Compassion, Peace, Freedom and Justice . . ." and ended his speech with this prayer: "I pray to you to hasten the emergence of your last repository, the promised one, that perfect and pure human being, the one that will fill this world with justice and peace."[26] The "promised one" in Ahmadinejad's prayer was a reference to the Twelfth Imam, a figure in Shi'ite teaching that parallels the figure of Al-Mahdi in Sunni teaching. In essence, both of these titles refer to the Islamic messiah who is yet to come.

Shi'ia Islam believes that the Twelfth Imam can appear only during a time of worldwide chaos. This explains many of Ahmadinejad's defiant actions—why he presses forward with his nuclear program in spite of world censure and why he is adamant about destroying Israel. In an infamous speech in Tehran on October 25, 2005, he said, "Israel must be wiped off the map," and he warned leaders of Muslim nations who recognized the state of Israel that they would "face the wrath of their own people."[27] With these defiant and divisive actions, Ahmadinejad is fomenting the chaotic environment that he believes will induce the Islamic messiah to come. In a televised speech in January 2008, Ahmadinejad reiterated: "What we have right now is the last chapter . . . Accept that the life of Zionists will sooner or later come to an end."[28] On March 14, 2008, Ahmadinejad "swept the nationwide ballot with about 70 percent support."[29]

The world as a whole seems to be starting to take Ahmadinejad seriously, but the people of Israel are totally convinced. They understand that he is determined to destroy them. And the prophet Ezekiel backs up that understanding. He tells us that the hatred Iran bears (Iran being the current name of the biblical Persia) toward the Jewish nation will play an important role in a major end-time battle. John Walvoord summarizes the scenario:

The rise of Islamic terror is setting the stage for the events in Ezekiel 38–39. These chapters prophesy an invasion of Israel in the end times by a vast coalition of nations, all of whom are Islamic today except Russia. Israel has said that a new "axis of terror"—Iran, Syria, and the Hamas-run Palestinian government—is sowing the seeds of the first world war of the twenty-first century. The rise of Islam, and especially radical Islamic terrorism, strikingly foreshadows Ezekiel's great prophecy.[30]

Even though the hope for an Islamic messiah is surely futile, the chaos radical Islamic leaders are creating to bring about that hope is all too real and deadly. So deadly that much of the biblical prophecies concerning the end times will be brought about by the beliefs and actions of radical Islam. And we are beginning to feel the pressure of those impending events in the rise and rapid spread of Islamic radicalism in our own time.

Responding to the Islamic Threat

How are we responding to the rise of Islamic radicalism? Not too well, I fear. On the whole, those who shape our culture and policies seem to bear out General Sada's observation that we "fail to understand the true nature of this enemy." In our rush to be democratic, tolerant, and inclusive, we are inadvertently accommodating the radical agenda of Islamic conquest. We must stop being deceived about this threat. We must stand our ground and affirm truths that many seem all too willing to give up in the name of tolerance and accommodation. If you are looking for a beginning place, here are two truths on which I see much confusion today. It is critical that we affirm these truths to maintain a clear understanding of the vast chasm between Christianity and Islam.

"Allah" Is Not Another Name for the God of the Bible

In mid-August 2007, Fox News instigated a blogger's field day when it reported that seventy-one-year-old Dutch Catholic Bishop

Muskens of Breda "wants everyone to call God 'Allah.'" Fox quoted from Muskens's interview on a Dutch TV program in which he said, "Allah is a very beautiful word for God. Shouldn't we all say that from now on, we will call God 'Allah'?" The bishop further added, "What does God care what we call him?" Fox's Roman Catholic news analyst disagreed with the bishop, stating, "Words and names mean things. Referring to God as Allah means something."[31]

Indeed they do! As journalist Stan Goodenough reminded his *Jerusalem Newswire* readers, in the name of Allah, people hijack planes and use them to wreak unspeakable devastation, blow themselves up in crowded public venues to annihilate innocent people, and in the name of Allah, "millions of people pray for the destruction of Israel and the United States." Goodenough observed that when God introduced Himself to Moses, He gave His name as YHWH—Jehovah. He went on to say, "He also has many other names describing aspects of His nature and character. 'Allah' is not one of them."[32]

Bishop Muskens surely knows the biblical names for God, so what was he thinking when he urged Christians to call God Allah? As he explained, "If Muslims and Christians address God with the same name, this contributes to harmonious living between both religions."[33] When Islamic leaders heard this, their mosques must have rung with the slaps of high fives. Their policy of *fatah* was working beautifully. And they must have ascended into unspeakable ecstasies when the spokesman for the Council on American-Islamic Relations immediately embraced Muskens's proposal, saying, "It reinforces the fact that Muslims, Christians and Jews all worship the same God."[34]

We hear this appalling claim often these days, but nothing could be farther from the truth. Allah and God are emphatically not the same! To claim otherwise is nothing short of a slander against the one true God. As Hal Lindsey explains:

The doctrine of Satan is that all religions are equally valid, that all paths lead to God, that God is impersonal, unknowable, and it is therefore irrelevant to Him what we call Him or how we worship Him. If Allah and God are one and the same, then wouldn't the worship of the Hindu chief gods, Vishnu and Shiva, also be the worship of Allah and God, only by a different name? Pretty soon, everybody is God ... Which is the same as saying that nobody is.[35]

The God of the Bible and the Allah of the Qu'ran are nothing alike. The differences are vast and allow no possibility of synthesis. The God of the Bible is knowable. According to the Qu'ran, Allah is so exalted that he cannot be known. The God of the Bible is a personal being with intellect, emotion, and will. Muslim theology tells us Allah is not to be understood as a person. The God of the Bible is a spirit. To Muslims, such a thought is blasphemous and demeaning to Allah. The God of the Bible is one God in three persons. The Qu'ran denies the Trinity and views it as a major heresy. The God of the Bible is a God of love. Allah does not have emotional feelings toward man. The God of the Bible is a God of grace. According to the Qu'ran, there is no savior or intercessor. Clearly the God of the Bible and Allah are not at all the same and should never be equated with one another![36]

The Qu'ran Is Not a Divine Book on Par with the Bible

Just as many say the God of the Bible and Allah are the same, many also say that we should consider the Qu'ran to be on the same level as the Bible. Actually, the Muslims believe the Qu'ran to be the mother of all books and the Bible as subservient to it. A comparison of the two books will show the absurdity of such a claim. The Bible is a masterpiece of cohesion, depth, literate quality, and consistency. God inspired more than 40 men over a period of 1,400 years to write the God-breathed words that carry His unified message from Genesis to Revelation (2 Timothy 3:16).

The Qu'ran, on the other hand, is a self-contradicting book supposedly given by the angel Gabriel to Mohammad. Since Mohammad could neither read nor write, the sayings were translated and collected from the memories of those who had heard him.

Objective readers who have read both the Bible and the Qu'ran are immediately able to tell the difference between the quality and comprehensibility of the two books. Historian Edward Gibbon (1737–1794) is an example of such a reader. He could hardly be accused of being a Christian, yet he described the Qu'ran as "an incoherent rhapsody of fable, and precept, and declamation, which sometimes crawls in the dust, and sometimes is lost in the clouds."[37]

Muslims Are Not Beyond the Reach of God's Grace

Recently I saw a bumper sticker that made me stop and consider. It read, "Have You Prayed for Osama Bin Laden Today." I must admit I had not. Yet Peter reminds us that "the Lord is . . . not willing that any should perish but that all should come to repentance" (2 Peter 3:9). I am absolutely certain that the "any" of this verse includes Muslims. We may find it hard to pray for avowed enemies who threaten our destruction, but one of the characteristics of Christlikeness given by Jesus Himself is to "love your enemies, bless those who curse you, do good to those who hate you, and pray for those who spitefully use you and persecute you" (Matthew 5:44). I believe that includes Osama bin Laden and his radical Islamic counterparts.

We have good evidence that such prayers are effective. Through the miracle of satellite delivery, our weekly television program, *Turning*

Point, is now available in almost every Arab country. We routinely get e-mail and letters from individuals who have come to Christ through the ministry of God's Word beamed into their lives via satellite TV. Recently we received a letter from an Arab country. The writer told us that he had accepted Christ into his heart and expressed great gratitude for the encouragement of God's truth. A note at the bottom of the letter pleaded with us not to send any materials to his address. That postscript made us vividly aware of the courage it takes for a Muslim in an Islamic country to confess Christ as Savior.

God is at work in the Islamic world. We have reports that many Muslims are being confronted with the gospel in their dreams. Here is the testimony of one Saudi Arabian who was born close to Mecca and grew up going to the mosque five times a day. For many nights he had a terrifying nightmare in which he was being taken down into hell. This dream, always vivid and horrifying, destroyed the man's peace night after night. Suddenly one evening, Jesus appeared in his dream and said, "Son, I am the way, the truth, and the life. And if you would give your life to Me, I would save you from the hell that you have seen."

This young man knew something of Jesus from the distorted teachings of the Qu'ran, but he didn't know the Jesus of the New Testament. So he began searching for a Christian who could help him. Since Christianity is banned in Saudi Arabia, and a Christian caught witnessing to a Muslim could be beheaded, the young man's search took time. But the Lord eventually led him to an Egyptian Christian who gave him a Bible. He began reading, and when he got into the New Testament, he was moved to give his life totally to Jesus Christ.

Soon afterward, an opponent of the young man discovered his conversion and accused him of being a Christian. The authorities arrested and imprisoned him. In jail, he was tortured and eventually sentenced to death by beheading. But on the morning of his scheduled execution, no one showed up to escort him from the cell. Two days later the authorities threw open his cell door and screamed at him: "You demon! Get out of this place!"[38]

The man learned later that his execution had not taken place because on the very day he was to be beheaded, the son of his accuser had mysteriously died. The new Christian is now quietly working to bring other Muslims to faith in Christ.

In this chapter we have explored one of the unsettling events that is going on in today's world—the rising threat of radical Islam. In the true story I related above, we have the key to the Christian response to this threat. As Abraham Lincoln said, "The best way to destroy an enemy is to make him a friend." The best way to counter the threat of Islam is to make Christians out of Muslims. I don't claim that this will turn away prophecies of events sure to come, but it does give you a role in the drama to be played. Our prayers, our testimonies, our love and care for our Islamic neighbors may not turn the inevitable tide for the world, but they can turn the tide for individuals and allow them to escape the wrath to come. And that is definitely worth doing.

FIVE

Vanished Without a Trace

ONE OF THE MORE POPULAR CBS TV SHOWS IS THE FICTIONAL drama *Without a Trace*. It is set in New York City's special FBI missing persons unit. Each episode is devoted to finding one missing person, and, usually, one of the agents assigned to the case develops a strong emotional interest that carries the story along. In reality, the FBI has no dedicated missing persons unit; investigations into disappearances are assigned to agents on a case-by-case basis. At the end of each episode, however, the show does touch on reality by providing public service information to help the FBI locate real-life missing persons.

Another TV show built on the theme of missing persons was the Fox Broadcasting drama *Vanished*. The plotline centered on a Georgia senator whose wife apparently vanished into thin air. That series failed to attract enough viewers to survive the season, provoking anger among those who had become hooked when the thirteen aired episodes never resolved the mystery.

And mystery is exactly what the word *vanished* implies. Headlines about people who vanish rivet our attention: "Relatives Wait for Word of Vanished Sailors"; "Man Vanishes After Concert"; "Search Continues for Woman Who Vanished"; "Police Say Man Vanished Without a Trace." We read such headlines with eerie wonder: *What could have happened to the missing person? How could he have simply been there one moment and not the next?*

According to the Bible, a time is coming when this very thing will happen on a massive, global scale. A day is coming when a billion people will suddenly vanish from the face of the earth without a trace! And when that event occurs, calling in the FBI will be of no use. A TV series based on the mystery would never have a conclusion, for these vanished people will never again be seen until the Lord Himself returns. What will this worldwide phenomenon be like? That is a question in the minds of many who—through popular novels, sermons, or religious writings—have heard of this event but don't understand it. They know that Christians call it the Rapture, yet they have little idea what it means or what in the world is going on that could bring it about. In this chapter I will seek to resolve this common confusion.

The Great Disappearance

Some of us are familiar with massive evacuations, which leave large areas empty and desolate, as if their inhabitants had simply vanished. As I mentioned in a previous chapter, I pastor a church located in the fire zone of Southern California. In October 2007, we witnessed the largest evacuation of homes in California history, and the largest evacuation for fire in United States history. Emergency personnel evacuated 350,000 homes, displacing 1 million Californians as sixteen simultaneous fires swept through our community.[1]

Imagine a person who missed the call to evacuate, waking up after everyone was gone and stumbling through the acrid smoke and empty streets, confused and amazed, wondering why he had been left behind. That person's reaction would be nothing compared to the shock of those who witness the coming worldwide evacuation.

The Bible tells us that on that day, millions of people will disappear from the face of the earth in less than a millisecond. And the purpose of that evacuation is similar to that of the emergency evacuation of Southern Californians: to avoid horrific devastation. This evacuation will remove God's people from the disastrous effects of coming earthquakes, fire, and global chaos. As Bruce Bickel and Stan Jantz explain, the evacuation itself will create considerable chaos and destruction:

Jumbo jets plummet to earth as they no longer have a pilot at the controls. Driverless buses, trains, subways, and cars will cause unimaginable disaster. Classrooms will suddenly be without teachers . . . Doctors and nurses seem to abandon their patients in the middle of surgical operations, and patients will vanish from operating tables. Children disappear from their beds. People run through the streets looking for missing family members who were there just moments ago. Panic grips every household, city and country.[2]

Attempting to put realism into this event for my first youth group as a fledgling pastor, I utilized the idea of an imaginary newspaper covering the recent Rapture. The lead article read:

At 12:05 last night a telephone operator reported three frantic calls regarding missing relatives. Within fifteen minutes all communications were jammed with similar inquiries. A spot check around the nation found the same situation in every city. Sobbing husbands sought information about the mysterious disappearance of wives. One husband reported, "I turned on the light to ask my wife if she remembered to set the clock, but she was gone. Her bedclothes were there, her watch was on the floor . . . she had vanished!" An alarmed woman calling from Brooklyn tearfully reported, "My husband just returned from the late shift . . . I kissed him . . . he just disappeared in my arms."

These two descriptions of the coming disappearance are quite disturbing. Considering the devastation, loss, grief, and confusion the event will cause, it may seem strange that it is called the Rapture. According to my online dictionary, the word *rapture* means "an expression or manifestation of ecstasy or passion," and "being carried away by overwhelming emotion."[3] Everyone wants that kind of euphoric delight, which is why marketing experts have made *rapture* a popular term in today's culture.

There's a perfume called Rapture, and also a well-known New York City-based rock band. Many novels and movies carry the word *rapture* in their titles. A concert-promoting agency calls itself Planet Rapture. One sporting goods company even sells a set of golf clubs called Rapture! The world is looking for rapture, so marketers offer it everywhere.

So why would Christians use *Rapture*, of all terms, to denote a chaotic event when a billion people will suddenly disappear from the earth? The word *Rapture* is the Latin version of a phrase the Bible uses to describe the catching away of all Christians before the end times.

The focus is on looking at the event not from the viewpoint of those who remain, but from that of those who are evacuated. All true Christians will be caught up from the earth and raptured into the presence of the Lord before the seven-year period of evil, the Tribulation, breaks throughout the earth. This will fulfill the promise He made to His disciples in John 14:1–3:

> Let not your heart be troubled; you believe in God, believe also in Me. In My Father's house are many mansions; if it were not so, I would have told you. I go to prepare a place for you. And if I go and prepare a place for you, I will come again and receive you to Myself; that where I am, there you may be also.

Followers of Christ who are raptured will be spared the trauma of death and the coming disasters that will occur when the Tribulation breaks out upon the earth. That is indeed a cause for true rapture on the part of those who love the Lord and long to be with Him.

One morning recently I spoke about the Rapture during a series of messages on prophecy. Later I was told that on the way out of church, a girl expressed confusion to her mother about something I had said. "Dr. Jeremiah keeps talking about all the signs that are developing concerning the Lord's return. And then in the next breath he says that nothing needs to happen before Jesus comes back to take us home to be with Him. I don't understand!" It seemed to this girl that I had contradicted myself. First, I seemed to say that certain prophesied signs would occur before the coming of Christ; then I seemed to say that nothing needed to occur before Jesus comes to claim His own. The girl's honest confusion deserves to be addressed because I believe she speaks for many who are similarly puzzled about events relating to the Rapture.

Most of the misunderstanding comes from confusing two events: the Rapture and the Second Coming. When we talk about the signs that signal the return of Christ, we speak not of the Rapture but of the Lord's ultimate return to the earth with all His saints. According to the book of Revelation, this coming of Christ occurs after the Rapture and differs from it in at least two ways: First, the Rapture will be a "stealth event" in which Christ will be witnessed by believers only. His second coming, on the other hand, will be a public event. Everyone will see Him. "Behold, He is coming with clouds, and every eye will see Him, even they who pierced Him. And all the tribes of the earth will mourn because of Him" (Revelation 1:7; see also Zechariah 14:1, 3–5; Revelation 19:11–21).

Second, all believers are raptured. He will immediately take them back into heaven with Him. But when Christ returns to earth seven years later in the Second Coming, He is coming to stay. This return, usually referred to as "the Second Advent," will take place at the end of the Tribulation period and usher in the Millennium—a thousand-year reign of Christ on this earth. So, first, the Rapture will occur seven years before the Second Advent. At that time Christ will take us to be with Him in heaven, immediately before the seven-year tribulation period. Then second, we will return to earth with Him at His Second Advent.

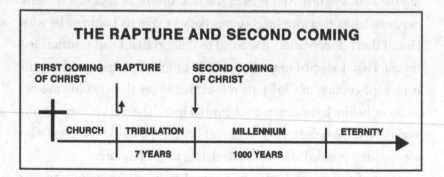

There is another important difference. There are no events that must take place before the Rapture occurs. It's all a matter of God's perfect timing. When I preached that signs are developing concerning the Lord's return, I referred to events that must yet occur before the return of Christ in the Second Advent.

The prophecies I spoke of concern the Second Advent, but that does not mean that the Rapture doesn't figure into prophecy. Future events cast shadows that are precursors to their coming. Since the Rapture takes place seven years before the Second Advent, the signs that point to the Second Advent cast shadows that clue us in to the imminent Rapture. The fact that the Rapture precedes the Second Advent makes the signs portending the Advent all the more immediate and ominous. For those who are left behind, the Rapture will give irrefutable confirmation of end-time events, seven years before they come to pass.

The New Testament indicates that the Rapture of those who have put their trust in Christ is the next major event on the prophetic calendar. In other words, the Rapture awaits us on the horizon—it could happen at any moment. This is the clear message of the Bible, and it is a truth I have taught consistently for more than thirty years.

Unraveling the Rapture

The apostle Paul was the first to reveal the details of the Rapture. He wrote of it in his first letter to the Corinthians, but it was in his first letter to the church in Thessalonica that he presented his most concise teaching on the subject.

Like many today, the Christians in that city were confused about the events that would take place in the future. They, too, wondered what in the world was going on. While they believed that Jesus was coming back someday, they could not figure out what would happen to their Christian parents and loved ones who had already died. So Paul wrote to instruct them concerning God's plan for both the living and the dead in the Rapture. In this writing, he explained in detail exactly what the Rapture is all about.

> But I do not want you to be ignorant, brethren, concerning those who have fallen asleep, lest you sorrow as others who have no hope. For if we believe that Jesus died and rose again, even so God will bring with Him those who sleep in Jesus.
>
> For this we say to you by the word of the Lord, that we who are alive and remain until the coming of the Lord will by no means precede those who are asleep. For the Lord Himself will descend from heaven with a shout, with the voice of an archangel, and with the trumpet of God. And the dead in Christ will rise first. Then we who are alive and remain shall be caught up together with them in the clouds to meet the Lord in the air. And thus we shall always be with the Lord. Therefore comfort one another with these words. (1 Thessalonians 4:13–18)

This passage tells us all we need to know about the Rapture. Let's look more deeply into what Paul said, point by point. First, he wrote: "But I do not want you to be ignorant, brethren, concerning those who have fallen asleep, lest you sorrow as others who have no hope" (1 Thessalonians 4:13). In this statement, the apostle addressed the ignorance of the Thessalonians concerning the state of those who had died believing in Christ. The word he used to describe that state has great significance for every believer today. Paul said that they had fallen asleep. For the word translated *asleep*, he used the Greek word *koimao*, which has as one of its meanings, "to sleep in death." The same word is used to describe the deaths of Lazarus, Stephen, David, and Jesus Christ (*emphasis added in the following examples*):

Lazarus: "These things He said, and after that He said to them, 'Our friend Lazarus *sleeps*, but I go that I may wake him up.'" (John 11:11)

Stephen: "Then he [Stephen] knelt down and cried out with a loud voice, 'Lord, do not charge them with this sin.' And when he had said this, he *fell asleep*." (Acts 7:60)

David: "For David, after he had served his own generation by the will of God, *fell asleep*, was buried with his fathers, and saw corruption." (Acts 13:36)

Jesus Christ: "But now Christ is risen from the dead, and has become the firstfruits of those who have *fallen asleep*." (1 Corinthians 15:20)

This concept of death is emphasized in the wonderful word early Christians adopted for the burying places of their loved ones. It was the Greek word *koimeterion*, which means "a rest house for strangers, a sleeping place." It is the word from which we get our English word *cemetery*. In Paul's day, this word was used for inns or what we would call a hotel or motel. We check in at a Hilton Hotel or a Ramada Inn, expecting to spend the night in sleep before we wake up in the morning refreshed and raring to go. That is exactly the thought Paul expressed in words such as *koimao* and *koimeterion*. When Christians die, it's as if they are slumbering peacefully in a place of rest, ready to be awakened at the return of the Lord. The words have great import, for they convey the Christian concept of death, not as a tragic finality, but as a temporary sleep.

In the next part of the Thessalonian passage, we find Paul affirming their hopes that their loved ones will live again. He did this by tying that hope to the Resurrection and the Rapture: "lest you sorrow as others who have no hope. For if we believe that Jesus died and rose again, even so God will bring with Him those who sleep in Jesus" (1 Thessalonians 4:13c–14). Here Paul tells the Thessalonians (and us) that God's plan for our future gives us such a new perspective on death that when someone we love dies, we are not overcome with sorrow and despair, for on that day when those who are alive in Christ are raptured, those who died in Christ will be raised to be with Him.

Paul reasoned that Christians can believe this promise of resurrection because it is backed up by the resurrection of Christ Himself. The logic is simple: if we believe that Jesus died and rose again, is it hard to believe His promise that He can perform the same miracle for us and those we love?

Paul did not forbid us to grieve; it is natural to feel sorrow when a loved one passes away, even when that loved one is a Christian. We miss the person terribly, and as Tennyson put it, we long for "the touch of a vanished hand and the sound of a voice that is still."[4] Jesus Himself wept by the tomb of Lazarus. But because of our Lord's promise of resurrection, we are not to grieve the way non-Christians do—as people to whom death is the ultimate tragedy—for they have no grounds for hope.

Tim LaHaye is the coauthor of the famous Left Behind series, which at last count had sold more than sixty-five million books. He became fascinated with the doctrine of the Rapture as a nine-year-old boy at his father's grave. He wrote:

My love for second-coming teachings, particularly the Rapture of the church, was sparked as I stood at my father's grave at the age of nine. His sudden death of a heart attack left me devastated. My pastor, who also was my uncle, pointed his finger toward heaven and proclaimed, "This is not the last of Frank LaHaye. Because of his personal faith in Christ, one day he will be resurrected by the shout of the Lord; we will be translated to meet him and our other loved ones in the clouds and be with them and our Lord forever." That promise from Scripture was the only hope for my broken heart that day. And that same promise has comforted millions of others through the years.[5]

As Dr. LaHaye said, the promise of the Rapture has comforted millions, and it is right that it should, for it is a promise we can depend on to be utterly sound.

The Chronological Program of the Rapture

As Paul continued in his letter to the Thessalonians, he wrote: "For this we say to you by the word of the Lord" (1 Thessalonians 4:15a).

Here Paul affirms that what he is about to say is by divine authority. He is authorized to say it "by the word of the Lord." This bold assertion suggests that what followed was not to be taken lightly because it was a revelation given directly to the apostle by God himself. In 1 Corinthians, Paul referred to the Rapture as a "mystery" (15:51). And the biblical definition of a mystery is "a truth that has not been revealed before."

Having established his authority to reveal what had formerly been a mystery, Paul went on to explain the first of the sequence of events that make up the Rapture.

There Will Be an Order of Priority

Paul then told the Thessalonians, "we who are alive and remain until the coming of the Lord will by no means precede those who are asleep" (1 Thessalonians 4:15b). Here Paul was saying that not only will those who have died in Christ be present at the return of the Lord, but they will actually have a place of priority. He said that those who are alive at the Rapture will not be taken up to Christ ahead of "those who are asleep," which means all believers who have died prior to the Rapture.

There is a linguistic root we need to examine here. The Greek word *phthano* in this verse means "come before, precede." When the Greek was translated into the English of the King James era, the word "prevent" was used because it then carried the meaning "to go or arrive before." Over many years, *prevent* has come to mean "to keep from happening." The emphatic point of this verse is that we will "by no means precede those who are asleep" in Christ. Those who have died believing in Christ will take precedence over us in the Rapture.

There Will Be a Return

Paul continued by saying, "For the Lord Himself will descend from heaven with a shout, with the voice of an archangel, and with the trumpet of God" (1 Thessalonians 4:16a).

As you read these words, the Lord Jesus Christ is seated in the heavens at the right hand of the Almighty Father. But when the right moment comes, He will initiate the Rapture by literally and physically rising from the throne, stepping into the corridors of light, and actually descending into the atmosphere of planet Earth from which He rose into the heavens over the Mount of Olives two thousand years ago. It is not the angels or the Holy Spirit but the Lord Himself who is coming to draw believers into the heavens in the Rapture.

The details of this passage paint an amazingly complete sensory picture of the Rapture. Paul even gave the sounds that will be heard—a shout, the voice of an archangel, and the trumpet of God. The purpose and relationship of these three sounds have generated considerable discussion. Some have claimed that the shout is for the church, the archangel's voice is for the Jews, and the trumpet is for all gentile believers. But these claims are mistaken. The three allusions to sounds are not to be taken as coordinate but rather as subordinate. Paul was not describing three separate sounds; he was describing only one sound in three different ways.

This sound will be like a shout, ringing with command authority like the voice of an archangel. It will also be like the blare of a trumpet in its volume and clarity. And the sound will be exclusively directed—heard only by those who have placed their trust in Christ. When Jesus raised Lazarus from the dead, he shouted "Lazarus, come forth!" (John 11:43). I've heard Bible students speculate as to what might have happened had Jesus forgotten to mention Lazarus's name. Would all the dead within the range of His voice have emerged from their graves? At the Rapture that is exactly what will happen. His shout of "Come forth!" will not name a single individual, but it will be heard by every believer in every grave around the world. All those tombs will empty, and the resurrected believers will fly skyward.

This arising from the grave was the hope that Winston Churchill movingly expressed in the planning of his own funeral. Following the prayer by the archbishop of Canterbury and the singing of "God Save the Queen," a trumpeter perched in the highest reaches of the dome of St. Paul's Cathedral sounded "The Last Post" (or "Taps" as we know it). As the last sorrowful note faded, "high in another gallery, sounded the stronger blaring 'Reveille.'"[6] The call to sleep was followed by a call to arise.

There Will Be a Resurrection

As Paul continued his writing to the Thessalonians, he asserted that the expectation expressed by believers such as Churchill is not vain. The coming resurrection is a reality. Paul wrote, "And the dead in Christ will rise first" (1 Thessalonians 4:16*b*). As he indicates here, the call to resurrection at the Rapture will not summon all the dead, but believers only. A time will come much later when *all* the dead will be raised to stand before the white throne in judgment. But at this first call, our believing loved ones who have already died will arise to take first place in the program of the Rapture.

There Will Be a Rapture

Paul explained the next event in the Rapture sequence: "Then we who are alive and remain shall be caught up" (1 Thessalonians 4:17*a*). The words *caught up* are translated from a Greek word that has as one of its meanings "to snatch out or away speedily." This word emphasizes the sudden nature of the Rapture. Paul described this suddenness in his letter to the Corinthians: ". . . in a moment, in the twinkling of an eye, at the last trumpet. For the trumpet will sound, and the dead will be raised incorruptible, and we shall be changed" (1 Corinthians 15:52).

In a split second the Lord will call all believers to Himself to share in His glory; not one will remain behind. It is hard to imagine just what that will be like, but I read a paragraph recently that created this vivid picture:

Millions of people from all parts of the earth feel a tingling sensation pulsating throughout their bodies. They are all suddenly energized. Those with physical deformities are healed. The blind suddenly see.

Wrinkles disappear on the elderly as their youth is restored. As these people marvel at their physical transformation, they are lifted skyward. Those in buildings pass right through the ceiling and roof without pain or damage. Their flesh and bones seem to dematerialize, defying all known laws of physics and biology. As they travel heavenward, some of them see and greet those who have risen from their graves. After a brief mystical union . . . they all vanish from sight.[7]

Lest such pictures as this lead us to think the Rapture is a fanciful, futuristic dream, we find such experiences validated historically. Throughout the Bible, we have records of several people who had actual experiences very similar to the Rapture:

Enoch: "By faith Enoch was taken away so that he did not see death, 'and was not found, because God had taken him'; for before he was taken he had this testimony, that he pleased God." (Hebrews 11:5)

Elijah: "Then it happened, as they continued on and talked, that suddenly a chariot of fire appeared with horses of fire, and separated the two of them; and Elijah went up by a whirlwind into heaven." (2 Kings 2:11)

Paul: "I know a man in Christ who fourteen years ago—whether in the body I do not know, or whether out of the body I do not know, God knows—such a one, was *caught up* to the third heaven. And I know such a man—whether in the body or out of the body I do not know, God knows—how he was *caught up* into Paradise and heard inexpressible words, which it is not lawful for a man to utter." (2 Corinthians 12:2–4, *emphasis added*)

I find it significant that twice in this passage Paul used the words *caught up*, which are translated from the word meaning "rapture" in the Greek language.

Jesus Christ: "And while they looked steadfastly toward heaven as He went up, behold, two men stood by them in white apparel, who also said, 'Men of Galilee, why do you stand gazing up into heaven? This same Jesus, who was taken up from you into heaven, will so come in like manner as you saw Him go into heaven.'" (Acts 1:10–11)

These records affirm the utter reality of the Rapture by providing us with prototypes of sorts to show that God can accomplish this coming event He promises to His people.

There Will Be a Reunion

Paul continued his explanation of the Rapture: "Then we who are alive and remain shall be caught up together with them [the believing dead who have arisen] in the clouds to meet the Lord in the air. And thus we shall always be with the Lord" (1 Thessalonians 4:17). Note that Paul began here with the word *then*, which is an adverb indicating sequence. It connects the previous events of the Rapture that we have already considered with this final event in a definite order of sequential reunions as follows:

1. Dead bodies reunited with their spirits

2. Resurrected believers reunited with living believers

3. Resurrected believers and raptured believers meet the Lord

As Paul pointed out, the ultimate consequence of this reunion with the Lord is that there will be no subsequent parting. After His return, our union and communion with Him will be uninterrupted and eternal. This glorious fact alone shows us why the word *rapture* is an altogether appropriate term for this event.

The Comforting Purpose of the Rapture

After completing his description of the Rapture to the Thessalonians, Paul wrapped up the passage with this practical admonition: "Therefore comfort one another with these words" (1 Thessalonians 4:18).

Here the apostle was telling both the Thessalonians and believers today that it's not enough simply to passively understand what was just explained about the Rapture, Christian death, and the Resurrection. Our understanding should spur us toward a certain action—to "comfort one another." And in the preceding verses he gave exactly the kind of information that makes true comfort possible. When believers suffer the loss of family members or dearly loved friends, we have in Paul's descriptions of Christian death and resurrection all that is needed to comfort each other in these losses. Christian death is not permanent; it is merely a sleep. A time is coming when we and our loved ones will be reunited in a rapturous meeting, when Christ Himself calls us out of this world or out of our graves to be with Him forever in an ecstatic relationship of eternal love. Nineteenth-century Bible teacher A. T. Pierson made this interesting observation about these things:

It is a remarkable fact that in the New Testament, so far as I remember, it is never once said, after Christ's resurrection, that a disciple died—that is, without some qualification: Stephen *fell asleep*. David, after he had served his own generation by the will of God *fell asleep and was laid with his father*. Peter says, "Knowing that I must shortly *put off this my tabernacle* as the Lord showed me." Paul says, "*the time of my departure is at hand.*" (The figure here is taken from a vessel that, as she leaves a dock, throws the cables off the fastenings, and opens her sails to the wind to depart for the haven) . . . The only time where the word "dead" is used, it is with qualification: "the *dead in Christ*," "the *dead which die in the Lord*."[8]

As Pierson implies, Christ abolished death so completely that even the term *death* is no longer appropriate for believers. That is why Paul wrote that we should comfort one another with reminders that for Christians, what we call death is nothing more than a temporary sleep before we are called into our uninterrupted relationship with Christ forever.

Today as never before, we are beginning to see the signs of our Lord's impending return. Some of these signs we have already covered—the rebirth of Israel as a nation, the growing crises over oil, the reformation of Europe in accordance with Daniel's prophecy, and the growth of militant, radical Islam. All these developments point toward that day when our Lord will come to rapture His followers out of this world.

I believe it is the Rapture that will trigger the cataclysmic upheavals that will ravage the earth for the seven years that follow it. The Tribulation will come about by the law of natural consequences. According to Jesus, Christians are the salt and light of the world (Matthew 5:13–14). Salt prevents decay; light proclaims truth. When all the Christians in the entire world are removed from the earth in one day, all the salt and all the light will suddenly be gone. The result is predictable. You may think the world today is degenerating into rampant greed and immorality, and indeed it is. But as bad as things are becoming, we can hardly overstate the horror that will occur when society loses the tempering influence of Christians.

As the Bible teaches, every believer in Christ is indwelt by the Holy Spirit. This means the Holy Spirit ministers to today's world through followers of Christ. When all Christians are removed from the earth, the restraining ministry of the Holy Spirit will be completely absent. No salt! No light! No indwelling Spirit of God! The result will be horrific. Jesus himself described what will happen next: "For then there will be great tribulation, such as has not been since the beginning of the world until this time, no, nor ever shall be. And unless those days were shortened, no flesh would be saved" (Matthew 24:21–22).

As these dire words are being fulfilled during the Tribulation period, we who are followers of Christ will have already been raptured to heaven. This is another source of great comfort for Christians. No promise has been more precious to believers than the one made to the church of Philadelphia in Revelation: "Because you have kept My command to persevere, I also will keep you from the hour of trial which shall come upon the whole world, to test those who dwell on the earth" (Revelation 3:10).

Please note that our Lord's promise is not merely to keep us *in* the hour of trial, but rather *from* the hour of trial. As Paul wrote, "God did not appoint us to wrath, but to obtain salvation through our Lord Jesus Christ" (1 Thessalonians 5:9). The promise is that we who are believers will not experience the horrors of the Tribulation, and this is an enormous source of comfort.

How Shall We then Live?

We have been given two directives as to how we should live as we anticipate Christ's return. We should be looking for Him and living for Him.

We Should Be Looking for the Lord

Paul warned us in three of his letters to be alert and watchful for the Lord's return:

Looking for the blessed hope and glorious appearing of our great God and Savior Jesus Christ. (Titus 2:13)

For our citizenship is in heaven, from which we also eagerly wait for the Savior, the Lord Jesus Christ. (Philippians 3:20)

And to wait for His Son from heaven, whom He raised from the dead, even Jesus who delivers us from the wrath to come. (1 Thessalonians 1:10)

Wayne Grudem suggests that the degree to which we are actually longing for Christ's return is a measure of our spiritual condition. As he explains:

The more Christians are caught up in enjoying the good things of this life, and the more they neglect genuine Christian fellowship and their personal relationship with Christ, the less they will long for His return. On the other hand, many Christians who are experiencing suffering or persecution, or who are more elderly and infirm, and those whose daily walk with Christ is vital and deep, will have a more intense longing for His return.[9]

As Dr. Grudem suggests, the idea is not merely to watch for Jesus' coming as we might watch for a storm in a black cloud, but rather to anticipate it as something we look forward to and long for.

We Should Be Living for the Lord

The three great apostles, Paul, Peter, and John, all had something to say about how we should live in the face of Christ's impending return:

For the grace of God that brings salvation has appeared to all men, teaching us that, denying ungodliness and worldly lusts, we should live soberly, righteously, and godly in the present age, looking for the blessed hope and glorious appearing of our great God and Savior Jesus Christ, who gave Himself for us, that He might redeem us from every lawless deed and purify for Himself His own special people, zealous for good works. (Titus 2:11–14)

Therefore, since all these things will be dissolved, what manner of persons ought you to be in holy conduct and godliness. (2 Peter 3:11)

Beloved, now are we children of God; and it has not yet been revealed what we shall be, but we know that when He is revealed, we shall be like Him, for we shall see Him as He is. And everyone who has this hope in Him purifies himself, just as He is pure. (1 John 3:2–3)

You would think it obvious that since signs tell us that Christ is coming soon, people would take extra care to live as God would have them live—lives of purity and holiness. If you know that guests are coming soon to your home but you don't know exactly when they will arrive, you will keep your house swept, picked up, and dusted in anticipation. You don't want them ringing your doorbell with your dishes piled in the sink, beds unmade, and mud prints tracking the carpet. The admonitions of Paul, Peter, and John to stay ready by living pure and holy lives are hardly more than just plain common sense. But common sense does not always prevail in the lives of fallen humans, and that is why these apostles felt it worthwhile to admonish us to live as if Jesus could come at any moment. The fact is He can.

Two years after the wildfires of 2003, San Diego regional authorities installed Reverse 9-1-1. The early warning system was first used to warn residents of the approaching wildfires of 2007. Some home owners, however, did not receive a call or had phone systems that screened out the warning call as an unrecognized number. Others received the call but chose to ignore it. Some of those who did not hear the warning did not vacate their homes and, as a result, lost their lives.[10]

God has sounded the warnings loudly and clearly. They have come through His prophets in the Old Testament, through New Testament writers, and even through Jesus Himself. The firestorm is coming in the form of the seven years of tribulation, when no Christian influence will temper the evil that will plunge the earth into a cauldron of misery and devastation. But you can avoid the destruction and be evacuated. You can enter your name on the list of those who will hear the trumpet call of the Rapture by turning to Christ and beginning to live the pure and holy life that characterizes those who will enter heaven. As the apostle John wrote: "But there shall by no means enter it [the heavenly city of God] anything that defiles, or causes an abomination or a lie, but only those who are written in the Lamb's Book of Life" (Revelation 21:27).

If your name is not in that book, when the Rapture occurs you will be left behind to experience horrors worse than anything the world has yet seen. I hope you will not wait another day; turn to Jesus Christ now, before it is too late, and become one of those who will hear His call on that great and terrible day.

SIX

Does America Have a Role in Prophecy?

EVERY DAY WHEN THE SUN RISES OVER WASHINGTON DC, ITS first rays fall on the eastern side of the city's tallest structure, the 555-foot Washington Monument. The first part of that monument to reflect the rising sun is the eastern side of its aluminum capstone, where these words are inscribed: *Laus Deo*, Latin for "Praise be to God." This compact prayer of praise, visible to the eyes of heaven alone, is tacit recognition of our nation's unique acknowledgment of the place of God in its founding and its continuance.[1]

Were these words merely a grandiose but empty claim to national piety, or do they reflect a true reality? In the introduction to the book *The Light and the Glory*, authors Peter Marshall and David Manuel ask a very profound question:

What if Columbus' discovering of America had not been accidental at all? What if it were merely the opening curtain of an extraordinary

119

drama? Did God have a special plan for America? . . . What if He dealt with whole nations like He dealt with individuals? What if in particular He had a plan for those He would bring to America, a plan which saw this continent as a stage for a new era in the drama of mankind's redemption?[2]

President Ronald Reagan believed that God did have a plan for our nation. He wrote, "I have always believed that this anointed land was set apart in an uncommon way, that a divine plan placed this great continent here between the oceans to be found by people from every corner of the earth who had a special love of faith and freedom."[3]

The Sovereignty of God in the Founding of America

I am convinced that references such as the preceding three are not in vain. It seems clear that God *does* have a plan for America. It is true that we have no direct reference to that plan in the Old or New Testament, but that does not discount the evident fact that God has a sovereign purpose for America in His redemptive plan.

As authors Marshall and Manuel suggest, God's hand on America began with its discoverer. In the rotunda of the Capitol Building is a great painting entitled *The Landing of Columbus,* depicting his arrival on the shores of America. As Marshall asserts, the great explorer discovered the New World "by accident," but yet *not* by accident. God had His hand upon the wheel of the ship and brought it here.

Columbus was not oblivious to God's providence in his discovery. In his journal, Columbus expressed his literal belief that "his voyages were ushering in a millennial age . . . and initiat[ing] a messianic period." He was firmly convinced that Isaiah's words, "so shall they fear the name of the LORD from the west" (Isaiah 59:19), referred to the lands west of Europe that had not yet been discovered. The journal from his first voyage shows that the primary purpose of his explorations was to take the message of salvation through Jesus Christ to the people in this unknown land.[4]

Throughout our nation's history we see America's leaders turning to God for guidance. We see Washington kneeling in the snow of Valley Forge. We see our Founding Fathers on their knees at the first Continental Congress. We see the gaunt Lincoln praying in the hour of national crisis. We see Woodrow Wilson reading his Bible late at night by the White House lights. Washington summarized this national dependence on God, which was evident before his time and continued after him, when he said, "No people can be bound to acknowledge and adore the invisible hand which conducts the affairs of man more than those of the United States."[5]

Clearly America did not become the land of the free and the home of the brave by blind fate or a happy set of coincidences. A benevolent God was hovering over this nation from her very conception so that today, although America has only 5 percent of the world's population, she has more than 50 percent of the modern luxuries that characterize civilization.

Why has God blessed this nation above all other lands? Why has America in her short history outstripped the wealth, power, and influence of all ancient and modern civilizations? Can God have blessed a nation so richly without having for her a pivotal purpose? What is God's plan for America? What is its place in end-time prophecy? These are questions many people are asking today as they watch events coalesce toward world crises. They wonder how America fits into what is going on in the world.

In order to understand America's place in end-time prophecy, we must first answer the question we raised in the previous paragraph: Why has America been blessed above all other lands? Let's explore the reasons for God's favor on America, and then we will show what this means in terms of coming events.

America Has Been the Force Behind World Missions

"To the United States belongs the distinction of providing three-fourths of the missionaries of the last century and approximately the same amount of money and material aid."[6] This means that 75 percent of all missionaries have come from a country boasting only 5 percent of the total world population. God blesses those who make His priorities their priorities. The church I pastor in California is a case in point. More than fifteen years ago that church committed to give to world missions the first 20 percent of every dollar received in offerings. When we started that program back in the early '90s, our missions budget was not quite $250,000 per year. Today it is well over ten times that figure. God loves the world. He loves the people who are yet to hear the gospel. When we love whom He loves, He blesses us. And I believe that principle applies to our nation as well as to our church.

God has blessed America because we have been the launching pad of the world's great missionary movement. In the aftermath of World War II, Americans started 1,800 missions agencies and sent out more than 350,000 missionaries.[7] And as a result, "today, 95 percent of the world's population have access, not only to some portion of Scripture in their language, but also to Christian radio broadcasts, audio recordings, and the *Jesus* film."[8] That achievement is due largely to the missionary zeal of churches in the United States.

America Has Been a Friend to the Jewish People

Ever since the turn of the twentieth century, Jews have made up 3 percent of the total population of the United States, where they have been protected from harassment and anti-Semitism. America has given Jews opportunity for economic, educational, and cultural advancement without fear of losing their religious freedom.

America's historic support of Israel is based not so much on efforts by Jewish lobbyists in Washington or the presence of Jewish groups in our society, but on the Judeo-Christian heritage of our nation. President Truman's determination to recognize Israel as a modern state was fueled by his lifelong belief that in the book of Deuteronomy, God had given the land of Israel to the Jewish people for all time.

At the founding of the modern state of Israel, surrounding Arab nations immediately declared war on the new nation. Few felt Israel could survive, and western nations did not want to become embroiled in the conflict. Truman was under pressure not to intervene. In a dramatic speech to seek support before the United Nations, the Jewish statesman Abba Eban said:

Israel is the product of the most sustained historic tenacity which the ages recall. The Jewish people have not striven toward this goal for twenty centuries in order that, having once achieved it, it will surrender it in response to an illegitimate and unsuccessful aggression. Whatever else changes, this will not. The state of Israel is an immutable part of the international landscape. To plan the future without it is to build delusions on the sand.[9]

In spite of Eban's eloquent plea, the young nation was in great danger. Both US and UN recognition of Israel were in serious doubt.

Following his speech, Eban flew to Paris to meet with an American delegation regarding recognition. Secretary of State George Marshall, whose support of Israel was tepid at best, had to return home for medical treatment. His deputy, John Foster Dulles, assumed leadership of the delegation.

Eban later wrote that Dulles held the key to the success of the talks. "Behind a dry manner, redolent of oak-paneled courtrooms in the United States, there *was a curious strain of Protestant mysticism* which led him to give the Israel questions a larger importance that its geopolitical weight would indicate"[10] (*emphasis added*).

What Eban called "a curious strain of Protestant mysticism" is actually the historic love that Christians have for the land and people of Israel, based upon their shared religious heritage and scriptures. This, more than anything else, has cemented the friendship between America and Israel for more than sixty years.

As we discovered in the first chapter of this book, God has promised to bless those who bless Israel (Genesis 12:1–3). He has amply fulfilled that promise. America has been abundantly blessed as a nation because we have blessed the Jews.

America Has Been a Free Nation

In my studies of both the Old and New Testaments, I have observed that the principles of freedom are united with the tenets of Christianity. America today is the laboratory where those blended principles can grow and develop and become an example to all the world. The Bible says, "You shall know the truth, and the truth shall make you free" (John 8:32).

Freedom can never be taken for granted in our world. In early 2007, Freedom House released its annual survey, *Freedom in the World*, which stated that 3 billion people—46 percent of the world's population—live in a free to partly free country. Conversely, 54 percent—or more than half the population of the world—do not live in freedom.[11] In fact, the tendency in a fallen world is always away from freedom and toward despotism and tyranny.

In his 1981 inaugural address, President Ronald Reagan spoke of our freedom in these stirring words: "Above all, we must realize that no arsenal or no weapon in the arsenals of the world is so formidable as the will and moral courage of free men and women. It is a weapon our adversaries in today's world do not have. It is a weapon that we as Americans do have. Let that be understood by those who practice terrorism and prey upon their neighbors."[12]

America has learned what our repressive and terrorist adversaries do not understand: that liberty without law is anarchy, liberty to defy law is rebellion, but liberty limited by law is the cornerstone of civilization. We Americans have tried to share what we have learned by exporting freedom wherever we have gone in the world. We have tried to help people understand that freedom is what creates the life God intended us to have from the very beginning.

America has become the paradise of human liberty, a great oasis in a global desert of trouble, suffering, repression, and tyranny. Our nation is a dramatic exclamation point to the assertion that freedom works!

Today our precious heritage of freedom is being challenged internally by the erosion of our culture. As long-held freedoms come under fire, some Americans, especially those with wealth, are deciding that the United States is no longer the best place to live. According to the book *Getting Out: Your Guide to Leaving America*, some three hundred thousand Americans a year are choosing to leave the country. This is the first time in history that the number of people exiting this nation has become large enough to be significant, and the emergence of such a trend calls our attention to the degenerating character of America. If our culture continues to jettison the principles that made our nation great, we can hardly expect the blessing of Almighty God to continue.

America Has Been Founded on God and His Word

It is no mystery why America's founders insisted on the principle of freedom. Their dependence on the God of the Bible led them to subject themselves to Him as the ultimate authority for law rather than set themselves up as autocrats with the audacity to control the lives of their subjects. And because they submitted to God's authority, He has blessed this nation as none has ever been blessed. The Psalmist wrote, "Blessed is the nation whose God is the LORD, the people He has chosen as His own inheritance" (Psalm 33:12). The book of Proverbs adds, "Righteousness exalts a nation, but sin is a reproach to any people" (14:34).

I opened this chapter with a brief look at how America's founders and early leaders exhibited humble reliance on Almighty God. Now I want to show how that godly dependence characterized our governmental philosophy through several generations and resulted in God's blessings on our nation. Our leaders stabilized government with a lifeline between their country and their God, with authority and blessing flowing downward as dependence and thanksgiving flowed upward.

George Washington set the tone for the nation's governmental authority when he said, "It is impossible to rightly govern the world without God and the Bible."[13] That philosophy remained intact through the time of Abraham Lincoln, who is quoted as saying, "God is my witness that it is my constant anxiety and prayer that both myself and this nation should be on the Lord's side."[14]

Benjamin Franklin explained why he requested that each day of the Constitutional Convention be opened in prayer, saying: "The longer I live, the more convincing proofs I see of the truth—that God governs in the affairs of Men. And," he continued, "without His aid, we shall succeed in this political building no better than the builders of Babel."[15]

Henry Wilson (1812–1875) was a US senator and vice president under Ulysses S. Grant from 1873 to 1875. On December 23, 1866, he spoke to a YMCA gathering in Natick, Massachusetts, where he said:

> Remember ever, and always, that your country was founded, not by the "most superficial, the lightest, the most irreflective of all European races," but by the stern old Puritans who made the deck of the *Mayflower* an altar of the living God, and whose first act on touching the soil of the new world was to offer on bended knees thanksgiving to Almighty God.[16]

In 1911, President Woodrow Wilson said:

> The Bible . . . is the one supreme source of revelation of the meaning of life, the nature of God and spiritual nature and needs of men. It is the only guide of life which really leads the spirit in the way of peace and salvation. America was born a Christian nation. America was born to exemplify that devotion to the elements of righteousness which are derived from the revelations of Holy Scripture.[17]

Today as I write these words, our heritage of national dependence on God is under fire. Forces within our nation threaten its divine lifeline. The attitude of many in our culture today seems symbolized by the powerful legal tides now trying to remove the words *under God* from the Pledge of Allegiance. Those two words were inserted into the pledge in 1954, partly to distinguish our nation from the atheistic communism of the Soviet Union. But while these words came late to the pledge, they certainly reflected what had been a part of America's heritage from the beginning.

For example, on July 2, 1776, General George Washington wrote in the general orders to his men that day, "The fate of unborn millions will now depend, *under God*, on the courage and conduct of this army."[18] Almost a hundred years later, Abraham Lincoln consecrated the military cemetery on the battlefield of Gettysburg, saying: "We here highly resolved that these dead shall not have died in vain; that this nation, *under God*, shall have a new birth of freedom; and that government of the people, by the people, for the people, shall not perish from the earth" (*emphasis added*).[19]

This recognition that our nation was founded on godly principles of freedom and divine authority continued to be the basic assumption of government through the middle of the twentieth century. Our leaders realized that once America failed to acknowledge that we were under God, our basis for freedom and equitable government would come crashing down. President Calvin Coolidge said it well: "The foundation of our society and our government rests so much on the teachings of the Bible that it would be difficult to support them if faith in these teachings would cease to be practically universal in our country."[20] In other words, when America turns from its position of being under God, we can no longer expect His blessings on this nation to continue. We will have broken our lifeline.

As I've been writing this book, two attempts to hack through that lifeline were exposed. At a Dallas-area elementary school, one parent complained that the national motto, "In God We Trust," was painted on a wall in the gym. The school board promptly had the offending words painted over. When several parents complained about its abrupt removal, Texas law and Texas Education Code prevailed, causing a school district representative to admit the district had "made a mistake" and announced, "'In God We Trust' will be repainted on the wall."[21]

Do you remember the capstone of the Washington Monument I wrote about at the beginning of this chapter? Since the actual inscription is not visible at its stately height, the National Park Service has maintained a replica capstone in an exhibit at the 490-foot level. Located near a wall detailing the construction of the monument, the capstone case was positioned such that the public could see the inscription. However, late last year, the display was changed. The case was repositioned against the wall and turned so the east side inscription *Laus Deo* was no longer viewable. A previous reference to that inscription was also omitted from the new description tag on the exhibit. When some citizens complained of the unacceptable modifications, an NPS official responded by saying, "We made a mistake and we are fixing it."[22]

More than a mistake, these removals are an assault. Almost routinely these days, attacks are made on any public reminder of our dependence on God's grace for our national existence. I fear our lifeline is fraying.

The Silence of the Bible on the Future of America

Dr. Tim LaHaye wrote, "One of the hardest things for American prophecy students to accept is that the United States is not clearly mentioned in Bible prophecy, yet our nation is the only superpower in the world today."[23] Indeed, no specific mention of the United States or any other country in North or South America can be found in the Bible. One reason may be that in the grand scheme of history, the United States is a new kid on the block. As a nation, it is less than 250 years old—much younger than the nations of Bible times that are featured in biblical prophecy. In fact, the Bible makes no mention of most nations in the modern world. The ancient prophets were primarily concerned with the Holy Land and its immediate neighbors. Areas remote from Israel do not figure in prophecy and are not mentioned in the Bible.

Dr. LaHaye went on to raise this question:

"Does the United States have a place in end time prophecy?" My first response is no, there is nothing about the U.S. in prophecy. At least nothing that is specific. There is an allusion to a group of nations in Ezekiel 38:13 that could apply, but even that is not specific. The question is why? Why would the God of prophecy not refer to the supreme superpower nation in the end times in preparation for the one-world government of the Antichrist?[24]

The question has no one, simple answer, but it will help us understand what is going on in the world today if we look at some of the best thinking that students of prophecy have given us on why America is absent from end-time prophecies.

America Will Be Incorporated into the European Coalition

Our first answer comes from noted prophecy expert John Walvoord, who wrote:

Although the Scriptures do not give any clear word concerning the role of the United States in relation to the revived Roman Empire, it is clear this will be a consolidation of the power of the West. Unlike the coalitions led by the United States, this coalition will be led by others—the Group of Ten . . . Most citizens of the United States of America have come from Europe, and their sympathies would more naturally be with a European alliance than with Russia, Asia, and Africa . . . Europe and America may be in formal alliance with Israel in opposition to the radical Islamic countries of the Middle East.[25]

According to this theory, though America is not mentioned by name in prophecy, it will be in the mix of the political realignments that foreshadow the end of time. And we can see signs of such realignments taking place today.

With the usual presidential fanfare, President Bush welcomed EU Commission president Jos Barroso and the serving president of the European Council, German chancellor Angela Merkel, in the Rose Garden of the White House in April 2007. The president thanked the two for their part in "the trans-Atlantic economic integration plan that the three of us signed today. It is a statement of the importance of trade. It is a commitment to eliminating barriers to trade. It is a recognition that the closer that the United States and the EU become, the better off our people become. So this is a substantial agreement and I appreciate it."[26] The president went on to say, "I believe it's in this country's interests that we reject isolationism and protectionism and encourage free trade."

The agreement these three leaders signed is called "Framework for Advancing Transatlantic Economic Integration between the United

States of America and the European Union"—an appropriately long title for what one would expect to be a long process. But things moved swiftly. In less than seven months the Transatlantic Economic Council held its first official meeting in Washington DC. In a joint statement it was announced, "Since April, the United States and the European Union have made substantial progress in removing barriers to trade and investment and in easing regulatory burdens."[27]

On the surface there seems to be nothing ominous about such an agreement; it appears to be simply about freeing up economic trade between nations. But a similar, less publicized meeting was held in March 2008 at the State Department, which focused on linking the United States, Mexico, and Canada in a "North American community with the European Union" in anticipation of the "creation of a 'Transatlantic Economic Union' between the European Union and North America."[28] One participant—whose identity is protected by the Chatham House Rule, which permits information to be disseminated without attribution to guarantee confidentiality—made this revealing statement:

> North America should be a premiere platform to establish continental institutions. That's why we need to move the security perimeters to include the whole continent, especially as we open the borders between North American countries for expanding free trade.[29]

Statements such as this reveal an intention toward union that has implications far beyond mere economic trade. And considering the speed at which leaders are pushing union between nations, it appears that it will not be long before we see such a union instituted. What does this mean for America?

America Will Be Invaded by Outside Forces

Perhaps the silence of Scripture on the future of America indicates that by the time the Tribulation period arrives, America will have lost her influence in the world and will no longer be a major player. As we have noted, America's thirst for oil and our inability to close the gap between supply and demand could cripple our ability to defend our borders and protect our nation. Once again John Walvoord addresses the issue:

> Some maintain that the total absence of any scriptural reference to America in the end time is evidence that the United States will have been crippled by a nuclear attack, weapons of mass destruction, or some other major catastrophe . . . In the post 9/11 world the detonation of a dirty bomb, nuclear device, or biological weapon on U.S. soil is a dreaded yet distinct possibility. Such an attack could kill millions of people and reduce the United States to a second rate power overnight.[30]

Since the deployment of the first atomic bomb on the city of Hiroshima in August 1945, America has enjoyed a certain fear based aura of invincibility. We now had the big stick, and we were the king of the hill. Both friends and enemies knew that we would use any and all weapons in our formidable arsenal to protect our nation. Even today, according to Ed Timperlake, who served in the Office of the Defense Secretary under Ronald Reagan, "Air Force and Navy personnel continue to stand vigilant 24 hours a day, seven days a week inside the strategic triad of bombers, land-based ICBMs and submarine 'boomers.'"[31]

In today's world, however, such power and vigilance may no longer deter enemies determined to attack the United States. In a truly frightening column in *The Washington Times*, Timperlake went on to observe: "a totally new dimension has emerged regarding a nuclear attack on America. The great tragedy of the murder of Benazir Bhutto brought the world's attention to the possibility of loose nukes falling into the hands of fanatics who would use them." In other words, the political instability in Pakistan could lead to nuclear warheads falling into the hands of radical Islamic jihadists. "It is certain," continued Timperlake, "that a nuclear weapon in the hands of fanatical jihadists will be used. The only current deterrence against its use is a worldwide hunt for the device before Israel, London, New York, or D.C. disappears in a flash."[32]

Timperlake went on to say that jihadists are not our only threat from a rogue nation armed with nuclear weapons. "What about the criminal state of North Korea or the vitriolic anti-Semitic nation of Iran?" he asked. "Either country for many perverse reasons can slip a device to a terrorist group."[33] As if to underscore his point, in late March of 2008, North Korea "test-fired a battery of short-range missiles" only one day after they "expelled South Korean officials from a joint industrial complex north of the border." The three "ship-to-ship missiles [were] launched into the sea."[34]

These enemies have different agendas, but they share a common disregard for human life and a burning hatred for the United States. While we would like to close our ears to predictions of impending disaster, experts such as Timperlake and others see a major attack on our country in the near future as virtually inevitable.

America Will Be Infected with Moral Decay

The average lifespan of all the world's greatest civilizations from the beginning of history has been about two hundred years. During that two-century span, each of these nations progressed through the following sequence: from bondage to spiritual faith; from spiritual faith to great courage; from courage to liberty; from liberty to abundance; from abundance to complacency; from complacency to apathy; from apathy to dependence; and from dependence back into bondage.[35]

At what point is America in this cycle? Popular blogger La Shawn Barber answered this question in an article titled, "America on the Decline." She wrote:

> In *The Decline and Fall of the Roman Empire*, author Edward Gibbon discusses several reasons for the great civilization's demise, including the undermining of the dignity and sanctity of the home and the decay of religion. America has been compared to the Roman Empire in secular and religious ways. Regardless of its ultimate legacy, America is a civilization on the decline. A couple of centuries from now (or sooner), someone will lament the loss of a once-great civilization that brought prosperity to the world and tried to make it safe for democracy. The glory that was the United States will lay in ruins, brought down not by terrorists but its own debauchery and complacency.[36]

Barber's analysis is right on the money with one exception: given the present situation in our world, another "couple of centuries" for America is not in the equation. Nevertheless, her analysis is perceptive, and she continues it by referencing an expert from decades past. In 1947, forward-looking sociologist Dr. Carle Zimmerman wrote a text called *Family and Civilization*. He identified eleven "symptoms of final decay" observable in the fall of both the Greek and Roman civilizations. See how many characterize our society:

1. No-fault divorce

2. "Birth Dearth"; increased disrespect for parenthood and parents

3. Meaningless marriage rites/ceremonies

4. Defamation of past national heroes

5. Acceptance of alternative marriage forms

6. Widespread attitudes of feminism, narcissism, hedonism

7. Propagation of antifamily sentiment

8. Acceptance of most forms of adultery

9. Rebellious children

10. Increased juvenile delinquency

11. Common acceptance of all forms of sexual perversion[37]

One cannot read lists such as these and doubt that America is throwing away its treasured position as the most blessed nation ever on the face of the earth. Remember, as we noted earlier, God blessed this country for a reason: our nation was founded on submission to Him. But now as the reasons for His blessings upon America are eroding, we can expect the blessings themselves to fade as well. It's a simple matter of cause and effect: remove the cause, and the effect ceases. Once, we invited God into our nation. From the first moments of our existence, we opened our national doors to Him and made Him welcome as our most honored guest. But now our culture seems bent on shutting Him out, as author Mike Evans laments:

Most can remember the classic painting of Jesus standing outside a door waiting to be allowed entry. That poignant portrayal of Christ on the outside, wanting to fellowship with His creation, has never been more powerful than it is today. Prayer has been excised from schools, suits have been filed to force Congress to remove "under God" from the Pledge of Allegiance, displays of the Ten Commandments have been removed from public buildings, and the motto, "In God We Trust," is in danger of extinction. Teachers have been forbidden even to carry a personal Bible in view of students, Christian literature has been removed from library shelves, religious Christmas carols have been banned from school programs, and "spring break" has replaced Easter vacation.[38]

Almost six decades ago, former president Herbert Hoover wrote a warning that I fear America has not heeded. After calling attention to several new programs and concepts, including "New Freedom" and "New Religion," Hoover stated, "We have overworked the word 'new' . . . The practical thing we can do, if we want to make the world over, is to try out the word 'Old' for a while. There are some 'old' things that made this country . . . Some old things are slipping badly in American life and if they slip too far, the lights will go out of America!" Among the old things he listed: "Old Virtues of religious faith, integrity and whole truth . . . honor in public office, economy in government, individual liberty . . . willingness to sacrifice . . . Our greatest danger is not from invasion by foreign armies. Our dangers are that we may commit suicide from within by complaisance with evil."[39]

It saddens me to say it, but I believe the signs make it certain that America is now infected with the deadly disease of moral decay. And as that infection eats away at our foundations, we can expect the law of cause and effect to come into play. Scripture often warns us that even a long-suffering God will not forever strive with men. If we ignore divine directives, we cannot expect God's blessing. A limb that cuts itself off from the trunk will not continue to live.

America Will Be Impotent Because of the Rapture

If the Rapture were to happen today and all the true believers in Jesus Christ disappeared into heaven in a single moment, America as we know it could be obliterated. It is estimated that at the Rapture, America will lose millions of citizens—all its Christians and their small children.[40] This means that not only would the country lose a minimum of 25 percent of her population, but she would also lose the very best, the "salt" and "light" of the nation. Who can imagine the chaos in our country when all the godly people disappear—enough to populate many vast cities—leaving only those who have rejected God? It is not a pretty picture. We who love Christ will be blessed by the Rapture in more ways than one. We not only will know the joy of being with our beloved Lord but also will be spared the horrors that the world will suffer through the evil of people left in the wake of the Rapture. It's like a reverse surgical operation—one in which all the healthy cells are removed and only the cancerous ones are left to consume one another.

Yet as we look back at all we have been learning, we who will be rescued cannot help but feel a sense of tension in our hearts. Yes, God will save us, but things we've never experienced are about to happen, and changes such as we've never imagined loom on the horizon. It is important to realize that God understands this internal tension. We do not sin by feeling uneasy. Perhaps it's a little like getting married. We anticipate the event with joy but also with butterflies in the stomach. It's not a matter of dread or wanting to draw back; it's merely a matter of our natural discomfort when facing new experiences. But in spite of the uneasiness, we approach with confidence the events we are anticipating because we know they were put into play by the Creator of the universe. He knows the end from the beginning, and because we are His friends, He is letting us in on the eternal secrets of His determined will.

In an article about the United States in prophecy, Herman A. Hoyt made a fine statement that makes a fitting conclusion to this chapter. He wrote:

> Since the promise of Christ's coming for the Church has always been held out to His people as an event that could take place at any moment, surely the events of the present hour in relation to the United States ought to give new stimulus to watch momentarily for His coming. In these days of crisis, our trust should not rest in a nation that may shortly disappear, but in Him who works all things after the counsel of His own will.[41]

Dr. Hoyt is right; what do we have to worry about? Our trust has never been in governments, civilizations, or cultures. By the standards of eternity, these institutions last but a moment, crumbling into dust to be swept away by the winds of history. They are helpful while they are here, but they have never been worthy of our trust. We have always put our trust in the One who stands above institutions, above history, and even above time itself—the One by whose power and permission these things exist, and who knows their times and the ends of their days. Only He is worthy of our ultimate allegiance.

SEVEN

When One Man Rules the World

WHEN I FIRST BEGAN STUDYING PROPHECY NEARLY FORTY YEARS ago, I encountered the Bible's prediction that one man would eventually take control of the entire world. Frankly, I could not imagine how such a thing would ever happen. But since the Bible presented this as a major part of the end-time landscape, I believed it, and I preached it even though I could not comprehend it.

Today it is much easier to envision the possibility of such a world ruler. Technology has given us instant global communication. CNN is seen everywhere in the world. The Internet and satellite cell phones reach every country on the face of the earth. Air transportation has shrunk the planet to the point where we can set foot on the soil of any nation in a matter of hours. I am told that there are now missiles that can reach any part of the world in fewer than thirty minutes. Men and nations no longer live in isolation.

There are also other factors that make the ascendance of a global

leader more plausible than ever before. The Bible predicts that worldwide chaos, instability, and disorder will increase as we approach the
end of this age. Jesus Himself said that there would be wars, rumors
of wars, famines, and earthquakes in various places (Matthew 24:6–7).
Just before these tensions explode into world chaos, the Rapture of
the church will depopulate much of the planet. As many as seventy
million people could suddenly disappear from our nation alone.

The devastation wrought by these disasters will spur a worldwide
outcry for relief and order at almost any cost. That will set the stage
for the emergence of a new world leader who will, like a pied piper,
promise a solution to all problems. He will negotiate world peace and
promise order and security. This leader, who will emerge out of the
newly formed European Union, is commonly referred to in the Bible
as the Antichrist.

The very word *antichrist* sends a shudder through the hearts of
Christians. All have heard or read of him, and the fear that some feel
at the mention of his name comes largely from misunderstandings
and confusion about who he is, when he will appear, and what powers
he can exercise over God's people. In this chapter I want to dispel those
fears and clear up the confusion. I want to show you what is going on
in the world as it relates to the biblical predictions and descriptions of
the Antichrist and his work.

The word *antichrist* is used four times in the New Testament, each
time by the apostle John, and it is found only in his epistles (1 John
2:18, 22; 4:3; and 2 John 7). As the word suggests, the Antichrist is a
person who is against Christ. The prefix *anti* can also mean "instead
of," and both meanings will apply to this coming world leader. He will
overtly oppose Christ and at the same time pass himself off as Christ.

The Antichrist will aggressively live up to his terrible name. He will be Satan's superman, who persecutes, tortures, and kills the people of God and leads the armies of the world into the climactic Battle of Armageddon. He will be the most powerful dictator the world has ever seen, making Caesar, Hitler, Mao, and Saddam seem weak and tame by comparison.

Even though the Antichrist is identified by that name only four times in the Bible, he appears many more times under various aliases. He is also called:

- "the prince who is to come" (Daniel 9:26 NKJV)

- a "fierce" king (Daniel 8:23 NKJV)

- "a master of intrigue" (Daniel 8:23 NIV)

- "a despicable man" (Daniel 11:21 NLT)

- a "worthless shepherd" (Zechariah 11:16–17 NLT)

- "the one who brings destruction" (2 Thessalonians 2:3 NLT)

- "the lawless one" (2 Thessalonians 2:8 NKJV)

- "the evil man" (2 Thessalonians 2:9 NLT)

- the "beast" (Revelation 13:1 NKJV)

As a study of these references shows, the Antichrist is introduced and described in great detail in the Bible, yet his identity is not revealed. That lack of specific identification, however, has not stopped speculation on who he might be and even the outright naming of certain individuals. Many names have been suggested. When you google "Who is Antichrist?" you get about 1.5 million hits. Some of the Web sites post incredibly long and detailed articles—a sign of the extreme fascination generated by this sensational subject.

In the late 1930s and early 1940s, when Hitler was moving through Europe and swallowing up whole nations, many believed that he was the coming Antichrist.

Hitler offered himself as a messiah with a divine mission to save Germany. On one occasion he displayed the whip he often carried to demonstrate that "in driving out the Jews I remind myself of Jesus in the temple." He declared, "Just like Christ, I have a duty to my own people." He even boasted that just as Christ's birth had changed the calendar, so his victory over the Jews would be the beginning of a new age. "What Christ began," he said, "I will complete." . . . At one of the Nuremberg rallies, a giant photo of Hitler carried the caption, "In the beginning was the Word."[1]

I have a pamphlet in my file called *The Beast: The False Prophet and Hitler*. It was published in 1941, the year I was born. This pamphlet presented the formula for identifying Hitler as the Antichrist by showing how the letters in the word *Hitler* link him numerologically with the "number of the beast" given in Revelation 13:16–18:

He causes all, both small and great, rich and poor, free and slave, to receive a mark on their right hand or on their foreheads, and that no one may buy or sell except one who has the mark or the name of the beast, or the number of his name. Here is wisdom. Let him who has understanding calculate the number of the beast, for it is the number of a man: His number is 666.

The pamphlet bases its conclusion on a numerologic formula. Numerologists believe that meaning can be assigned to numbers.

Some biblical numerologists tell us that the number 666, when worked out through a transposition of number assignments to alphabetical letters, will identify the name of a certain man. In the Revelation passage we have only three numerals—666—but according to numerology, through these numbers we can find the man's name. The first step is to numeralize the alphabet: you let 100 stand for A, 101 for B, 102 for C, and so on through the rest of the letters. Then you take Hitler's name and give each letter its numerical value: H=107, I=108, T=119, L=111, E=104, R=117. Now, add up these six numbers, and voilà! The total is 666! So obviously Hitler must be the Antichrist.

Now, to get the most fun out of the game of "Who is the Antichrist?" you must play by these three rules: If the proper name does not reach the necessary total, add a title. If the sum cannot be found in English, try Hebrew, Greek, or Latin. Don't be too particular about the spelling.

And above all, be persistent. If you keep working at it, you can make anybody the Antichrist!

If numerology doesn't work for you, don't despair. There are other ways to identify the Antichrist, as we see by looking at another favorite candidate for the role: President John F. Kennedy. What signs pointed to him? He went through "death" and "resurrection" as a PT boat commander in the South Pacific during World War II. At the Democratic convention in 1956, he received 666 votes. He was also elected president and shot through the head, which is what the Bible says will happen to this future dictator. There were some who expected that as President Kennedy lay in state in the rotunda of the Capitol, he would come out of his casket and assert himself as the ruler of the world . . . which, of course, he failed to do. So, in spite of the elaborate and contrived reasons for believing that these two men and several others in history were to have been the Antichrist, all efforts to identify him have failed.

And they will continue to fail. As I noted above, the Bible does not tell us who the Antichrist will be. In fact, Paul tells us in the second chapter of Thessalonians that this coming world ruler will not be revealed until after the Rapture of the church. "So if you ever reach the point where you think you know who he is, that must mean you have been left behind."[2]

Yet while it is not possible to know the identity of the future world ruler, it is possible to know what kind of a man he will be, for the Bible gives us a wealth of information about him. Let's explore some of that information and learn a little more about the Antichrist.

The Personality of the Coming World Ruler

He Will Be a Charismatic Leader

The prophet Daniel described the Antichrist in these graphic terms: "After this I saw in the night visions, and behold, a fourth beast . . . And there . . . were eyes like the eyes of a man, and a mouth speaking pompous words. . . . He shall speak pompous words against the Most High" (Daniel 7:7–8, 25).

In these passages Daniel gives us one of the characteristics of the coming world ruler—his charismatic personality enhanced by his speaking ability, which he will use to sway the masses with spellbinding words of power and promise. We little realize the power of good speaking ability. An actor who is not classically handsome, such as James Earl Jones, can land great parts and charm audiences simply by the power of his resonant and articulate voice. Often Americans are swayed by political candidates who have little to offer, but they offer it in the beautiful package of their smooth intonation and syntax. As Daniel says, the coming world leader will be renowned for this kind of eloquence, which will capture the attention and admiration of the world.

Daniel goes on to tell us that this golden-tongued orator not only will speak in high-blown terms but also will utter pompous words against God. The apostle John described him in a similar fashion in the book of Revelation: "And he was given a mouth speaking great things and blasphemies" (Revelation 13:5).

Considering these and other prophecies, it's not hard to understand why Hitler has often been pegged as the prototype of the Antichrist. Hitler was a man of charisma, great oratory, and pomp. In his now classic book, *Kingdoms in Conflict*, Charles Colson described the well-orchestrated events that were played out in countless crowded halls as Hitler manipulated the German people:

> Solemn symphonic music began the set-up. The music then stopped, a hush prevailed, and a patriotic anthem began and "from the back, walking slowly down the wide central aisle," strutted Hitler. Finally, the Fuhrer himself rises to speak. Beginning in a low, velvet voice, which makes the audience unconsciously lean forward to hear, he speaks his love for Germany ... and gradually his pitch increases until he reaches a screaming crescendo. But his audience does not think his rasping shouts excessive. They are screaming with him.[3]

Hitler's pomp and charisma were not the only parallels between him and biblical prophecy.

The Bible predicts that a world ruler will arise in Europe who will promise peace while preparing for war. He will mesmerize the world, demanding the worship of the masses in exchange for the right to buy bread. He, like Hitler, will be indwelt by demonic forces, most likely by Satan himself. The parallels are so striking that Robert Van Kampen in his book *The Sign* says that he believes the Antichrist will actually be Hitler raised from the dead. Though this supposition is unlikely, Hitler does provide us a sneak preview showing in miniscule format the kind of man the Antichrist is likely to be.[4]

Daniel continued his description of the Antichrist by telling us he is a man "whose appearance was greater than his fellows" (Daniel 7:20). In terms of his outward appearance, this man will be a strikingly attractive person. The combination of magnetic personality, speaking ability, and extreme good looks will make him virtually irresistible to the masses. When he comes on the scene, people will flock to him like flies to honey, and they will fall over themselves to do anything he asks.

He Will Be a Cunning Leader

Daniel was given a picture of this world leader in his famous dream recorded in the seventh chapter of his book. Here is what he reported: "I was considering the horns, and there was another horn, a little one, coming up among them, before whom three of the first horns were plucked out by the roots" (Daniel 7:8).

If we read carefully and understand the prophetic symbol of the horns, we learn from this verse that the coming world leader subdues three other kings by plucking them out by their roots. This man will squeeze out the old to make room for the new. He will take over three kingdoms, one by one, not by making war but by clever political manipulation. He begins as the little horn, but then he succeeds in uprooting three of the first horns and thus abrogates their power to himself. Daniel reiterated this event in the eleventh chapter of his prophecy, telling us that this future world leader "shall come in peaceably, and seize the kingdom by intrigue" (Daniel 11:21). The Antichrist will be a political genius, a masterful diplomat, and a clever leader. Arthur W. Pink wrote of him:

Satan has had full opportunity afforded him to study fallen human nature . . . The devil knows full well how to dazzle people by the attraction of power . . . He knows how to gratify the craving for knowledge . . . He can delight the ear with music and the eye with entrancing beauty . . . He knows how to exalt people to dizzying heights of worldly greatness and fame, and how to control the greatness so that it may be employed against God and His people.[5]

In today's world, every leader wants to be the one who solves the perpetual crisis in the Middle East. American presidents dream of adding that distinction to their legacy. Jimmy Carter thought he had achieved it at Camp David. Bill Clinton tried frantically to eke out a settlement during the final months of his administration. Today, in a renewal of that shuttle diplomacy, President Bush also seeks to broker such a peace agreement. If this attempt fails, and if campaign speeches are any indication, the next US president appears likely to join the pursuit to complete the "road map to world peace."

Perhaps no diplomat worked harder at this goal than secretary of state Henry Kissinger during the Nixon and Ford years. Kissinger was himself a Jew whose family had escaped Germany during the Nazi years and who negotiated the end of the Yom Kippur War. In September 1970, Kissinger managed a Middle Eastern crisis between

Israel, Jordan, and Syria, during which he virtually lived in the White House Situation Room. One top US official who was involved in the sessions was asked if Dr. Kissinger enjoyed the manipulation of American power. "'Enjoy?' exclaimed the official. 'Henry adores power, absolutely adores it. To Henry, diplomacy is nothing without it.'" A Pentagon aid related how Kissinger leaned over large maps, moving toy battleships and aircraft carriers from one end of the Mediterranean to the other, arguing with admirals, expounding on military tactics and then picking up the phone to order the Joint Chiefs of Staff to change the deployment of the Sixth Fleet. The World War II sergeant had become all at once a general and an admiral and, during that crisis, a kind of deputy commander in chief.[6]

Because Kissinger was a European-born Jew of great brilliance who became the most powerful voice in world politics in the 1970s, some people speculated that he might be the Antichrist. He wasn't, of course, nor was he able to resolve the Israeli-Arab conflict. But Kissinger's love for power gives us a snapshot of one characteristic of the coming world ruler. One day a cunning superleader—a man who adores power—will arise and use his manipulative ability to succeed where all other diplomats have failed. He will resolve the Israeli-Arab conflict.

He Will Be a Cruel Leader

Once again we turn to the writings of Daniel to understand the personality of this coming tyrant.

Thus he said: "The fourth beast shall be a fourth kingdom on earth, which shall be different from all other kingdoms, and shall devour the whole earth, trample it and break it in pieces . . . He shall speak pompous words against the Most High, shall persecute the saints of the Most High, and shall intend to change times and law. Then the saints shall be given into his hand for a time and times and half a time." (Daniel 7:23, 25)

Here Daniel tells us that the Antichrist is going to devour the whole world; he will tread the world down. He will break it in pieces. These words hint at something utterly horrific. What will happen to agitate the Antichrist to unleash this immense cruelty? Although all the believers of the present age will be taken to heaven before the reign of this man, new converts will come to Christ during the years of tribulation. This will infuriate the Antichrist, and he will take out his wrath on those new Christians. Many followers of Christ will be martyred for their faith.

The word *persecute* in Daniel 7:25 literally means to "wear out." The same word is used to describe the wearing out of garments. The use of the word here indicates a slow, painful wearing down of the people of God—a torturous, cruel persecution reminiscent of the horrors Nero inflicted on Christians in ancient Rome, but even worse. It would be easier for the saints during the Tribulation if they were simply killed outright, but instead they will be "worn out"—mercilessly tortured by this unthinkably cruel man.

Again, we find a prototype of what is to come in the regime of Hitler. Charles Colson gives us a chilling description of what went on in Nazi concentration camps:

The first Nazi concentration camp opened in 1933. In one camp, hundreds of Jewish prisoners survived in disease-infested barracks on little food and gruesome, backbreaking work. Each day the prisoners were marched to the compound's giant factory, where tons of human waste and garbage were distilled into alcohol to be used as a fuel additive. Even worse than the nauseating smell was the realization that they were fueling the Nazi war machine.[7]

Colson goes on to say that as the result of the humiliation and drudgery of their lives, "dozens of the prisoners went mad and ran from their work, only to be shot by the guards or electrocuted by the fence."[8]

Hitler and the Nazis did not annihilate the Jews all at once; they deliberately and systematically wore down their souls. And that gives us a picture of what will happen in the Tribulation when the Antichrist is in power. He will be a cruel, blood-shedding leader, taking out his wrath on the saints who come to Christ under his regime.

The Profile of the Coming World Ruler

In the twelfth chapter of Revelation we read of the dragon, or Satan, being thrown out of heaven in a great war. Then in the thirteenth chapter we discover that the dragon comes to earth to begin his program by embodying his agent, the Antichrist. When we link this chapter with verses from Daniel, we get a good profile of this leader by looking at how he comes to power from several different viewpoints. Each of these viewpoints—the political, the national, the spiritual, and the providential—give us a good picture of what he will be like. So let's briefly explore what the Bible tells us about how the Antichrist comes to power.

He Will Be Politically Inconspicuous

Daniel 7 tells us that the Antichrist will not make a big splash when he arrives on the political scene. He will not enter with a fanfare, announcing, "I am here! I will now take over!" Instead, he will squeeze his way in, little by little, beginning as one among many minor political leaders. In prophetic imagery, he is the little horn who grows to be the big horn. He will attract little attention as he methodically begins to grasp more and more power.

John the apostle emphasized this fact when he wrote that this ominous personality will arise from among the mass of ordinary people. "Then I stood on the sand of the sea. And I saw a beast rising up out of the sea, having seven heads and ten horns, and on his horns ten crowns, and on his heads a blasphemous name" (Revelation 13:1). The *sea* in biblical imagery stands for the general mass of humanity or, more specifically, the gentile nations. We find confirmation of that meaning for the sea in Revelation 17: "Then he said to me, 'The waters which you saw, where the harlot sits, are peoples, multitudes, nations, and tongues'" (v. 15).

What we learn in these passages is that at first the Antichrist will not be obvious. He will not burst onto the scene in all his power and glory, but rather he will rise out of the sea of common humanity, or emerge inauspiciously from among ordinary people, as did Napoleon and Hitler.

He Will Emerge from a Gentile Nation

From what nation will the coming world ruler emerge? Often we hear that he must come from the Jewish nation. Since he will make a covenant with the nation of Israel, many people reason that perhaps he will be the Jew that Israel anticipates as her messiah. But the Bible gives us no evidence for determining that the Antichrist is a Jew. In fact, we have strong evidence for believing the opposite. Dr. Thomas Ice weighed in on the ethnicity of the Antichrist and concluded:

A widely held belief throughout the history of the church has been the notion that Antichrist will be of Jewish origin. This view is still somewhat popular in our day. However, upon closer examination we find no real Scriptural basis for such a view. In fact, the Bible teaches just the opposite . . . that Antichrist will be of Gentile descent.[9]

As we saw in an earlier chapter, some form of the Roman Empire must be revived before the end times, and this appears to be coming about through the formation of the European Union. The Antichrist will emerge from one of the unified European nations. John's revelation affirms that the world ruler will arise from the masses within a gentile nation.

He Will Be Spiritually Blasphemous

Daniel said of this world leader, "He shall speak *pompous* words against the Most High, shall persecute the saints of the Most High, and shall intend to change times and law" (Daniel 7:25, *emphasis added*). In his second letter to the Thessalonians, Paul described him as one "who opposes and exalts himself above all that is called God or that is worshiped, so that he sits as God in the temple of God, showing himself that he is God" (2 Thessalonians 2:4).

As Paul wrote in Romans 1, and as the history of ancient Israel warns us over and over, it is a terrible thing to worship a *creature* instead of the *Creator*. Yet as Daniel warned, this man will defy God and demand to be worshipped instead of Him. And his demand will be met. As John wrote, "All who dwell on the earth will worship him, whose names have not been written in the Book of Life of the Lamb slain from the foundation of the world" (Revelation 13:8).

As if declaring himself to be God gives him power over nature and human nature, this ruler will also attempt to change the moral and natural laws of the universe. In the early days of the French Revolution, the new leaders tried to get control of the masses by changing everything that grew out of Christianity or Christian tradition. They set up a new calendar by which years were numbered, not from the birth of Christ but from the date of the revolution. They issued decrees to change all Christian churches to "temples of reason" and to melt down church bells for the metal. They actually tried to replace the seven-day week established by God with a ten-day week.[10] Such extreme actions showing hostility to everything related to God will characterize the coming world leader. No doubt he would even change the length of a year if he could somehow gain control of the earth's rotation!

While the Antichrist is pictured as "the beast rising up out of the *sea*," John wrote that the beast, "that ascends out of the bottomless *pit*," the one who will again be remanded to the bottomless pit until the end of the Millennium, is none other than Satan himself (Revelation 9:11; 11:7; 20:1–3, *emphasis added*). The Antichrist, with his seven heads, ten horns with their ten crowns, and his blasphemous mouth . . . whom all the world marveled at and followed, was given his power by Satan (Revelation 13:1–4).

He Will Be Limited Providentially

As both Daniel and John show us, the Antichrist is a terrifying person. He is the epitome of evil, the ultimate negation of everything good, the avowed enemy and despiser of God. Every follower of Christ ought to bow before God at this moment and give thanks that he or she will not be on this earth during the reign of the Antichrist. At the same time, we must not forget that this satanic creature is not equal to God. He does not have absolute power or anything close to it. God has him on a chain. In fact, in Revelation 13, we are reminded repeatedly that the Antichrist can only do what he is allowed to do.

Twice in this chapter, we find the little phrase, *and he was given.* "And he was given a mouth speaking great things and blasphemies, and he was given authority to continue for forty-two months" (v. 5). We also find in this chapter, "It was granted to him to make war with the saints and to overcome them. And authority was given him over every tribe, tongue, and nation" (v. 7). As in the story of Job, Satan (and his puppet, the Antichrist) will be able to do only that which God allows. The Antichrist will be able to create terrible havoc and chaos, but ultimately God is still God, and no enemy of His will go beyond the boundaries He sets.

He Will Have an Intimidating Presence

The four major kingdoms depicted in Daniel's other prophetic vision were likened to certain animals: Babylon was like a lion, Medo-Persia was like a bear, Greece was like a leopard, and Rome was like the ten-horned beast (Daniel 7). In the descriptions of the beast in Revelation, we have all of these characteristics combined into one horrific creature (Revelation 13:2). This likeness of the Antichrist to ferocious beasts is meant to show us the intimidating presence of this satanic creature. He combines in his person all of the threatening characteristics of the kingdoms which have gone before him. Dr. W. A. Criswell wrote:

Think of the golden majesty of Babylon. Of the mighty ponderous massiveness of Cyrus the Persian. Think of the beauty and the elegance and the intellect of the ancient Greek world. Think of the

Roman with his laws and his order and his idea of justice. All of these glories will be summed up in the majesty of this one eventual *Antichrist* who will be like Nebuchadnezzar, like Cyrus, like Tiglath Pileser, like Shalmanezer, like Julius Caesar, like Caesar Augustus, like Alexander the Great, like Napoleon Bonaparte, like Frederick the Great and Charlemagne, all bound up into one.[11]

It's no wonder that people will follow this man and even fall down and worship him. We see in our own political campaigns how quickly people gravitate to charisma and power. Give us a fine-looking candidate with a golden voice, a powerful presence, and the ability to enthrall people with vague rhetoric about an undefined better future, and we follow like sheep as the media bleats the candidate's praises. Completely overlooked is the substance of the man's program. The presence and charisma of the Antichrist will be similar, making his rise to power inevitable.

The Program of the Coming World Ruler

One of the first acts of this world leader will be to make peace with Israel. And he will keep this covenant during the first three and a half years of his rule. At that point, however, he will change his tactics. He will drop all pretensions of peace and adopt a program of crushing power. He will break his covenant with Israel and subject the Jews to great persecution (Daniel 9:27; Isaiah 28:18).

Then will come the leader's most sensational moment. The Antichrist will actually be killed, but to the astonishment of all the world, he will be raised back to life by the power of Satan in a grotesque counterfeit of the Resurrection of Jesus Christ (Revelation 13:3–4).

After his death and satanic resurrection, the Antichrist will assassinate the leaders of three countries in the European Union, and all other nations will immediately relinquish their power to him. It is then that he will set himself up to be worshipped by all the people of the world. Through his associate, the false prophet, the mark of the beast will be placed upon all those who will follow him. Anyone who does not bear this mark will be unable to buy or sell in the world's economy.

In times past, the idea of a mark that would individually identify everyone in the world for governmental control seemed a far-fetched fantasy possible only in science fiction. No one today, however, questions the possibility of such an identification process. New methods of identification are being invented every day. Recently I became acquainted with RFID, or Radio Frequency Identification. RFID is on the crest of the current wave of technology. The system involves the implantation of a tiny chip (0.05 by 0.05 millimeters) into retail items to thwart shoplifters. They have also been implanted into pets to track them should they stray, and more recently into Alzheimer's patients. These microchips can also be used as personal identity markers surgically implanted under your skin and loaded with tons of recorded information about you.[12] The Antichrist will have available to him this technology and many other options when it comes to implementing the mark of the beast.

In a final act of rebellion against God, this vile person will set himself up in Jerusalem and desecrate the rebuilt temple in what is called the "abomination of desolation." He will then attempt to annihilate every Jew on earth, thus sounding the first ominous note in the prelude to the Battle of Armageddon.

This despot of all despots will be ultimately destroyed when Jesus Christ comes to battle against the Antichrist and his armies. In that climactic war the Antichrist will be killed, and his forces will be .

destroyed. The victorious Christ will assume His throne as rightful king and ruler of the universe.

More important than speculating about the identity of the Antichrist is remembering that his power broker, Satan, is not the equal opposite of Almighty God. Only God knows the day, the hour, the millisecond that will usher in Satan's reign on earth as Christ raptures the church. Like us, Satan can only look for the signs and wait. Throughout the millennia of his waiting, it is likely that he has been reading scouting reports and evaluating some choice candidates and maybe even issuing a few letters of intent so he will be ready when his hour does come.

Is the Antichrist lurking somewhere out there in the masses of humanity right now? Is his darkened mind already plotting the evils that he will inflict in the last days? I believe it is entirely possible, if not highly probable.

Gary Frazier gives us a possible scenario:

> Somewhere at this moment there may be a young man growing to maturity. He is in all likelihood a brooding, thoughtful young man. Inside his heart, however, there is a hellish rage. It boils like a caldron of molten lead. He hates God. He despises Jesus Christ. He detests the Church. In his mind there is taking shape the form of a dream of conquest. He will disingenuously present himself as a friend of Christ and the Church. Yet . . . He will, once empowered, pour out hell itself onto this world. Can the world produce such a prodigy? Hitler was once a little boy. Stalin was a lad. Nero was a child. The tenderness of childhood will be shaped by the devil into the terror of the *antichrist*.[13]

I realize that the picture of the future I've presented in this chapter is not a pretty one. Yet I am so often questioned about the identity of the Antichrist, and there is so much spurious and false information about him floating around, that I felt compelled to address the question. Christians need to know what is going on in the world concerning this dreaded person. But of much greater importance than looking for the Antichrist, we are to be "looking for the blessed hope and glorious appearing of our great God and Savior Jesus Christ" (Titus 2:13).

Jesus told us what to do during this time of waiting. We are to keep our hearts from being unnecessarily troubled. If we believe in Him, He will one day take us to that home He has been preparing for us, and we will be with Him! There is only one way to have that assurance. Jesus said, "I am the way, the truth, and the life. No one comes to the Father except through Me" (John 14:6).

Giving your life to Christ is the only absolute and certain guarantee that when He comes, you will be saved from personally experiencing the evil of the Antichrist by that daring air rescue called the Rapture. You will be taken out of the world into His glorious presence, never to experience the horrors Daniel and John described in their prophecies.

Keep looking up!

EIGHT

The New Axis of Evil

ON JANUARY 29, 2002, IN HIS STATE OF THE UNION ADDRESS, President George W. Bush used the term *Axis of Evil* for the first time. He identified Iran, Iraq, and North Korea as "states . . . [who are] arming to threaten the peace of the world . . . These regimes," he said, "pose a grave threat and growing danger. They could provide these arms to terrorists, giving them the means to match their hatred."[1] President Bush was roundly criticized for calling these nations *evil*, but as we will see in this chapter, his description was more than accurate.

On May 6, 2002, US ambassador to the United Nations John Bolton gave a speech titled "Beyond the Axis of Evil," in which he added three more rogue states to the axis: Libya, Syria, and Cuba. Today the term *Axis of Evil* includes all six states.

One nation on this Axis of Evil list is of special interest to us because we find that it is also on God's list. That nation and that list are found in the thirty-eighth and thirty-ninth chapters of Ezekiel. These chapters, written some twenty-six hundred years ago, give us one of the most important and dramatic prophecies in all Scripture.

It is commonly referred to as the prophecy against Gog and Magog, and it is the most detailed prophecy concerning war in the entire Bible. The prophecy predicts an invasion of Israel in the last days—an invasion comprised of enormous masses of troops from a coalition of nations led by Russia and Iran.

It is likely that this invasion will occur shortly after Israel signs a covenant with the new leader of the European Union. Because of this agreement, Israel will be at peace with her Islamic neighbors. The people of Israel will believe that the European powers will protect them from any outside aggressor or invader . . . especially from Russia, which will have joined forces with Iran to develop weapons for the purpose of utterly destroying Israel.

The Identity of the Nations

Now the word of the LORD came to me, saying, "Son of man, set your face against Gog, of the land of Magog, the prince of Rosh, Meshech, and Tubal, and prophesy against him, and say, 'Thus says the Lord GOD: "Behold, I am against you, O Gog, the prince of Rosh, Meshech, and Tubal. I will turn you around, put hooks into your jaws, and lead you out, with all your army, horses, and horsemen, all splendidly clothed, a great company with bucklers and shields, all of them handling swords. Persia, Ethiopia, and Libya are with them, all of them with shield and helmet; Gomer and all its troops; the house of Togarmah from the far north and all its troops— many people are with you. Prepare yourself and be ready, you and all your companies that are gathered about you; and be a guard for them."'" (Ezekiel 38:1–7)

Here we see that Ezekiel's prophecy begins with a list of proper names. Many of these names identify certain grandchildren and great-grandchildren of Noah who were the fathers of nations that for a time bore their names (Genesis 10). These nations, which today no longer have those original names, will ultimately form a coalition that will march against Israel. As we identify these nations by their present names and locate them on today's world map, we can see how the stage is being set for this predicted Russian/Islamic invasion of Israel.

Gog is an exception on Ezekiel's list. Gog is not one of the descendants of Noah listed in Genesis 10. This name, however, is found twelve times in Ezekiel 38–39. It is not the name of a nation, but rather the title of a ruler. In fact, the word means "ruler," or "the man on top." It is clear that Gog is an individual rather than a nation because God addresses him as such in this prophecy (Ezekiel 38:14; 39:1). Furthermore, Gog is explicitly called "the prince" in Ezekiel 38:2 and 39:1.

The next name in Ezekiel's prophecy is Magog. In his book, *The Nations in Prophecy,* John F. Walvoord wrote, "Magog is best identified with the Scythians . . . The ancient historian Josephus makes that identification and we have no reason to question it. The Scythians apparently lived immediately to the north of . . . Israel, then some of them emigrated north, going all the way to the Asiatic Circle."[2] Interestingly, Herodotus records that these Scythians were of Indo-Aryan heritage and spoke an Iranian language related to Persian.[3] Using these clues, we can identify Magog today as being made up of nations that were formerly parts of the Soviet Union: Kazakhstan, Kyrgyzstan, Uzbekistan, Turkmenistan, Tajikistan, Azerbaijan, Georgia, and possibly Afghanistan.

The next name on Ezekiel's list is Rosh, which is found in the Old Testament more than six hundred times. During Ezekiel's time, the word *Rosh* identified a nation that included people living north of the Black Sea. In the prophecies of Ezekiel, we are told three times (38:6, 15; 39:2) that part of the force that invades Israel will come from the "distant north," or "the remotest parts of the north." The land that is most distantly north and remote to Israel is Russia.

John F. Walvoord wrote:

If one takes any map of the world and draws a line north of the land of Israel he will inevitably come to the nation of Russia. As soon as the line is drawn to the far north beyond Asia Minor and the Black Sea it is in Russia and continues to be Russia for many hundreds of miles all the way to the Arctic Circle . . . On the basis of geography alone, it seems quite clear that the only nation which could possibly be referred to as coming from the far north would be the nation of Russia.[4]

When the Soviet Union collapsed in the 1990s, many thought that Russia's days of prominence and power were over. But fewer than two decades later we find a resurgent Russia seeking to reclaim the strategic ground she lost. Someone has said that since the days of the collapse of the Soviet Union, the great Russian bear has been like a mother bear robbed of her cubs.[5] If Magog includes the countries of the collapsed Soviet Union, Rosh specifically identifies the nation of Russia, which is presently trying to reassemble its lost empire.

Edward Lucas, a journalist who has covered Eastern Europe for the *Economist* for more than twenty years, has recently written a frightening book titled *The New Cold War*. He warns that Russia is rising again as a hostile power. It is reasserting its military muscle, intensely pursuing global energy markets, coercing neighboring nations back into the old Soviet orbit, silencing journalists and dissidents, and laying the groundwork with modernized weaponry for reestablishing its former power and influence. The West, wrote Lucas, is asleep to the growing danger and is losing the New Cold War. I would have to agree.

His Web site gives some very insightful examples:

> Russia's vengeful, xenophobic, and ruthless rulers have turned the sick man of Europe into a menacing bully. The rise to power of Vladimir Putin and his ex-KGB colleagues coincided with a tenfold rise in world oil prices. Though its incompetent authoritarian rule is a tragic missed opportunity for the Russian people, Kremlin, Inc. has paid off the state's crippling debts and is restoring its clout at home and abroad. Inside Russia it has crushed every constraint, muzzling the media, brushing aside political opposition, castrating the courts and closing down critical pressure groups.[6]

So successful is Russia's return to the world stage that *Time* magazine chose Russian president Vladimir Putin as its 2007 Person of the Year for "taking Russia from chaos to a position of importance in the world today."[7] Although the Russian leader appears to have quelled chaos within his own country by use of autocratic power, he seems intent on fomenting chaos on the world stage by advancing a new cold war. He "accused the West of encroaching on Russia's borders and starting a new arms race,"[8] and "the United States of trying to impose its will on the world by military force."[9]

Attempting to justify his hostility toward the West, Putin said, "We [Russians] are striving to create a fairer world based on the principles of equality . . . Time has shown our views find support in Arab and other Muslim states."[10] In fact, "Russia is determined to further enhance its relations with Muslim countries . . . We are all allies of the kingdom in working to meet the world's need for energy."[11]

In October 2007, during Putin's first ever visit to Iran, an Iranian newspaper reported that he "reassured Iran that the Bushehr nuclear reactor, a billion-dollar energy project being built by Russia and dogged by delays, would be completed." The report went on to suggest, "Maybe the most important result of Putin's trip is to show the independence of Russia toward America and the West."[12] Putin made other first-time-ever visits of a Russian leader to the Muslim nations of Saudi Arabia, Qatar, Jordan, United Arab Emirates, Indonesia, and most currently, Libya. By all reports, his visits were successful financially, resulting in lucrative agreements and contracts for further joint efforts in the production of oil and the exploration of natural gas reserves.

Apparently the Russian president was successful politically as well. In Libya, President Gadhafi and Putin agreed that the United Nations "needs to be reformed in order to face an 'imbalance of forces' internationally," and especially "the Security Council with which we can work together to resolve problems."[13]

Europe is not blind to what is going on in Russia. European leaders have taken note of Russia's resurgence with growing alarm and dismay. According to a former German foreign minister, "Today, it is the Kremlin that sets the agenda for EU–Russia relations, and it does so in a manner that increasingly defies the rules of the game."[14] According to one source, "Russia appears to be winning the energy dominance game, signing individual deals with EU member states and moving forward with . . . pipelines."[15] Among these EU member states are several of Russia's former cubs. As the mother bear regains her strength, she is actively seeking to draw her brood back into her den.

Meshech and Tubal, the next names on Ezekiel's list, are usually mentioned together when they appear in the Bible. In the past, it has been widely assumed that these were ancient names for the modern cities of Moscow and Tobolsk. But very few scholars today identify Meshech and Tubal as Russian cities. One reason is Ezekiel's assertion that they were trading partners with ancient Tyre: "Javan, Tubal, and Meshech were your traders. They bartered human lives and vessels of bronze for your merchandise" (Ezekiel 27:13). It is highly unlikely that ancient Tyre (modern Lebanon) would be trading with Moscow and the Siberian city of Tobolsk. The more probable identification of Meshech and Tubal is as part of the present nation of Turkey.

The next country Ezekiel names is Persia, a name that appears thirty-five times in the Old Testament. Persia is easy for us to identify because it retained the name it had held since ancient times until March 1935, when it became the nation of Iran. Nearly four and a half decades later, Iran officially changed its name to the Islamic Republic of Iran. Today, with its population of 70 million people, Iran has become the hotbed of militant Islam and anti-Semitic hatred.

Iran's government is officially a theocratic republic whose ultimate political authority resides in the supreme leader, currently Ayatollah Ali Khamenei. This fact surprises many people who assume that the persistently vocal and visible president Mahmoud Ahmadinejad is the top man in Iran. But despite his virulent verbalizing, threats, and saber rattling, Ahmadinejad is only a figurehead under Khamenei. Iran's geographical location on the Persian Gulf and the vital Strait of Hormuz gives her great power. According to CIA reports in 2007, vast oil reserves and the upwardly spiraling price of crude oil gave Iran sixty billion dollars in foreign exchange reserves. Yet her people continue to live with high unemployment and inflation. Iran is identified as a prime player in the human trafficking trade. It is also a "key transshipment point" for heroin into Europe and has the "highest percentage of the populations in the world using opiates."[16] Additionally, the United States has identified Iran as a state sponsor of terrorism.

In a cat-and-mouse game that's been going on since August 2002, world governments have been in a continual on-again, off-again confrontation with Iran over its uranium enrichment capabilities. But world opinion seems to have no more effect on Iran than water on the back of a duck. As a US State Department spokesman recently commented, "the Iranian regime is continuing on a path of defiance of the international community."[17] Despite two rounds of sanctions and the possibility of a third, in February 2008 a defiant Ahmadinejad thumbed his nose at the UN Security Council's demand that Iran suspend uranium enrichment. He said, "With the help of Allah, the Iranian nation with its unity, faith, and determination stood and defeated the world powers and brought them to their knees."[18]

In a surprising reversal, the United States announced in early December 2007 that while Iran did have a secret nuclear weapons program at one time, the program had been abandoned, and Iran was no longer pursuing nuclear capabilities. Perhaps emboldened by the US announcement, in January 2008, five armed Iranian boats menaced three US Navy vessels in the Strait of Hormuz. The tense confrontation prompted a White House warning: "We urge the Iranians to refrain from such provocative actions that could lead to a dangerous incident in the future."[19]

The Iranian regime is well known for its hatred of Israel and its desire to eliminate her. In October 2005, the newly elected president Ahmadinejad declared to the World Without Zionism audience, "As the imam said, Israel must be wiped off the map . . . Anybody who recognizes Israel will burn in the fire of the Islamic nation's fury." He went on to say that any Islamic leader "who recognizes the Zionist regime means he is acknowledging the surrender and defeat of the Islamic world."[20]

Iran's militant influence extends beyond her own borders. In March 2008, Hezbollah chief Hassan Nasrallah railed, "The presence of Israel is but temporary and cannot go on in the region. We will see you killed in the fields, we will kill you in the cities, we will fight you like you have never seen before."[21] Hezbollah leaders do not have the authority to make such threats on their own. Hezbollah is an Islamic fundamentalist group, and though its base of operations is Lebanon, its authority comes from a source higher in the Islamic hierarchy. As Hezbollah's deputy chief, Sheikh Naim Qassem has said, "Even when it comes to firing rockets on Israeli civilians, that decision requires an in-principle permission from [the ruling jurisprudent]."[22] In this case the ruling jurisprudent would be the supreme leader of Iran— Ayatollah Ali Khamenei. "We ask, receive answers, and then apply. This is even true for acts of suicide for the sake of Allah—no one may kill himself without a jurisprudence permission [from Khamenei]."[23] Thus we can see that the aggressive and threatening influence of Iran infects and controls other Islamic terrorist organizations.

In reply to the Iranian-Hezbollah verbal bullying, UN secretary-general Ban Ki-Moon stated, "I am concerned by the threats of open war against Israel by the secretary general of Hezbollah."[24] Such deadly threats and utter disdain for world opinion is pretty convincing evidence that our national leaders are right on target in including Iran as a member of the Axis of Evil.

The next nation Ezekiel lists is Ethiopia. Some Bible translations render this nation as Cush, who is identified as a grandson of Noah, the first of Ham's four sons. "The sons of Ham were Cush, Mizraim, Put, and Canaan" (Genesis 10:6). In the verses that follow, we learn that the descendants of Cush settled in Arabia, Mesopotamia, and Assyria. The Cushites themselves, however, were established in Africa where they occupied a territory much larger than the modern Ethiopia, for the Ethiopia of ancient times included the present-day Sudan. This fact is significant to us, as Sudan is hardly a friend to the West. Sudan supported Iraq in the Gulf War and also harbored Osama bin Laden.

The next nation identified by Ezekiel is Libya. Some Bible translations render this nation as Put, which we find in Genesis 10 to be the name of another grandson of Noah. There is no ambiguity about the present identity of this nation, for ancient maps show that the territory occupied in Ezekiel's time by the nation of Put is now the modern nation of Libya. Since 1969, Libya has been under the dictatorial control of Colonel Mu'ammar al Gadhafi. It is an Islamic nation seething with a great hatred for Israel and, ominously, has recently formed a new alliance with Russia.

Gomer is next on Ezekiel's list. Gomer is mentioned in Genesis 10 as one of Japheth's sons. Genesis 10:3 helps us identify Gomer further by telling us that one of Gomer's relatives is Ashkenaz. Today, Israelis describe Jews from Germany, Austria, and Poland as *Ashkenazim*. This gives us a clue to Gomer's present-day identity, as this term associated with Gomer has likely been passed down through generations, retaining the identify of the people even as the name of the country has changed. Gibbon, in *The Decline and Fall of the Roman Empire*, said, "Gomer is modern Germany."[25] The modern nation identified as the ancient land of Gomer is usually thought to be either Germany or Turkey.

Ezekiel 38:6 refers to Gomer with "all its troops" (NKJV), or "all his bands" (KJV), or "all its hordes" (ASV), indicating that this nation will provide a powerful army in the assault on Israel. If ancient Gomer is part of the modern Turkey, as I believe it to be, it is a country with a growing allegiance to Russia. If we listen to the nightly news, we know that this nation has a strong military presence on the northern border of Iraq—quite possibly the "hordes" that Ezekiel refers to—and is already involved in the conflict over the control of the Middle East.

At the end of his list, Ezekiel added the house of Togarmah or, as it is rendered in some translations, Beth Togarmah (which is the same thing since the word *beth* is the Hebrew word for *house*). Secular historians usually place Beth Togarmah in the geographic location of Phrygia, a western kingdom in Asia Minor. Like Meshech, Tubal, and Gomer, Beth Togarmah was a part of the geographical area we currently call Turkey.

Thus Ezekiel completed his list of specifically identified nations that will come against Israel in the last days. And what a formidable list it is! Yet as if those nations were not enough, Ezekiel added that many more nations will also join the coalition to crush Israel: "many people are with you," he wrote. This is a reference to many smaller countries that have become allied with the more significant nations that Ezekiel specifically identifies. Nearly all of these nations are either Islamic or pro-Islamic. When this formidable mass of armies comes against Israel, there will be no possible human defense for the Israelis.

In a verse that follows this prophecy, Ezekiel spoke of some nations that will not be involved in the invasion of Israel: "Sheba, Dedan, the merchants of Tarshish, and all their young lions will say to you, 'Have you come to take plunder? Have you gathered your army to take booty, to carry away silver and gold, to take away livestock and goods, to take great plunder?'" (v. 13). Most Bible scholars believe that Sheba and Dedan refer to the peoples of the Arabian Peninsula, including modern-day Saudi Arabia, Yemen, Oman, and the Gulf countries of Kuwait and the United Arab Emirates.

Tarshish was a term that in ancient times described the western-most part of human civilization. Many scholars believe that "the merchants of Tarshish" and its "villages" and "young lions" refer to the market-based economies of Western Europe. Some scholars have even dared to be more specific. Dr. David L. Cooper wrote, "When all the historical statements are examined thoroughly, it seems that the evidence is in favor of identifying Tarshish as England."[26] Another scholar, Theodore Epp, agrees with this identification. He points out that the lion is a symbol for Britain and suggests that Britain's colonies, many of which have spun off to become nations of their own, are the cubs, or "young lions" in Ezekiel's prophecy. He said, "Great Britain's young lions, such as Canada, Australia, New Zealand, the African colonies, and the United States are strong enough to make an exhibit of disfavor in that day."[27]

If Theodore Epp and Dr. Cooper are right, it seems that the West in general will not participate in the invasion of Israel. What interests us in this study is that Ezekiel's prophecy of the alignment of nations, showing which ones will and which will not rise to crush Israel, squares very closely with the alignment of nations we see shaping up in the world right now. Thus we find that Ezekiel's ancient prophecy, written some twenty-six hundred years ago, informs us as to what is going on in the world today right before our very eyes.

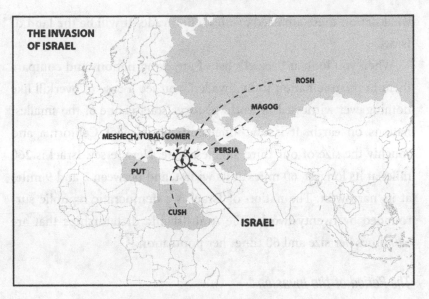

THE INVASION
OF ISRAEL

ROSH

MAGOG

MESHECH, TUBAL, GOMER

PERSIA

PUT

CUSH

ISRAEL

The Invasion of Israel

The Place of the Invasion

Ezekiel clearly identifies Israel as the land that will be invaded by the nations named on the map above. He stresses this fact at least five times in chapter 38—sometimes obliquely, giving us some characteristic of the people to be invaded, and sometimes explicitly, identifying the land by name: "you will come into the land of those brought back from the sword and gathered from many people on the mountains of Israel, which had long been desolate; they were brought out of the nations, and now all of them dwell safely" (v. 8); "a land of unwalled villages; I will go to a peaceful people, who dwell safely, all of them dwelling without walls, and having neither bars nor gates" (v. 11); "a people gathered from the nations" (v. 12); "'On that day when My people Israel dwell safely'" (v. 14); "'You will come up against my people Israel'" (v. 16). There can be no question about what nation these amassed armies will invade. It will be the land of Israel.

When you look at Ezekiel's list of attacking nations and compare them to the one nation to be invaded, you see a case of overkill like nothing ever witnessed in world history. Israel is one of the smallest nations on earth. It is one-nineteenth the size of California and roughly the size of our third smallest state, New Jersey. Israel is 260 miles at its longest, 60 miles at its widest, and between 3 and 9 miles at its narrowest. The nation of Israel is a democratic republic surrounded by twenty-two hostile Arab/Islamic dictatorships that are 640 times her size and 60 times her population.[28]

The Period of the Invasion

Ezekiel does not give a specific date for the invasion, but he does give us ways to identify the time when it will occur: "'After many days . . . in the latter years . . .'" (Ezekiel 38: 8); "'On that day when My people Israel dwell safely . . .'" (v. 14); "'It will be in the latter days that I will bring you against My land'" (v.16).

The prophet tells us that the invasion of Israel will take place sometime in the future (latter years). It will happen at a time when Israel is dwelling in peace and safety and not involved in conflict with other nations.

Has there ever been such a time in Israel's history? No, there has not! Is today such a time? No! When will there be such a time? The only period in Israel's life likely to meet this requirement comes immediately following the Rapture of the church when the Antichrist and the European Union make a treaty with Israel to guarantee her peace and security. When this treaty is signed, the people of Israel will relax the diligence they have been forced to maintain since the founding of their nation in 1948. They will rely on the treaty and turn their attention away from defense to concentrate on increasing their wealth. Israel will truly be a land of unwalled villages. Her defenses will be down, and she will be woefully unprepared for the invasion by the armies of Russia and the coalition.

The Purpose of the Invasion

The nations in the battle of Gog and Magog will come down on the nation of Israel, pursuing three primary goals. The first goal will be to seize her land. As Ezekiel puts it, "to stretch out your hand against the waste places which are again inhabited" (Ezekiel 38:12). The second goal of the invaders will be to steal Israel's wealth: "To take plunder and to take booty, to stretch out your hand . . . against a people gathered from the nations, who have acquired livestock and goods, who dwell in the midst of the land . . . to carry away silver and gold, to take away livestock and goods, to take great plunder" (vv. 12–13).

And there is plenty of wealth to be plundered in modern Israel, as we can see by the following quote from a recent article in the *Jerusalem Post*: "Despite a population of only slightly more than 7 million people . . . Israel is now home to more than 7,200 millionaires . . . Of the 500 wealthiest people in the world, six are now Israeli, and all told, Israel's rich had assets in 2007 of more than 35 billion dollars . . . Israel's GDP is almost double that of any other Middle East country."[29]

Success and wealth in the high-tech industry has replaced earlier agricultural kibbutzim and started her on "the extraordinary road . . . from the socialist experiment of defiant European Jews to the high-tech revolution that has created a Silicon Valley in the Middle East, second only to the United States in start-ups.[30] In 2007, venture capitalists invested 1.76 billion dollars in start-up companies in developing "advanced telecom equipment" in Israel's "Silicon Wadi."[31]

According to one prosperity index, Israel exported goods and services of more than $70 billion last year, including $34.2 billion from the technology sector alone. "Israel is the highest-ranking Middle Eastern country in the index."[32] In 2007, she had a per capita gross domestic product index of $28,800, which compared favorably with the much larger European Union at $32,900.[33] Any way you measure it, Israel has become prosperous, and despite a recent recession and military conflict, her economy has continued to grow.

Finally, the invading nations have as their ultimate goal the wholesale slaughter of Israel's people: "I will go to a peaceful people, who dwell safely, all of them dwelling without walls, and having neither bars nor gates . . . to stretch out your hand . . . against a people gathered from the nations . . . You will come up against My people Israel like a cloud, to cover the land" (vv. 11–12, 16). The historical accumulated hatred for the Jews will drive these armies forward with the assurance that this time, the people of Israel will not escape death.

The Particulars of the Invasion

"You will ascend, coming like a storm, covering the land like a cloud, you and all your troops and many peoples with you . . . Then you will come from your place out of the far north, you and many peoples with you, all of them riding on horses, a great company and a mighty army. You will come up against My people Israel like a cloud, to cover the land." (Ezekiel 38:9, 15–16)

In these passages Ezekiel tells us that the coalition of massive armies will gather from all the attacking nations and assemble on the mountains of Israel. One writer helps us understand the strategy of invading from these mountains:

> The mountains of Israel are mainly located on the country's north-ern borders with modern-day Syria, Lebanon, and northern Jordan (notably the strategically important Golan Heights). Since the Russian-Iranian coalition is described by the prophet as coming pri-marily from the north, it is reasonable to conclude that Syria and Lebanon are participants in the coalition. Jordan maybe as well, though this is not entirely clear.[34]

Now that we have set the stage for the invasion of the assembled armies against Israel by identifying the place, the timing, the purpose, and some of the particulars, let's look next at what will happen when this invasion actually begins.

The Intervention of God

When the massive Russian-Islamic armies assemble on the northern mountains of Israel, ready to come against that tiny country, it will appear to be the most grossly mismatched contest in military history. The Israelis will be so outnumbered that there will be no human way they can win this war. Only intervention by God himself could pos-sibly save them. And that is exactly what will happen. As Ezekiel tells us: "'And it will come to pass at the same time, when Gog comes against the land of Israel,' says the Lord GOD, 'that My fury will show in My face. For in My jealousy, and in the fire of My wrath I have spoken'" (Ezekiel 38:18–19a).

How will God accomplish this miraculous feat? What will be the results of His intervention? These are questions we can answer by continuing to explore Ezekiel's prophecy, and the answers will enable us to understand how today's events will play out to fulfill God's purposes in the near future.

The Arsenal of Weapons

When God goes to war, He uses weapons unique to Him—weapons that render the arsenals of men as ineffective as a water pistol against a nuclear bomb. God will save His people Israel by employing four of these weapons simultaneously. First, he will rout the armies of Israel's attackers with massive convulsions in the earth. As Ezekiel explains:

> "For in My jealousy and in the fire of My wrath I have spoken: 'Surely in that day there shall be a great earthquake in the land of Israel, so that the fish of the sea, the birds of the heavens, the beasts of the field, all creeping things that creep on the earth, and all men who are on the face of the earth shall shake at My presence. The mountains shall be thrown down, the steep places shall fall, and every wall shall fall to the ground.'" (38:19–20)

God will follow these convulsions of the earth with His second weapon, which will be to create such confusion among the attacking troops that they will panic and begin killing one another: "'I will call for a sword against Gog throughout all My mountains,' says the Lord GOD. 'Every man's sword shall be against his brother'" (Ezekiel 38:21).

In the seventh and eighth chapters of Judges, we see a similar event reported. We are told that 135,000 Midianites had gathered against Israel. Gideon and his little band of three hundred men, under the direction of God and through the power of God, threw the enemy into total confusion, and the Lord set every man's sword against his brother. As a result, 120,000 Midianite soldiers died, largely by what today we would call "friendly fire."

In Ezekiel we can see how God's first two weapons work together in a one-two punch. A sudden earthquake in the mountains of Israel would certainly panic an army. With the ground moving like sea waves, the upheaval of the earth generating dense clouds of dust, it would be impossible for warriors to distinguish an enemy from an ally, and in their blind terror they would kill anything that moved.

The third divine weapon will be the contagion of disease: "And I will bring him to judgment with pestilence and bloodshed," asserts the Lord (38:22a). He will infect the invading troops with some debilitating disease that will render them incapable of carrying out an effective attack. God will follow this contagion with his fourth and final weapon: calamities from the sky. "I will rain down on him, on his troops, and on the many peoples who are with him, flooding rain, great hailstones, fire, and brimstone" (v. 22b).

We find the prototype for this strategy in God's judgment upon Sodom and Gomorrah, where the two decadent cities were forever buried under the briny waters of the Dead Sea by a storm of fire and brimstone. One man has written: "Every force of nature is a servant of the Living God, and in a moment can be made a soldier, armed to the teeth. Men are slowly discovering that God's forces stored in nature are mightier than the brawn of the human arm."[35] When God goes to war, no army on earth can stand against His formidable arsenal. The

armies that come against Israel in the last days will learn that truth
the hard way.

The Aftermath of War

First, there will be a feast. There is strong irony in using the term
feast for what will happen immediately following the destruction of
Israel's enemies. It will not be a feast of victory for the rescued Israelis;
it will be a feast for vultures and predators feeding on the incredible
masses of bodies strewn across the battlefield. Here is how Ezekiel
described the grisly banquet:

> "You shall fall upon the mountains of Israel, you and all of your
> troops and the peoples who are with you; I will give you to birds of
> prey of every sort and to the beasts of the field to be devoured. You
> shall fall on the open field; for I have spoken," says the Lord GOD . . .
> "And as for you, son of man, thus says the Lord GOD, 'Speak to every
> sort of bird and to every beast of the field:
>
>> "Assemble yourselves and come;
>> Gather together from all sides to My sacrificial meal
>> Which I am sacrificing for you,
>> A great sacrificial meal on the mountains of Israel,
>> That you may eat flesh and drink blood.
>> You shall eat the flesh of the mighty,
>> Drink the blood of the princes of earth,
>> Of rams and lambs,
>> Of goats and bulls,
>> All of them fatlings of Bashan.
>> You shall eat fat till you are full,

And drink blood till you are drunk,

At My sacrificial meal

Which I am sacrificing for you.

You shall be filled at My table

With horses and riders,

With mighty men

And with all the men of war,'" says the Lord GOD. (Ezekiel 39:4–5,

17–20)

This chilling prophecy uses the language of a feast—what God calls His "sacrificial feast"—to show how the intervention of God will result in a gruesome spectacle of uncountable bodies littering the landscape like debris from a tornado, creating a bountiful banquet for His guests, the birds of the air and the beasts of the field.

The second event that will occur after the destruction of Israel's enemies is a great funeral. Ezekiel described it:

It will come to pass in that day that I will give Gog a burial place there in Israel, the valley of those who pass by east of the sea; and it will obstruct travelers, because there they will bury Gog and all his multitude. Therefore they will call it the valley of Hamon Gog. For seven months the house of Israel will be burying them, in order to cleanse the land . . . They will set apart men regularly employed, with the help of a search party, to pass through the land and bury those bodies remaining on the ground, in order to cleanse it. At the end of seven months they will make a search. The search party will pass through the land; and when anyone sees a man's bone, he shall set up a marker by it, till the buriers have buried it in the Valley of Hamon Gog. (Ezekiel 39:11–12, 14–16)

Here Ezekiel painted another chilling and macabre picture of the horrendous death and destruction inflicted on Israel's invaders. This war will produce so many casualties that it will take seven months to bury all the bodies. In fact, the task will be so enormous that a special detachment of soldiers will be assigned to carry it out. According to the Old Testament, an unburied corpse is a reproach to God and causes a land to be defiled (Deuteronomy 21:23). Thus the Israelis will feel compelled to clean up the bloody battlefield and bury all the dead.

The third aftermath of the war against Israel will be a great and long-burning fire. Here's how Ezekiel explained the fire and its purpose:

> "Then those who dwell in the cities of Israel will go out and set on fire and burn the weapons, both the shields and bucklers, the bows and arrows, the javelins and spears; and they will make fires with them for seven years . . . They will not take wood from the field nor cut down any from the forests, because they will make fires with the weapons; and they will plunder those who plundered them, and pillage those who pillaged them," says the Lord God. (Ezekiel 39:9–10)

This passage indicates that the arsenal of weaponry and military equipment brought against Israel by the coalition of nations will be utterly staggering. While it will take seven months to bury the bodies, which is astonishing enough, it will take *seven years* to burn the weapons.

Some readers of Ezekiel are troubled that the prophet described these as weapons of ancient origin, whereas a battle that is yet to occur in the future will surely employ modern weaponry and highly sophisticated military equipment—guns, tanks, planes, bombs, missiles, and possibly even nuclear weapons. But we must allow common sense to prevail in our reading of Ezekiel. He did what all prophets have done: he spoke of the future using terms and descriptions that he and the people of his day would understand. If he had written of tanks and missiles and bombs, those living in his time would have been utterly mystified, and his message would have had no meaning to them.

The burial of the bodies and the burning of the weapons comprise what Ezekiel calls the "cleansing of the land" from the defilement of death and destruction wrought upon it by the enemies of God's people. These massive cleanup operations in the aftermath of the war give us an eye-opening picture of the enormity of the destruction predicted in Ezekiel's end-time prophecy. As we try to comprehend these cataclysmic events, we can only shake our heads in wonder and ask, "What in the world is going on?" I believe Ezekiel helps us to answer that question as we look further into his prophecy.

The Sovereignty of God's Plan

The Inevitable Accomplishment of God's Purpose

To understand what is going on in the war and destruction described in Ezekiel's prophecy, we must first consider the sovereignty of God's plan. Throughout this book we have observed that even in the most devastating of times, God is still in control. In fact, He often orchestrates events to bring about His purposes. He tells us what He will do to Israel's enemies in no uncertain terms: "I will turn you around, put hooks into your jaws, and lead you out, with all your army, horses, and horsemen" (Ezekiel 38:4); "It will be in the latter days that I will bring you against My land" (v. 16); "and I will turn you around and lead you on, bringing you up from the far north, and bring you against the mountains of Israel" (39:2).

Passages such as these confuse many people because of the seeming implication that God leads men to be evil or to do evil things. But the Bible never says that God instills evil in the hearts of men. Some would attempt to refute this claim by pointing out that during the Exodus, the Bible explicitly says that God hardened Pharaoh's heart. It does say that, of course, but the statement speaks about the nature of Pharaoh's heart, not about God overriding man's free will. Some hearts are like clay; the sun's heat will harden them. Others are like wax; the sun will cause them to melt. It's not the sun's fault that it hardens one substance and melts the other; it all depends on the nature of the material. Pharaoh's heart was the sort that would harden when exposed to God's light. It had nothing to do with God coercing him to do evil.

The Old Testament, especially, is intended to show that God is the sovereign ruler over all. Even though men try to thwart His plan and wreak great destruction, God's purpose will always win out. When Ezekiel wrote that God will bring the enemy against His land, he was simply saying that God will bring these nations to the doom that their wickedness inevitably demands. Everyone accomplishes God's will in the end. Those who conform to His will accomplish it willingly; those who do not conform accomplish it inadvertently as an unwitting tool in His hands.

The Simplicity of God's Purpose

Secondly, let's look at the simplicity of God's purpose. As you read the following verses from Ezekiel's prophecy, you will have no difficulty picking out the defining purpose clauses:

I will bring you against My land, so that the nations may know Me, when I am hallowed in you, O Gog, before their eyes. (38:16)

Thus I will magnify Myself and sanctify Myself, and I will be known in the eyes of many nations. Then they shall know that I am the LORD. (38:23)

Then they shall know that I am the LORD. (39:6)

So I will make My holy name known in the midst of My people Israel, and I will not let them profane My holy name anymore. Then the nations shall know that I am the LORD. (39:7)

I will set My glory among the nations; all the nations shall see My judgment which I have executed, and My hand which I have laid on them. So the house of Israel shall know that I am the LORD their God from that day forward. (39:21–22)

It doesn't take a rocket scientist to figure out God's purpose in the cataclysmic battle of the last days. It is very clear and very simple. God intends for people to recognize Him as the Lord God of heaven, whose name is holy, whose glory fills the universe, and whom men must recognize as sovereign if they are to find the peace and joy He desires for His people.

The Salvation of God's People

Finally, note the sovereignty of God's plan in rescuing His people. Ezekiel tells us that the ultimate outcome of the battle of Gog and Magog will be the salvation of the Jewish people:

Therefore thus says the Lord GOD: "Now I will bring back the captives of Jacob, and have mercy on the whole house of Israel; and I will be jealous for My holy name—after they have borne their shame, and all their unfaithfulness in which they were unfaithful to Me, when they dwelt safely in their own land, and no one made them afraid. When I have brought them back from the peoples and gathered them out of their enemies' lands, and I am hallowed in them in the sight of many nations, then they shall know that I am the LORD their God, who sent them into captivity among the nations, but also brought them back to their land, and left none of them captive any longer. And I will not hide My face from them anymore; for I shall have poured out My Spirit on the house of Israel," says the Lord GOD. (39:25–29)

Thus Ezekiel ends his monumental prophecy on a high note, extolling God's tender love and compassion toward His people. No matter how great the evil in men's hearts, no matter how much destruction and death that evil brings about, God's ultimate purpose in confronting that evil, in revealing His glory among the nations, and in bringing His own from the lands of the enemy is always to accomplish the salvation of His people.

As Ezekiel shows us so vividly, God's destruction of the Axis of Evil in the last days will accomplish the salvation of his people, the nation of Israel. By identifying this Axis of Evil as modern nations who are unwittingly bent on fulfilling this devastating prophecy, we have answered another question about what is going on in the world today. We have shown how present events will lead to the ultimate accomplishment of God's purposes.

As I close this chapter, I think it is important to point out that there is, in a sense, the potential for an axis of evil within the heart of every one of us. As the apostle Paul tells us, each of us has in our heart that "sinful nature" we inherited from Adam—a propensity for selfish evil that, if not controlled by the presence of God's Spirit, can run rampant and produce destruction in our own lives and in the lives of those about us.

But thanks be to God, His salvation is not for Israel only. All men and women today can choose to be among God's people. You don't have to be a Jew to receive salvation, nor does being a Russian or an Iranian force one to be a part of the Axis of Evil. God in His infinite love pours out His Spirit on all who believe and turn to Him. With that wonderful transaction, and as His Spirit is poured out on the redeemed, the axis of evil in our hearts is transformed by God's love.

I will conclude this chapter by passing on to you a fine and touching example of this principle, which I recently found in a true incident reported by Robert Morgan:

Daniel Christiansen tells about a relative, a Romanian soldier in World War II, named Ana Gheorghe. It was 1941, and troops had overrun the Romanian region of Bessarabia and entered Moldavia. Ana and his comrades were badly frightened. Bullets whizzed around them, and mortar shells shook the earth. By day, Ana sought relief reading his Bible, but at night he could only crouch close to the earth and recall verses memorized in childhood.

One day during a spray of enemy fire, Ana was separated from his company. In a panic, he bolted deeper and deeper into the woods until, huddling at the base of a large tree, he fell asleep from exhaustion. The next day, trying to find his comrades, he moved cautiously toward the front, staying in the shadows of the trees, nibbling a crust of bread, drinking from streams. Hearing the battle closing in, he unslung his rifle, pulled the bolt, and watched for the enemy, his nerves near the breaking point. Twenty yards away, a Russian soldier suddenly appeared.

All my mental rehearsals of bravery served me nothing. I dropped my gun and fell to my knees, then buried my face in my sweating palms and began to pray. While praying, I waited for the cold touch of the Russian's rifle barrel against my head.

I felt a slight pressure on my shoulder close to my neck. I opened my eyes slowly. There was my enemy kneeling in front of me, his gun lying next to mine among the wildflowers. His eyes were closed in prayer. We did not understand a single word of the other's language, but we could pray. We ended our prayer with two words that need no translation: "Alleluia . . . Amen!"

Then, after a tearful embrace, we walked quickly to opposite sides of the clearing and disappeared beneath the trees.[36]

NINE

Arming for Armageddon

GENERAL DOUGLAS MACARTHUR STOOD TALL ON THE DECK OF the USS *Missouri* in Tokyo harbor. It was September 2, 1945, and this man who had engineered America's hard-fought victory in the Pacific had just witnessed the signatures of Japan's leaders ending the bloody global struggle known as World War II. On that day, this authentic American hero uttered a profound warning, which he later repeated in his famous farewell address before the United States Congress: "We have had our last chance," he said. "If we do not now devise some greater and more equitable system, Armageddon will be at our door."[1]

Shortly after he was inaugurated as the fortieth president of the United States, Ronald Reagan was astounded by the complexities of the Middle East. Israel, on its thin strip of land, was surrounded by well-armed Arab enemies who were splintered like broken glass into countless factions and divisions impossible to reconcile. On Friday, May 15, 1981, scribbling in his diary, Reagan noted the intractable problems involving Lebanon, Syria, Saudi Arabia, the Soviet Union, and Israel. "Sometimes I wonder," he wrote, "if we are destined to witness Armageddon."

Only three weeks later, on Sunday, June 7, he received news that Israel had bombed the Iraqi nuclear reactor. That afternoon, Reagan wrote in his diary: "Got word of Israel bombing of Iraq—nuclear reactor. I swear I believe Armageddon is near."[2]

Armageddon. The very word chills the soul. Probably there are few adults who are not familiar with that word and what it implies. Why have our national leaders, in the twentieth and twenty-first centuries, begun to use that doomsday word in their speaking and writing? I believe it is because they can see how modern weaponry and international tensions are showing how quickly global equilibrium could get out of control, leading to a cataclysmic war such as the world has never seen before.

Our nation is no stranger to war. According to the US Army Military Institute, the United States has been involved in twenty-nine wars or military conflicts. This averages out to one war for every eight years of America's history. This number includes not only the major conflicts, but also lesser-known engagements, such as the Seminole wars, America's involvement in the Boxer rebellion, and the invasion of Panama. Approximately 1,314,971 troops have died for their country in these wars. This includes 25,000 who died in the War of Independence; 623,026 in the Civil War; more than 400,000 in World War II; more than 58,000 in Vietnam; and nearly 4,000 in the current conflicts in Iraq and Afghanistan. (That number has increased to more than 4,000 since the report was published.)[3]

The Bible tells us that there is yet another war to be fought on this earth. This war, called Armageddon, makes all the wars America has fought to date look like minor skirmishes. This war will draw the final curtain on modern civilization. In this chapter we will lift the biblical veil to show what is going on in the world that will lead to Armageddon. In fact, preparations for that war are underway right now throughout the world. The only thing holding back its rapid approach is the yet-to-occur disappearance of all true believers in Jesus Christ, the event we know as the Rapture of the church.

The Preparation for the Battle of Armageddon

In the twelfth chapter of Revelation, the apostle John revealed how this conflagration will come about. "So the great dragon was cast out, that serpent of old, called the Devil and Satan, who deceives the whole world; he was cast to the earth, and his angels were cast out with him . . . Now when the dragon saw that he had been cast to the earth, he persecuted the woman who gave birth to the male Child" (vv. 9, 13).

These verses tell us that during the Tribulation, when Satan is cast out of heaven to the earth, he will begin immediately to persecute the woman who brought forth the male child. The "woman" is an obvious metaphor for Israel, through whom the child Jesus was born. Satan's first attempt at persecution will be the battle of Gog and Magog. As we learned in the previous chapter, this battle, which precedes the Battle of Armageddon, will be a massive, Russian-led coalition of nations coming against Israel like swarms of hornets against a defenseless child. As Revelation tells us, Satan will be the motivating force behind this invasion. But before he accomplishes his intended annihilation of Israel, she will be rescued by Almighty God.

The thwarting of the battle of Gog and Magog will be a setback to Satan, but he will not give up; he is relentless in his persecution of the

Jews. His purpose, beginning in the middle of the Tribulation period, is to destroy the Jewish people before Christ can set up His kingdom, thus wrecking God's prophesied rule over the earth. According to Revelation 16, Satan will employ two fearful personalities in these plans: "And I saw three unclean spirits like frogs coming out of the mouth of the dragon, out of the mouth of the *beast*, and out of the mouth of the *false prophet*" (v. 13, *emphasis added*).

Here John tells us that Satan will empower the beast, who is the head of the reestablished Roman Empire, and the false prophet, the head of the new world religious system. Thus Satan (the dragon), the Beast (the Antichrist), and the false prophet become the unholy trinity committed to the destruction of Israel. When the church of Jesus Christ is taken safely into heaven and the Tribulation period begins, the unrestrained satanic persecution of Israel will propel the entire world toward the Battle of Armageddon.

The Place of the Battle of Armageddon

"And they gathered them together to the place called in Hebrew, Armageddon" (Revelation 16:16).

As we noted previously, the word *Armageddon* is much bandied about these days. It has become a synonym for every kind of doomsday scenario. We hear talk of an impending *financial* Armageddon, an *ecological* Armageddon, an *environmental* Armageddon, and a *nuclear* Armageddon for which physicist Stephen Hawking tells us we should prepare by relocating ourselves "somewhere else in another solar system."[4] Obviously the popular imagination has captured the essence of the type of event that will occur at Armageddon, but people have missed the inherent meaning of the word by a country mile. Armageddon is not actually a battle; it is a place.

Given the enormous attention this word receives, it may surprise you that *Armageddon* is mentioned only once in the Bible—right here in the sixteenth chapter of Revelation. The Hebrew word *harmageddon* means "the mount of Megiddo." *Har* means mount, and *megiddo* means slaughter; so the meaning of *Armageddon* is "Mount of Slaughter." The mountain of Megiddo is an actual geographical feature located in northern Israel. It includes an extended plain that reaches from the Mediterranean Sea to the northern part of the land of Israel. Megiddo is about eighteen miles southeast of Haifa, fifty-five miles north of Jerusalem, and a little more than ten miles from Nazareth, the town where Jesus grew up.

While the word *Armageddon* is mentioned only once in the Bible, the mountain of Megiddo has a rich biblical history. It was at Megiddo that Deborah and Barak defeated the Canaanites (Judges 4–5). It was also there that: Gideon defeated the Midianites (Judges 7); Saul was slain during a war with the Philistines (1 Samuel 31); Ahaziah was slain by Jehu (2 Kings 9); and Josiah was slain by the invading Egyptians (2 Kings 23).

These are not by any means the only battles that have been fought on this bloody ground. Last year I stood at the top of Megiddo, overlooking the plain of Armageddon. If I could have watched past centuries fast-forward before my eyes, I would have seen a long succession of waged battles as great armies marched across the field one after the other—the Crusaders, the Egyptians, the Persians, the Druze, the Greeks, the Turks, and the Arabs. During World War I, British general Edmund Allenby led his army against the Turks in a fierce battle on the plain of Armageddon. According to scholar Alan Johnson, "More than 200 battles have been fought at or near there."[5] As you can see, Megiddo has earned its awful name: it is indeed a Mount of Slaughter.

Why Megiddo? Why will this be the location of the world's final conflict? One of the world's greatest military figures gives us the answer. In 1799, Napoleon stood at Megiddo before the battle that ended his quest to conquer the East and rebuild the Roman Empire. Considering the enormous plain of Armageddon, he declared: "All the armies of the world could maneuver their forces on this vast plain . . . There is no place in the whole world more suited for war than this . . . [It is] the most natural battleground on the whole earth."[6]

While it is no mystery why the earth's final battle will be fought at Armageddon, it is important to understand that the battle will be centralized on that field but not contained there. All the ancient prophets agree that this war will be fought throughout the entire land of Israel. In the book he edited on Armageddon, A. Sims wrote:

It appears from Scripture that this last great battle of that great day of God Almighty will reach far beyond Armageddon, or the Valley of Megiddo. Armageddon appears to be mainly the place where the troops will gather together from the four corners of the earth, and from Armageddon the Battle will spread out over the entire [country of Israel]. Joel speaks of the last battle being fought in the Valley of Jehoshaphat, which is close by Jerusalem and Isaiah shows Christ coming with blood-stained garments "from Edom," [present day Jordan]. So the battle of Armageddon, it seems, will stretch from the Valley of Megiddo in the north . . . through the Valley of Jehoshaphat, near Jerusalem, [and down to Jordan, south of Israel]. And to this agree the words of the prophet Ezekiel that the armies of this great battle will "cover the land" . . . But Jerusalem will no doubt be the center of interest during the battle of Armageddon, for God's Word says: "I will gather all nations against Jerusalem to battle."[7]

The words of the prophet Zechariah support Sims's view of Jerusalem as the center of conflict in the Armageddon war. "Behold, I will make Jerusalem a cup of drunkenness to all the surrounding peoples, when they lay siege against Judah and Jerusalem. And it shall happen in that day that I will make Jerusalem a very heavy stone for all peoples; all who would heave it away will surely be cut in pieces, though all nations of the earth are gathered against it" (Zechariah 12:2–3). So while we use the term *Armageddon* and localize the war to the plain of Megiddo, Scripture teaches that the battle will literally fill the whole land of Israel with war and bloodshed.

This war will be so horrific that the Bible says blood will flow in staggering torrents. "And the winepress was trampled outside the city, and blood came out of the winepress, up to the horses' bridles, for one thousand six hundred furlongs" (Revelation 14:20). If you translate these ancient measurements into the terminology of today, sixteen hundred furlongs is almost exactly two hundred miles—the distance from the northern to the southern tip of the land of Israel.

While that image may be hard for us to visualize, it is not unknown in human experience. Ancient historians Plutarch and Herodotus describe similar scenes during vicious battles of their days. Of the siege of Athens in 405 – 404 BC, Plutarch wrote:

About midnight Sylla entered the breach, with all terrors of trumpets and coronets sounding, with the triumphant shout and cry of an army let loose to spoil and slaughter, and scouring through the streets with sword drawn. There was no numbering the slain; the amount is to this day conjectured only from the space of ground overflowed with blood. For without mentioning the execution done in the other quarters of the city, the blood that was shed about the marketplace spread over the whole [public square] . . . and passed through the gate and overflowed the suburb.[8]

Similarly, writing of the fall of Jerusalem to the Roman hordes in AD 70, Josephus wrote:

> When they [Romans] went in numbers into the lanes of the city, with their swords drawn, they slew those whom they overtook, without mercy, and set fire to the houses wither the Jews fled . . . they ran every one through whom they met with, and obstructed the very lanes with their dead bodies, and made the whole city run down with blood, to such a degree indeed that the fire of many of the houses was quenched with these men's blood.[9]

We would actually be more accurate to refer to this conflict as the *"Campaign* of Armageddon." The word translated as *battle* in Revelation 16:14 is the Greek word *polemos,* which signifies a war or campaign. Armageddon will involve many battles fought throughout the entire land of Israel over a three-and-one-half-year period of time.

The Purpose of the Battle of Armageddon

Our sensibilities revolt when we read of the carnage the Bible pictures when describing the Battle of Armageddon. And the horrible scene raises all kinds of questions that many people find difficult to answer. We wonder what is going on, not only in the world but also in the mind of God. What is the purpose of this war in the plan of God? Let's address these questions in order to show God's purpose, plan, and intent in allowing the Battle of Armageddon to occur. Just what are His purposes?

To Finish His Judgment upon Israel

The Tribulation period is a time of divine indignation against the people of Israel, the people who rejected their Messiah and—time and time again after given the chance to return—failed to heed the corrective and punitive judgment of God. It is no accident that this future period of time is often referred to as "the time of Jacob's trouble" (Jeremiah 30:7).

To Finalize His Judgment upon the Nations that Have Persecuted Israel

Those nations that have persecuted the Jewish people are finally gathered together in the Battle of Armageddon, in the Valley of Jehoshaphat, giving God the perfect opportunity to deal with them finally and decisively.

> I will also gather all nations,
> And bring them down to the Valley of Jehoshaphat;
> And I will enter into judgment with them there
> On account of My people, My heritage Israel,
> Whom they have scattered among the nations;
> They have also divided up My land. (Joel 3:2)

To Formally Judge All the Nations that Have Rejected Him

"Now out of His mouth goes a sharp sword, that with it He should strike the nations. And He Himself will rule them with a rod of iron. He Himself treads the winepress of the fierceness and wrath of Almighty God" (Revelation 19:15).

This verse gives us another of God's purposes in bringing about Armageddon. Notice particularly that last phrase: "He Himself treads the winepress of the fierceness and wrath of Almighty God." To our time-bound senses, God's activity often seems so slow and ponderous that people pursuing ungodly goals tend to dismiss His judgment as a factor to be taken seriously. Thus the nations do not believe that a time is coming when God's judgment will inevitably descend. But be assured, He is storing up judgment against a day to come. The Bible is clear: one of these days God will have had enough, and His judgment will pour down like consuming fire against the world's wicked nations. "And men were scorched with great heat, and they blasphemed the name of God who has power over these plagues; and they did not repent and give Him glory" (Revelation 16:9).

This verse tells us just how incredibly wicked the nations will have become when God's judgment descends. Even when these men are writhing and screaming with the excruciating pain God inflicts upon them, they will continue to curse Him to His face. They will be so far gone, so given over to evil, that in their prideful defiance they will refuse to repent, even in the grip of fatal judgment.

The Particularities of the Battle of Armageddon

Just to be sure there is no confusion about the wars in the Tribulation period, I want to make it clear that we have identified two separate battles. In the previous chapter we learned about the first battle, the one that will occur at the beginning of the Tribulation period when Gog (Russia) assembles a mass of nations against Israel that are thwarted by God's intervention. In this chapter we are learning about a second battle, one that will end the Tribulation period. It is easy to confuse the two, but the Bible presents them as two distinct events. The battle of Gog and the Battle of Armageddon are separated by several years and involve different participants. Here are some of the differences that will help us keep the two battles separate in our minds:

- In the battle of Gog, Russia and at least five other nations are involved (Ezekiel 38:2–6). In the Battle of Armageddon, all the nations of the world are involved (Joel 3:2; Zechariah 14:2).

- In the battle of Gog, the invaders will attack from the north (Ezekiel 38:6, 15; 39:2). In the Battle of Armageddon, the armies come from the north, south, east, and west (Daniel 11:40–45; Zechariah 14:2; Revelation 16:12–16).

- In the battle of Gog, the purpose of the armies is to "take a spoil, and to take a prey" (Ezekiel 38:12 KJV). In the Battle of Armageddon, the purpose is to annihilate the Jews and to fight Christ and His army (Zechariah 12:2–3, 9; 14:2; Revelation 19:19).

- In the battle of Gog, Russia will be the leader of the nations (Ezekiel 38:13). In the Battle of Armageddon, the Antichrist will be the leader (Revelation 19:19).

- In the battle of Gog, God defeats the northern invaders with the convulsions of the earth, the confusion of the troops, the contagion of diseases, and calamities from the sky. In the Battle of Armageddon, the armies are defeated by the word of Christ—"a sharp sword" (Revelation 19:15; see also verse 21 NKJV).

- In the battle of Gog, Israel's enemies will perish upon the mountains of Israel and in the open field (Ezekiel 39:4–5). In the Battle of Armageddon, those slain by the Lord will lie where they fall, from one end of the earth to the other (Jeremiah 25:33).

- In the battle of Gog, the dead will be buried (Ezekiel 39:12–15). In the Battle of Armageddon, the dead will not be buried, but their carcasses will be totally consumed by the birds (Jeremiah 25:33; Revelation 19:17–18, 21).

- After the battle of Gog, war will continue among the nations involved (other than Israel) during the remainder of the Tribulation (Revelation 13:4–7). After the Battle of Armageddon, swords and spears will be beaten into plowshares and pruning hooks (Isaiah 2:4) and the nations will study war no more.[10]

The Participants in the Battle of Armageddon

As we have noted, all the nations of the world will be involved in the Battle of Armageddon, and they will be led by the Antichrist. But the Bible gives us many more details about the motives and actions of the participants in this battle. These are worth exploring, as they provide insights into the nature of the war and why it will be fought.

The Deal Between Israel and Antichrist

Referring specifically to the Antichrist, Daniel tells us that "he shall confirm a covenant with many for one week" (Daniel 9:27*a*). In prophetic language, this means a week of years, so the covenant will be made for seven years. Until recently I thought Israel would simply be duped into thinking this peace treaty would be a lasting agreement, because I couldn't imagine any national leader taking seriously a peace treaty that was openly proposed for a prescribed period of time. Until, that is, maverick peace broker and former president Jimmy Carter and the leadership of Hamas recently proposed a peace treaty, a *hudna*, to Israel with a ten-year time limit.[11] Apparently in the last days, Israel will be so wearied of continual threats of war that they will think any treaty, even one that gives them a short space of breathing room, will be better than no peace at all.

The Antichrist, who will at this time be the head of the European Union, will sign such a covenant with Israel, guaranteeing peace and security for seven years. Israel will view this man not as the evil Antichrist but as a beneficent and charismatic leader.

The Worship of the Antichrist

On the heels of the covenant with Israel, this self-appointed world ruler will begin to strengthen his power by performing amazing signs and wonders, including even a supposed resurrection from the dead (Revelation 13:3). Then with his grip on the world greatly enhanced, he will boldly take the next step in his arrogant defiance of God: "Then the king shall do according to his own will: he shall exalt and magnify himself above every god, shall speak blasphemies against the God of gods" (Daniel 11.36).

Daniel goes on to give us a further description of the Antichrist's insidious methods:

He shall regard neither the God of his fathers nor the desire of women, nor regard any god; for he shall exalt himself above them all. But in their place he shall honor a god of fortresses, and a god which his fathers did not know he shall honor with gold and silver, with precious stones and pleasant things. Thus he shall act against the strongest fortresses with a foreign god, which he shall acknowledge, and advance its glory; and he shall cause them to rule over many, and divide the land for gain. (Daniel 11:37–39)

The Antichrist will be the epitome of the man with a compulsion to extend his dominion over everything and everyone. To achieve this end, the Antichrist will bow to no god but the "god of fortresses." That is, he will build enormous military might and engage in extensive warfare to extend his power throughout the world.

Daniel then describes how the swollen megalomania of the Antichrist will drive him to take his next step in Daniel 11:36, quoted earlier. John expanded on Daniel's description of the Antichrist's blasphemous acts by telling us that every living person will be required to worship this man. "He was granted power to give breath to the image of the beast, that the image of the beast should both speak and cause as many as would not worship the image of the beast to be killed" (Revelation 13:15). Step by step, the Antichrist will promote himself from a European leader, to a world leader, to a tyrannical global dictator, and finally to a god.

The Decision to Fight Against the Antichrist

The Antichrist's grip on global power will not last long. The world will become increasingly discontented with the leadership of this global dictator, who has gone back on every promise he made. Major segments of the world will begin to assemble their own military forces and rebel against him.

The king of the south and his armies will be the first to come after the Antichrist, followed by the armies of the north. "At the time of the end the king of the South shall attack him; and the king of the North shall come against him like a whirlwind, with chariots, horseman, and with many ships" (Daniel 11:40). John Walvoord pinpoints the source of this army and describes the magnitude of the initial thrust against the Antichrist:

> Daniel's prophecy described a great army from Africa, including not only Egypt but other countries of that continent. This army, probably numbering in the millions, will attack the Middle East from the south. At the same time Russia and other armies to the north will mobilize another powerful military force to descend on the Holy Land and challenge the world dictator. Although Russia will have had a severe setback about four years earlier in the prophetic sequence of events, she apparently will have been able to recoup her losses enough to put another army in the field.[12]

The Antichrist will put down some of these first attempts at rebellion against him. But before he can celebrate and move on toward his goal of destroying Israel and Jerusalem, something will happen.

The Disturbing News from the East

"But news from the east and the north shall trouble him; therefore he shall go out with great fury" (Daniel 11:44). The Bible leaves no doubt as to the source of the news that so disturbs and enrages the Antichrist: "Then the sixth angel poured out his bowl on the great river Euphrates, and its water was dried up, so that the way of the kings from the east might be prepared" (Revelation 16:12).

The Euphrates is one of the greatest rivers in the world. It flows from the mountains of western Turkey, through Syria, and continues on right through the heart of Iraq, not far from Baghdad. It eventually unites with the Tigris to become the *Shatt el Arab*, and finally empties into the Persian Gulf. The entirety of the Euphrates flows through Muslim territory. In Genesis 15 and Deuteronomy 11, the Lord specified that the Euphrates would be the easternmost border of the promised land. It serves both as a border and a barrier between Israel and her enemies.

Is it possible that a river the size of the Euphrates could be dried up? According to author Alon Liel, it is not only possible, it has recently happened. He wrote:

> On one occasion recently, the Euphrates was cut off. The headwaters of both the Euphrates and Tigris Rivers, on which both Syria and Iraq so heavily depend, are located in Turkish Territory, which makes Turkey's relations with those nations all the more sensitive. Tensions mounted in early 1990 when Turkey stopped the flow of the Euphrates River for an entire month during the construction of the Ataturk Dam . . . Having already showed it can completely cut off this flow, Turkey has strengthened its bargaining position in its complex relationships with its southern neighbors.[13]

What is the significance of the drying up of the Euphrates River, and why will that event have such a disturbing effect on the Antichrist? For an explanation, let's turn once more to John Walvoord:

> The drying-up of the Euphrates is a prelude to the final act of the drama, not the act itself. We must conclude then, that the most probable interpretation of the drying-up of the Euphrates is that by an act of God its flow will be interrupted even as were the waters of the Red Sea and of Jordan. This time the way will open not for Israel but for

those who are referred to as the Kings of the East . . . The evidence points, then, to a literal interpretation of Revelation 16:12 in relation to the Euphrates.[14]

It's no wonder the world dictator is disturbed and frustrated. He has just put down rebellions by defeating armies from the south and the north, and just when it appears that he is about to gain control of everything, he gets word that the Euphrates River has dried up and massive armies of the east are crossing it to come against him. He had thought himself safe, as no army could cross this barrier and come into the Israeli arena where he fought. But now that barrier is down, and an army of unprecedented numbers is marching toward him.

Just how large is that army? Listen to what John tells us: "Now the number of the army of the horsemen was two hundred million; I heard the number of them" (Revelation 9:16). Suddenly the Antichrist must divert the major portion of his attention to defending himself against an amassed force the size of which the world has never seen.

Is an army of two hundred million soldiers really believable? Dr. Larry Wortzel, a retired US Army colonel, is a leading authority on China and served as the director of the Strategic Studies Institute of the US Army War College. In October 1998, he filed the following report: "China's standing armed force of some 2.8 million active soldiers in uniform is the largest military force in the world. Approximately 1 million reservists and some 15 million militia back them up. With a population of over 1.2 billion people, China also has a potential manpower base of another 200 million males fit for military service available at any time."[15] So an army of that size is not only possible, the potential for it exists even at this moment.

When this unprecedented army crosses the bed of the Euphrates against the Antichrist, the greatest war of all history, involving hundreds of millions of people, will be set in motion. The major battleground for that war will be the land of Israel.

As if this news is not frightening enough, John tells us that all these events are inspired and directed by the demons of hell: "For they are spirits of demons, performing signs, which go out to the kings of the earth and of the whole world, to gather them to the battle of that great day of God Almighty" (Revelation 16:14).

No doubt demonism in every shape and form will manifest itself more and more as the end draws near, until at last it all ends in Armageddon . . . But besides these hosts of human armies, there will also be present at Armageddon an innumerable host of supernatural beings . . . So Armageddon will truly be a battle of heaven and earth and hell.[16]

So just at the moment when the Antichrist is about to attack and destroy Israel and Jerusalem, a diversion occurs in the form of another massive army entering the field of conflict. Thus the stage is set for the last, stunning movement in the Battle of Armageddon.

The Descending Lord from the Heavens

If you are a follower of Christ, what happens next may instill an urge to stand up and shout like a football fan watching the star quarterback come onto the field.

Now I saw heaven opened, and behold, a white horse. And He who sat on him was called Faithful and True, and in righteousness He judges and makes war. His eyes were like a flame of fire, and on His head were many crowns. He had a name written that no one knew except Himself. He was clothed with a robe dipped in blood, and His name is called The Word of God. And the armies in heaven, clothed in fine linen, white and clean, followed Him on white horses. Now out of His mouth goes a sharp sword, that with it He should strike the nations. And He Himself will rule them with a rod of iron. He Himself treads the winepress of the fierceness and wrath of Almighty God. And He has on His robe and on His thigh a name written: KING OF KINGS AND LORD OF LORDS. (Revelation 19:11–16)

The great Lord Jesus, the captain of the Lord's hosts, the King over all kings will descend to defend and protect His chosen people and put a once-and-for-all end to the evil of the Antichrist.

Descending with His Saints

But the Lord Jesus, captain of the Lord's hosts, will not descend alone, as the following scriptures make abundantly clear:

Thus the LORD my God will come;
and all the saints with you. (Zechariah 14:5)

The coming of our Lord Jesus Christ with all His saints . . . (1 Thessalonians 3:13)

When he comes, in that Day, to be glorified in His saints and to be admired among all those who believe. (2 Thessalonians 1:10)

Behold, the Lord comes with ten thousands of His saints. (Jude 14)

All those who have died in the Lord, along with those who were raptured before the years of the Tribulation, will join with the Lord and participate in the battle to reclaim the world for the rule of Christ.

Descending with His Angels

The saints are not the only ones who will comprise the army of the Lord. Both Matthew and Paul tell us that the angels will also descend with Christ. "When the Son of Man comes in His glory, and all the holy angels with Him, then He will sit on the throne of His glory" (Matthew 25:31); "and to give you who are troubled rest with us when the Lord Jesus is revealed from heaven with His mighty angels" (2 Thessalonians 1:7).

How many angels are available for conscription into this army? The Bible shows their numbers to be staggering. In Matthew 26:52–53, Jesus told Peter in the Garden of Gethsemane, "Put your sword in its place . . . Do you think that I cannot call on My Father, and He will provide Me more than twelve legions of angels?" A Roman legion numbered about six thousand soldiers, so Jesus claimed instant access to the protection of seventy-two thousand angelic soldiers who would have rushed to His rescue had He but said the word. Revelation 5:11, at the very least, supports that number, saying, "I heard the voice of many angels around the throne, the living creatures, and the elders; and the number of them was ten thousand times ten thousand, and thousands of thousands." The Greek says literally, "numbering myriads of myriads and thousands of thousands." The New Living Translation renders the passage as "thousands and millions of angels."

Hebrews 12:22 sums it up by talking about innumerable angels in "joyful assembly" (NIV). Angels as far as the eye can see and the mind can imagine.[17]

This admixture of saints and angels calls to mind scenes from great fantasies such as *The Chronicles of Narnia* and *The Lord of the Rings*, where humans fight alongside other-worldly creatures to defeat the forces of evil. It's a thrilling picture to think of human saints side-by-side with God's angels doing battle.

The inception of the Battle of Armageddon has something of a historical precedent in miniature. Author Randall Price recounts the event:

The Yom Kippur War began at 2 P.M. on October 6, 1973. It was a surprise attack on Israel from the Arab nations of Egypt and Syria, which were intent on the destruction of the Jewish State. Overwhelming evidence of large-scale Arab military preparations on the morning of October 6 had compelled Chief of Staff David Elazar to ask the United States to help restrain the Arabs. U.S. Secretary of State Henry Kissinger urged Prime Minister Golda Meir to not issue a preemptive strike, but to trust international guarantees for Israel's security. To which Mrs. Meir, in her characteristic up-front manner, retorted, "By the time they come to save Israel, there won't be an Israel!"

When international intervention finally came in calling for cease-fire negotiations, Israel's casualties had mounted to 2,552 dead and over 3000 wounded. And it would have been much worse if Israel hadn't realized that if nobody was going to fight for them, they were going to have to fight for themselves. For that reason, Israel has come to rely upon their own defenses for their security. That attack is just a foretaste of what Israel can expect in the future, when the worst attack in its history will come and will be centered on Jerusalem. In that day there will be no allies, not even reluctant ones . . . But Scripture has prophesied otherwise. At the right time, Jerusalem's Savior will return.[18]

As Price tells us, Israel in this last war will be forced to rely on herself and not depend on assistance from allies. That is the similarity between the inception of the Battle of Armageddon and the Yom Kippur War, its miniature historical precedent. But what about the outcome? Will the end of the final war be anything like the end of Israel's Yom Kippur War? We will answer that question by telling the full story of the event in the next chapter.

We will close this chapter on a high note, (or perhaps on an acoustic guitar chord) by giving you the lyrics of an old country music song written by Roy Acuff and Odell McLeod and recorded by Hank Williams. The title is "The Battle of Armageddon":

There's a mighty battle coming and it's well now on its way.

It'll be fought at Armageddon, it shall be a sad, sad day.

In the book of Revelation, words in chapter sixteen say:

There'll be gathered there great armies for that battle on that day.

Refrain:

All the way from the gates of Eden to the battle of Armageddon

There's been troubles and tribulation, there'll be sorrow and despair.

He has said "ye not be troubled for these things shall come to pass."

Then your life will be eternal when you dwell with him at last.

Turn the pages of your Bible, in St. Matthew you will see,

Start with chapter twenty-four and read from one to thirty-three.

In our Savior's blessed words he said on earth, he prophesied,

For he spoke of this great battle that is coming by and by.

Refrain

There'll be nation against nation, there'll be war and rumor of war.

There'll be great signs in heaven, in the sun, the moon, the stars.

Oh, the hearts of men shall fail them, there'll be gnashing of the teeth.

Those who seek it will receive it, mercy at the Savior's feet.

Terrible and terrifying as the events we've discussed in this chapter may be, the last line of this old country song gives us the good news. We may be disturbed by the signs we see of coming catastrophic events. We may feel uneasy due to the continual reports of wars and wanton terrorism. We may quail at reports of nature turning against us. But the last line of this song is our bottom line: we who trust the Lord as our Savior need have no fear. He loves and protects His own, and whatever comes, if we seek Him and His will for our lives, we will be among those whom He saves from the wrath to come.

TEN

The Return of the King

IN A ROOM DECORATED FOR AN ALBANIAN FUNERAL, OUR missionary to Albania, Ian Loring, delivered a powerful Good Friday message about Christ's great sacrificial death. Afterward, he invited everyone to come back on Sunday to observe the "third day ritual." In Albanian culture, friends return three days after a funeral to sit with the family, drink bitter coffee, and remember the one who has died. More than three hundred people filled the room that Easter Sunday. Ian preached about the "not quite empty tomb," observing that Christ's empty grave clothes still bore His shape, but the napkin, which had been wrapped around His head, was placed away from the other grave clothes, folded. To Ian's congregation, that minor detail held great meaning and promise. In Albania, when a person has finished a meal and prepares to leave the table, he crumples up his napkin to indicate that he is finished. But if, instead, he leaves his napkin folded, it is a sign that he plans to come back. The application was obvious to the Albanians. Jesus is coming back!

The second coming of Christ is a central theme of much of the Bible, and it is one of the best-attested promises in all of Scripture. Christians can rest in the sure conviction that just as Jesus came to earth the first time, so He will return at the conclusion of the Great Tribulation.

As Christians, we are quite familiar with our Lord's first coming to earth because we accept the record of the four Gospels. It is history. The Bible clearly tells us that He is coming to earth again. Though the exact expression "the second coming of Christ" is not found in the Bible, it makes the assertion in many places. For example, the writer of Hebrews said: "And as it is appointed for men to die once, but after this the judgment, so Christ was offered once to bear the sins of many. To those who eagerly wait for Him *He will appear a second time,* apart from sin, for salvation" (9:27–28, *emphasis added*).

The Old Testament prophecies of Christ's first and second advents are so mingled that Jewish scholars did not clearly see them as separate events. Their perception of these prophecies was like viewing a mountain range from a distance. They saw what appeared to be one mountain, failing to see that there was another equally high mountain behind it, obscured from their sight through the perspective of distance. The prophets saw both comings of Christ either as one event or as very closely related in time. One Bible scholar has written: "Words spoken in one breath, and written in one sentence, may contain prophetic events millennia apart in their fulfillments."[1]

This mixing of two prophetic events into one may partially explain why the Jews as a whole rejected Christ. The prophecies speak of the Messiah both enduring great suffering and accomplishing a great conquest. They thought the suffering savior would become the conquering savior in one advent. They did not realize He would come a first time to suffer and then a second time to conquer.

It is evident that even Jesus' followers expected Him to fulfill the glorious promises relating to His second coming when He came the first time. Only after He ascended to heaven did they realize that they were living in the time period between His two appearances, as if on a plain between two mountains. Theologian John F. Walvoord explains:

> From the present day vantage point . . . since the first coming is history and Second Coming is prophecy, it is comparatively easy to go back into the Old Testament and separate the doctrine of Jesus' two comings. In His first coming He came as a man, lived among people, performed miracles, ministered as a prophet as the Old Testament predicted, and died on the cross and rose again. All these events clearly relate to His first coming. On the other hand, the passages that speak of His coming to reign, judging the earth, rescuing the righteous from the wicked, and installing His kingdom on earth relate to His second coming. They are prophecy, not history.[2]

Nothing could be more dramatic than the contrast between our Lord's first and second comings:

- In His first coming He was wrapped in swaddling clothes. In His second coming He will be clothed royally in a robe dipped in blood.

- In His first coming He was surrounded by cattle and common people. In His second coming He will be accompanied by the massive armies of heaven.

- In His first coming the door of the inn was closed to Him. In His second coming the door of the heavens will be opened to Him.

- In His first coming His voice was the tiny cry of a baby. In His second coming His voice will thunder as the sound of many waters.

- In His first coming, He was the Lamb of God who came bringing salvation. In His second coming, He will be the Lion of the tribe of Judah who comes bringing judgment.

Rapture / Translation	Second Coming/ Established Kingdom
1. Translation of all believers	1. No translation at all
2. Translated saints go to heaven	2. Translated saints return to earth
3. Earth not judged	3. Earth judged and righteousness established
4. Imminent, any moment, signless	4. Follows definite predicted signs, including the Tribulation
5. Not in Old Testament	5. Predicted often in Old Testament
6. Believers only	6. Affects all humanity
7. Before the day of wrath	7. Concluding the day of wrath
8. No references to Satan	8. Satan bound
9. Christ comes *for* His own	9. Christ comes *with* His own
10. He comes in the *air*	10. He comes to the *earth*
11. He claims His bride	11. He comes with His bride
12. Only His own see Him	12. Every eye shall see Him
13. Tribulation begins	

Courtesy of Thomas Ice and Timothy Demy

The Anticipation of Christ

Although Christians are most familiar with the first coming of Christ, it is the second coming that gets the most ink in the Bible. References to the Second Coming outnumber references to the first by a factor of eight to one. Scholars count 1,845 biblical references to the Second Coming, including 318 in the New Testament. His return is emphasized in no less than seventeen Old Testament books and seven out of every ten chapters in the New Testament. The Lord Himself referred to His return twenty-one times. The Second Coming is second only to faith as the most dominant subject in the New Testament. Let's look briefly at some of the most significant of these references.

The Prophets Foretold the Second Coming of Christ

While many of the Old Testament prophets wrote concerning the second coming of Christ, it is Zechariah who has given us the clearest and most concise prediction of it:

> Then the LORD will go forth
> And fight against those nations,
> As He fights in the day of battle.
> And in that day His feet will stand on the Mount of Olives,
> Which faces Jerusalem on the east.
> And the Mount of Olives shall be split in two,
> From east to west,
> Making a very large valley;
> Half of the mountain shall move toward the north
> And half of it toward the south. (Zechariah 14:3–4)

Notice how Zechariah deals in specifics, even pinpointing the geographic location to which Christ will return: "In that day His feet will stand on the Mount of Olives" (14:4). Like Armageddon, the Mount of Olives is an explicitly identifiable place that retains its ancient name even today. Recently I visited a Jewish cemetery that has been on this site since biblical times. The prophet's specificity gives us confidence that his prophecy is true and accurate. Unlike vague fortune-tellers and prophetic charlatans, this prophet dared to be explicit and specific so that the truth of his prophecy cannot be missed when the event occurs.

Jesus Himself Announced His Second Coming

Jesus, speaking from the Mount of Olives, affirmed His second coming to His disciples in dramatic and cataclysmic terms:

"For as the lightning comes from the east and flashes to the west, so also will the coming of the Son of Man be . . . Immediately after the tribulation of those days the sun will be darkened, and the moon will not give its light; the stars will fall from heaven, and the powers of the heavens will be shaken. Then the sign of the Son of Man will appear in heaven, and then all the tribes of the earth will mourn, and they will see the Son of Man coming on the clouds of heaven with power and great glory." (Matthew 24:27, 29–30)

The Angels Announced that Jesus Would Return

Immediately following Christ's ascension into heaven, two angels appeared to the stunned disciples and spoke words of comfort to them. "Men of Galilee," they said, "why do you stand gazing up into heaven? This same Jesus, who was taken from you into heaven, will so come in like manner as you saw Him go into heaven" (Acts 1:11). The next verse tells us "they returned to Jerusalem from the mount called Olivet" (v. 12). Did you catch that? Jesus ascended to heaven from the Mount of Olives. According to the angels, Christ will return to that very same spot—the Mount of Olives. The words of the angels conveyed both consolation for the disciples' present loss of Jesus and confirmation of His future return.

John the Apostle Foretold Jesus' Second Coming

The prophecies of Christ's return are like bookends to John's Revelation. In the first chapter he wrote: "Behold, He is coming with clouds, and every eye will see Him, even they who pierced Him. And all the tribes of the earth will mourn because of Him" (v. 7). And in the last pages of the last chapter—indeed, almost the last words of the New Testament—our Lord emphatically affirms His second coming: "He who testifies to these things says, 'Surely I am coming quickly.' Amen. Even so, come, Lord Jesus!" (22:20).

Obviously we have excellent reason to anticipate the return of Christ. The Bible affirms it throughout as a certainty, describing it in specific terms and with ample corroboration.

The Advent of Christ

Twice in the book of Revelation we are told that the door to heaven will be opened. It is first opened to receive the church into heaven at the time of the Rapture: "After these things I looked, and behold, a door standing open in heaven. And the first voice which I heard was like a trumpet speaking with me, saying, 'Come up here, and I will show you things which must take place after this'" (4:1). The door swings open a second time for Christ and His church to proceed from heaven on their militant march back to earth (19:11,14). The first opening is for the Rapture of the saints; the second is for the return of Christ!

When Jesus arrives on earth the second time, His landing will dramatically herald the purpose of His coming. The moment His feet touch the Mount of Olives, the mountain will split apart, creating a broad passageway from Jerusalem to Jericho. As you can imagine, this will be an unprecedented geological cataclysm. In describing it, Dr. Tim LaHaye wrote: "There will be a Stellar Event. Celestial. Cosmic. Greater than earth. Greater than the heavens. And it will suck the air out of humanity's lungs and send men and women and kings and presidents and tyrants to their knees. It will have no need of spotlights, fog machines, amplified music, synthesizers, or special effects. It will be real."[3]

Thus Christ's return will be amplified by a devastating spectacle that will make Hollywood disaster movies look like Saturday morning child's fare. The world will see and recognize its rightful Lord and King. Whereas He came the first time in humility and simplicity, this time His glory and majesty will be spectacularly displayed for all to see.

Let's look briefly at the Bible's description of the glory and majesty Christ will display at His second coming.

His Designation

In Revelation 19, the descending Lord is given three meaningful titles.

> Now I saw heaven opened, and behold, a white horse. And He who sat on him was called Faithful and True, and in righteousness He judges and makes war . . . He had a name written that no one knew except Himself . . . and His name is called The Word of God . . . And He has on His robe and on His thigh a name written: KING OF KINGS AND LORD OF LORDS. (vv. 11–13, 16)

These three names are not merely rhetorical embellishments or empty titles. Prophecy scholar Harry Ironside gives us insight into their significance:

> In these three names we have set forth first, our Lord's dignity as the Eternal Son; second, His incarnation—the Word became Flesh; and last, His second advent to reign as King of Kings and Lord of Lords.[4]

These three names encompass the entire ministry of the Lord Jesus Christ. The first name, the one known only to God, indicates His intimacy and oneness with the Father and thus His eternal existence, including His role in the Trinity as creator and sustainer of the world. The second name, the Word of God, harks back to the first chapter of John's gospel and indicates His incarnation when "the Word became flesh," walked as a man upon this earth, and revealed God to us. The third name, the majestic and towering syllables, King of kings and Lord of lords, is the title He will wear at His second coming, designating His role as the sovereign ruler over all the earth.

His Description

The eyes of the returning Christ are described as burning like a flame of fire, signifying His ability as a judge to see deeply into the hearts of men and ferret out all injustice (Revelation 1:14; 2:18; 19:12). His eyes will pierce through the motives of nations and individuals and judge them for what they really are . . . not for how they hope their masks of hypocrisy will make them appear!

The head of the returning Christ is crowned with many crowns (Revelation 19:12), testifying to His status as the absolute sovereign King of kings and Lord of lords—the undisputed monarch of the entire earth. Famed nineteenth-century London preacher Charles

Haddon Spurgeon described the comfort and security that we derive from the sovereignty of Christ:

> I am sure there is no more delightful doctrine to a Christian, than that of Christ's absolute sovereignty. I am glad there is no such thing as chance, that nothing is left to itself, but that Christ everywhere hath sway. If I thought that there was a devil in hell that Christ did not govern, I should be afraid that devil would destroy me. If I thought there was a circumstance on earth, which Christ did not over-rule, I should fear that that circumstance would ruin me. Nay, if there were an angel in heaven that was not one of Jehovah's subjects, I should tremble even at him. But since Christ is King of kings, and I am his poor brother, one whom he loves, I give all my cares to him, for he careth for me; and leaning on his breast, my soul hath full repose, confidence, and security.[5]

The robe of the returning Christ is dipped in blood, reminding us that He is the sacrificial Lamb of God. Earlier in Revelation, John described Him as "the Lamb slain from the foundation of the world" (13:8). In fact, Jesus will be represented to us as the Lamb of God throughout eternity. In a sense, eternity will be an extended Communion service as we remember forever with love and gratitude the sacrifice of Jesus Christ that united us with God and gave us an eternity of joy with Him.

The Armies of Christ

When Jesus returns to this earth to put down the world's ultimate rebellion, the armies of heaven will accompany him. John described these armies as "clothed in fine linen, white and clean, [following] Him on white horses" (Revelation 19:14).

In the short epistle that immediately precedes the book of Revelation, Jude described this epic event in verses 14 and 15:

> Now Enoch, the seventh from Adam, prophesied about these men also, saying, "Behold, the Lord comes with ten thousands of His saints, to execute judgment on all, to convict all who are ungodly among them of all their ungodly deeds which they have committed in an ungodly way, and of all the harsh things which ungodly sinners have spoken against Him."

In one short verse, Jude used the word *ungodly* four times. This repetition is not accidental. Jude was emphasizing the fact that when Christ comes the second time, His long-suffering patience will have run its course. He will come to impose judgment upon those who have defied Him, and that judgment will be massive. At this point the people on the earth will have rejected the ministry of the 144,000 preachers and the two witnesses that God sent to them for their salvation, just as the prophet Jonah was sent to the Ninevites. In His loving mercy, God endeavored to turn them away from their fatal rebellion. But unlike the Ninevites, the people in the last days will have hardened their hearts beyond repentance.

In his second letter to the Thessalonians, Paul wrote in chilling terms of the judgment that will descend on these rebels:

> The Lord Jesus is revealed from heaven with His mighty angels, in flaming fire taking vengeance on those who do not know God, and those who do not obey the gospel of our Lord Jesus Christ. These shall

be punished with everlasting destruction from the presence of the Lord and from the glory of His power, when He comes, in that Day, to be glorified in His saints and to be admired among all those who believe, because our testimony among you was believed. (1:7–10)

As we learned in the previous chapter, the armies of heaven that accompany Christ in His second coming will be made up of saints and angels—people like you and me standing side-by-side with heavenly beings of immense power. These legions are dressed not in military fatigues but in dazzling white. Yet they need not worry about their pristine uniforms getting soiled because their role is largely ceremonial and honorary; they will not fight. Jesus Himself will slay the rebels with the deadly sword darting out of His mouth.

The Authority of Christ

When the Lord returns to earth at the end of the Tribulation, the men and nations who have defied Him will no more be able to stand against Him than a spiderweb could stand against an eagle. His victory will be assured and His authority undisputed. Here is how John described the finality of His judgment and the firmness of His rule: "And he Himself will rule them with a rod of iron. He Himself treads the winepress of the fierceness and wrath of Almighty God. And He has on His robe and on His thigh a name written: KING OF KINGS AND LORD OF LORDS" (Revelation 19:15–16).

This grand title, King of kings and Lord of lords, identifies our Lord at His second coming. It speaks of His unassailable authority. At this name every king on earth will bow, and every lord will kneel. Don't be confused about the sword proceeding from Christ's mouth; it is not "the sword of the Spirit, which is the word of God" (Ephesians 6:17). This is an altogether different and fearful sword—the sword of judgment—a sharp instrument of war with which Christ will smite the nations into utter submission and establish His absolute rule.

When Christ returns the second time, He will finally fulfill the prophecy of Isaiah that we often quote and hear choirs sing to Handel's lofty music at Christmastime: "For unto us a Child is born, unto us a Son is given; and the government will be upon His shoulder. And His name will be called Wonderful, Counselor, Mighty God, Everlasting Father, Prince of Peace" (Isaiah 9:6). At His first coming, Jesus fulfilled the first part of Isaiah's prophecy, the heartwarming Christmas part. At His second coming, He will fulfill the second part—the part that reveals His iron-hard power and authority over all the nations. The government of the world will at last be upon His shoulder!

The Avenging of Christ

The book of Revelation is divided into three sections. At the beginning of the book we are introduced to the world ruined by Man. As we move to the latter half of the Tribulation period, we witness the world ruled by Satan. But now as we come to Christ's return at the end of the Tribulation period, we see the world reclaimed by Christ.

Reclaiming the earth, however, is not merely a simple matter of Christ's stepping in and planting His flag. Before the earth can be reclaimed, it must be cleansed. You wouldn't move back into a house infested with rats without first exterminating and cleaning it up. That is what Christ must do before He reclaims the earth. All rebellion must be rooted out. He must avenge the damage done to His perfect creation by wiping the rebels from the face of the earth. The last verses of Revelation 19 give us an account of this purging and cleansing, and each step in the process is a dramatic story within itself. Let's briefly examine these avenging acts that will cleanse and reclaim the earth.

The Fowls of Heaven

In the classic Alfred Hitchcock film *The Birds*, a coastal California town is terrorized by the escalating attacks of vicious birds. Throughout the film the terror increases to the point that birds merely sitting in rows on highline wires look ominous and foreboding. Instead of closing the film with his typical "The End," Hitchcock simply fades the screen to black, leaving the viewer with a lingering sense of terror as he drives from the theater and sees birds sitting on the high wires in his neighborhood. As horrifying as that story is, it pales in comparison to the grisly bird scene that John unveils.

> Then I saw an angel standing in the sun; and he cried with a loud voice, saying to all the birds that fly in the midst of heaven, "Come and gather together for the supper of the great God, that you may eat the flesh of kings, the flesh of captains, the flesh of mighty men, the flesh of horses and of those who sit on them, and the flesh of all people, free and slave, both small and great" . . . And all the birds were filled with their flesh. (Revelation 19:17–18, 21)

Words are hardly adequate to describe the horror of this appalling scene. The fowl of the earth's air all gather at Armageddon to feast upon the massive piles of human flesh that will litter the battlefield for miles upon miles. The word translated *fowl* or *birds* is found only three times in the Bible: twice here in Revelation 19 (verses 17 and 21), and once more in Revelation 18:2. It is the Greek word *arnin*, which designates a scavenger bird that is best translated into English as *vulture*.

In John's vision the angel is calling the vultures of the earth to Armageddon to "the supper of the Great God," where they will feast on the fallen carcasses of the enemies of the Lord. The text says that these corpses include both great and small, kings and generals, bond and free. As Harry Ironside wrote, "It is an awful picture—the climax of man's audacious resistance to God."[6]

The book of Revelation tells of another supper, one altogether different from that of the vultures on the field of Armageddon. In Revelation 19:7 we read, "Let us be glad and rejoice and give Him glory, for the marriage of the Lamb has come, and His wife has made herself ready." In verse 9, we read of the feast that will follow the wedding: "Then he said to me, 'Write: "Blessed are those who are called to the marriage supper of the Lamb!"'"

The marriage supper of the Lamb is a time of great joy, celebrating the wedding between the bridegroom Christ and His bride, the church. I am glad that I have a confirmed reservation for the marriage supper of the Lamb where I will feast at the table of heaven, for at the other supper—the supper of the Great God on the fields of Armageddon—the human participants will *be* the food.

I pause here to ask a few important questions: Which supper will you be attending? Have you made your reservation for the marriage supper of the Lamb? Have you accepted the saving work of the Lamb of God in your behalf? Have you confessed your sin and surrendered your will to the authority of the Lamb? I sincerely hope you have, for doing so secures your invitation to a celebration you don't want to miss.

Strangely, as W. A. Criswell pointed out, as glorious as this feast is, it is never described explicitly:

Concerning the marriage itself, is it not a strange narrative that God should omit to describe it? Nothing is said about it, no word is used to describe it. The Greek word here says, "*elthen* [aorist], the marriage is come . . ." and that is all. Just the fact of it. John just hears the Hallelujah chorus announcing it. He has a word to say about the wife, the bride of Christ, who has made herself ready. He describes the robe of our righteousness that shall be our reward at the Bema of Christ. But He never recounts the actual wedding itself. The event just happens and all heaven bursts into Hallelujahs concerning it.[7]

Yet in spite of the lack of description, John made it clear that this feast will be glorious through a writer's technique known as *indirection*. When an event is too wonderful for words, it is sometimes more effective to show the wonder through reactions to the event rather than through the event itself. Instead of describing the feast directly, John used the reactions of others to show its character indirectly. Thus, we are told of the glorious robe we'll wear, the loveliness of the bride, and finally of the hallelujahs that will spring from heaven expressing the pure joy of the occasion. Through these indirect impressions we can see that the marriage supper will be a celebration beyond anything we can imagine. I strongly urge you to RSVP immediately.

The Foes of Heaven

"And I saw the beast, the kings of the earth, and their armies, gathered together to make war against Him who sat on the horse and against His army" (Revelation 19:19). Could there be anything more futile than creatures fighting against their Creator? Than little men stuck on one tiny planet, floating in the immeasurable cosmos, striking back at the Creator of the universe? Yet futility is not beyond hearts turned away from God. John warned that the beast and the false prophet will persuade the armies of the earth to go to war against Christ and the armies of heaven. It's like persuading mice to declare war against lions. This final war will be the culmination of all of the rebellion that men have leveled against Almighty God from the beginning of time! And there's not one iota of doubt about the outcome.

The Fatality of the Beast and False Prophet

The Bible tells us that God simply snatches up the Antichrist beast and the false prophet and flings them into the fiery lake. "Then the beast was captured, and with him the false prophet who worked signs in his presence, by which he deceived those who received the mark of the beast and those who worshiped his image. These two were cast alive into the lake of fire burning with brimstone" (Revelation 19:20).

These two evil creatures have the unwanted honor of actually getting to that awful place before Satan, whose confinement occurs much later: "The devil, who deceived them, was cast into the lake of fire and brimstone where the beast and false prophet are. And they will be tormented day and night forever and ever" (Revelation 20:10). Satan does not join the beast and the false prophet there until the end of the Millennium, one thousand years later.

Once again I turn to Harry Ironside for an interesting sidelight concerning the nature of the punishment these two men experience: "'Note that two men, are taken alive' . . . These two men are 'cast alive into [the lake burning with fire and brimstone]' where a thousand years later, they are still said to be 'suffering the vengeance of eternal fire' (Jude 7)." He focuses our attention on two important truths from God's Word; the men are alive when they arrive, and they are still alive a thousand years later—and still experiencing suffering. He draws a profound conclusion: "the lake of fire is neither annihilation nor purgatorial because it neither annihilates nor purifies these two fallen foes of God and man after a thousand years under judgment."[8]

Hell has become an unpopular subject these days. As church historian Martin Marty noted, "Hell disappeared. And no one noticed."[9] There have been many attempts of late to soften the impact of this thoroughly biblical doctrine in favor of what C. S. Lewis called a grandfatherly God of indulgent kindness who would never consign anyone to hell, but says of anything we happen to like doing, "What does it matter so long as they are contended?"[10]

As God's judgment in Revelation clearly shows, God is not that soft. He intends to remake us in His own image, which is often a painful and self-denying process. If we refuse to be remade, we must endure the hellish consequence that choice brings. As John's vision shows us, hell is frightfully real. And it shows how deadly it is to be an enemy of the Almighty God. His power is infinite, and His justice is certain. No rebellion can stand against Him, and the consequences of such rebellion are terrible and eternal.

The Finality of Christ's Victory over Rebellion

"And the rest were killed with the sword which proceeded from the mouth of Him who sat on the horse" (Revelation 19:21). Here is how John F. Walvoord describes the victory:

When Christ returns at the end of the tribulation period, the armies that have been fighting with each other for power will have invaded the city of Jerusalem and will have been engaged in house-to-house fighting. When the glory of the second coming of Christ appears in the heavens, however, these soldiers will forget their contest for power on earth and will turn to fight the army from heaven (16:16; 19:19). Yet their best efforts will be futile because Christ will smite them with the sword in His mouth (19:15, 21), and they will all be killed, along with their horses.[11]

Again we see the utter futility of fighting against God. Not only will the leaders of the rebellion be flung into hell, but also all the armies that joined them will be slaughtered by the mighty strokes of Christ's deadly sword.

The Application of Christ's Second Coming

Throughout my years of ministry as a pastor and Bible teacher, I have talked to more than a few pastors and Christian leaders who expressed doubts concerning the relevance of Bible prophecy. They usually say something like this: "I don't preach on prophecy because it has nothing to do with the needs of my people today. I try to preach on more relevant topics. I leave prophecy to people like you, Dr. Jeremiah."

My response is that today there are few subjects more relevant than biblical prophecy. In fact, as we move into times that are so clearly depicted in the prophetic scriptures, some of my critics are beginning to get questions from their own congregants who are looking at today's headlines and asking, "What in the world is going on?" When I preached to my own church the messages that became the basis for this book, we recorded some of the highest attendance figures in the history of our congregation. I suspect that many had come to hear these messages because they were not getting meaningful answers from their own pastors. I cannot imagine being a pastor in today's cataclysmic world and not using the Word of God to give people God's perspective on world events.

In spite of the high value I place on understanding future events, I find that studying prophecy has an even higher and more practical value. It provides a compelling motivation for living the Christian life. The immediacy of prophetic events shows the need to live each moment in Christlike readiness. As revered Southern Baptist evangelist Vance Havner has put it, "The devil has chloroformed the atmosphere of this age." Therefore, in view of the sure promises of Christ's return, as believers, we are to do more than merely be ready; we are to be expectant. In our day of "anarchy, apostasy, and apathy," Havner suggests that expectant living means: "We need to take down our 'Do Not Disturb' signs . . . snap out of our stupor and come out of our coma and awake from our apathy."[12] Havner reminds us that God's Word calls to us to awake out of our sleep, and to walk in righteousness, in the light Christ gives us (Romans 13:11; 1 Corinthians 15:34; Ephesians 5:14).

Prophecy can provide the wake-up call that Dr. Havner calls for. When we have heard and understood the truth of Christ's promised return, we cannot just keep living our lives in the same old way. Future events have present implications that we cannot ignore. When we know that Christ is coming again to this earth, we cannot go on being the same people. From the New Testament epistles, I have gleaned ten ways in which we should be different as a result of our prophetic knowledge. For emphasis in each scripture quotation, I have italicized the words connecting the admonition with the promise of Christ's return.

1. *Refrain from judging others:* "Therefore judge nothing before the time, *until the Lord comes,* who will both bring

to light the hidden things of darkness and reveal the counsels of the hearts. Then each one's praise will come from God" (1 Corinthians 4:5).

2. *Remember the Lord's table:* "For as often as you eat this bread and drink this cup, you proclaim the Lord's death *till He comes*" (1 Corinthians 11:26).

3. *Respond to life spiritually:* "If then you were raised with Christ, seek those things which are above, where Christ is, sitting at the right hand of God. Set your mind on things above, not on things on the earth. For you died, and your life is hidden with Christ in God. *When Christ who is our life appears,* then you also will appear with Him in glory" (Colossians 3:1–4).

4. *Relate to one another in love:* "And may the Lord make you increase and abound in love to one another and to all, just as we do to you, so that He may establish your hearts blameless in holiness before our God and Father at *the coming of our Lord Jesus Christ* with all His saints" (1 Thessalonians 3:12–13).

5. *Restore the bereaved:* "But I do not want you to be ignorant, brethren, concerning those who have fallen asleep, lest you sorrow as others who have no hope. For if we believe that Jesus died and rose again, even so God will bring with Him those who sleep in Jesus. For this we say to you by the word of the Lord, that we who are alive and remain *until the coming of the Lord* will by no means precede those who are asleep. For the Lord Himself will descend from heaven with a shout, with the voice of an archangel, and with the trumpet of God. And the dead in Christ will rise first. Then we who are alive and remain shall be caught up together with them

in the clouds to meet the Lord in the air. And thus we shall always be with the Lord. Therefore comfort one another with these words" (1 Thessalonians 4:13–18).

6. *Recommit ourselves to the ministry:* "I charge you therefore before God and the Lord Jesus Christ, who will judge the living and the dead *at His appearing* and His kingdom: Preach the word! Be ready in season and out of season. Convince, rebuke, exhort, with all longsuffering and teaching" (2 Timothy 4:1–2).

7. *Refuse to neglect church:* "And let us consider one another in order to stir up love and good works, not forsaking the assembling of ourselves together, as is the manner of some, but exhorting one another, and so much the more *as you see the Day approaching*" (Hebrews 10:24–25).

8. *Remain steadfast:* "Therefore be patient, brethren, until the coming of the Lord. See how the farmer waits for the precious fruit of the earth, waiting patiently for it until it receives the early and latter rain. You also be patient. Establish your hearts, for *the coming of the Lord is at hand*" (James 5:7–8).

9. *Renounce sin in our lives:* "And now, little children, abide in Him, that *when He appears*, we may have confidence and not be ashamed before Him *at His coming*. If you know that He is righteous, you know that everyone who practices righteousness is born of Him" (1 John 2:28–29).

10. *Reach the lost:* "Keep yourselves in the love of God, *looking for the mercy of our Lord Jesus Christ* unto eternal life. And on some have compassion, making a distinction; but others save with fear, pulling them out of the fire, hating even the garment defiled by the flesh" (Jude 21–23).

Hoping and Longing for Christ's Return

One of the finest stories I've heard about men longing for their leader's return is that of explorer/adventurer Sir Ernest Shackleton. On Saturday, August 8, 1914, one week after Germany declared war on Russia, twenty-nine men set sail in a three-masted wooden ship from Plymouth, England, to Antarctica on a quest to become the first adventurers to cross the Antarctic continent on foot. Sir Ernest Shackleton had recruited the men through an advertisement: "Men wanted for hazardous journey. Small wages. Bitter cold. Long months of complete darkness. Constant danger. Safe return doubtful. Honour and recognition in case of success."

Not only was Shackleton an honest man, for the men did experience all that his handbill promised, but he was also an able leader and a certified hero. His men came to refer to him as "the Boss," although he never thought of himself that way. He worked as hard as any crew member and built solid team unity aboard the ship, aptly named *Endurance*. In January 1915, the ship became entrapped in an ice pack and ultimately sank, leaving the men to set up camp on an ice floe—a flat, free-floating slice of sea ice. Shackleton kept the men busy by day and entertained by night. They played ice soccer, had nightly songfests, and held regular sled-dog competitions. It was in the ice floe camp that Shackleton proved his greatness as a leader. He willingly sacrificed his right to a warmer, fur-lined sleeping bag so that one of his men might have it, and he personally served hot milk to his men in their tents every morning.

In April 1916, their thinning ice floe threatened to break apart, forcing the men to seek refuge on nearby Elephant Island. Knowing that a rescue from such a desolate island was unlikely, Shackleton and five others left to cross eight hundred miles of open Antarctic sea in a 22.5-foot lifeboat with more of a hope than a promise of a return with rescuers. Finally, on August 30, after an arduous 105-day trip and three earlier attempts, Shackleton returned to rescue his stranded crew, becoming their hero.

But perhaps the real hero in this story is Frank Wild. Second in command, Wild was left in charge of the camp in Shackleton's absence. He maintained the routine the Boss had established. He assigned daily duties, served meals, held sing-alongs, planned athletic competitions, and generally kept up morale. Because "the camp was in constant danger of being buried in snow . . . and become completely invisible from the sea, so that a rescue party might look for it in vain," Wild kept the men busy shoveling away drifts.

The firing of a gun was to be the prearranged signal that the rescue ship was near the island, but as Wild reported, "Many times when the glaciers were 'calving' and chunks fell off with a report like a gun, we thought that it was the real thing, and after a time we got to distrust these signals." But he never lost hope in the return of the Boss. Confidently, Wild kept the last tin of kerosene and a supply of dry combustibles ready to ignite instantly for use as a locator signal when the "day of wonders" would arrive.

Barely four days' worth of rations remained in the camp when Shackleton finally arrived on a Chilean icebreaker. He personally made several trips through the icy waters in a small lifeboat in order to ferry his crew to safety. Miraculously, the leaden fog lifted long enough for all the men to make it to the icebreaker in one hour.

Shackleton later learned from the men how they were prepared to break camp so quickly and reported: "From a fortnight after I had left, Wild would roll up his sleeping bag each day with the remark,

'Get your things ready, boys, the Boss may come today.' And sure enough, one day the mist opened and revealed the ship for which they had been waiting and longing and hoping for over four months." Wild's "cheerful anticipation proved infectious," and all were prepared when the evacuation day came.[13]

Shackleton's stranded crew desperately hoped that their leader would come back to them, and they longed for his return. But as diligent and dedicated as Shackleton was, they could not be certain he would return. He was, after all, a mere man battling elements he could not control, so they knew he might not make it back. Unlike that desperate crew, we have a certain promise that the Lord will return. Ours is not a mere longing or a desperate hope, as theirs was, for our Lord is the Creator and Master of all, and His promise is as sure as His very existence.

The prophets, the angels, and the apostle John all echo the words of promise from Jesus Himself that He will return. God's Word further amplifies the promise by giving us clues in prophecy to help us identify the signs that His return is close at hand. The signs that tell us the second coming of the Lord is drawing near should motivate us as never before to live in readiness. As we noted in chapter 5, the Rapture, which is the next event on the prophetic calendar, will take place seven years before the events we have discussed in this final chapter. Future events cast their shadows before them. As we anticipate His return, we are not to foolishly set dates and leave our jobs and homes to wait for Him on some mountain. We are to remain busy doing the work set before us, living in love and serving in ministry, even when the days grow dark and the nights long. Be encouraged! Be anticipating! We are secure; we belong to Christ. And as the old gospel song says, "Soon and very soon, we are going to see the King!"

APPENDIX A

Jewish Population Statistics

Country	1970	2007	Projected 2020
World	12,633,000	13,155,000	13,558,000*
Israel	2,582,000	5,393,000	6,228,000*
United States	5,400,000	5,275,000	5,200,000
France	530,000	490,000	482,000
Canada	286,000	374,000	381,000*
United Kingdom	390,000	295,000	238,000
Russia	808,000	225,000	130,000
Argentina	282,000	184,000	162,000
Germany	30,000	120,000	108,000

* indicates anticipated Jewish population growth

Source: Jewish People Policy Planning Institute, *Annual Assessment 2007* (Jerusalem, Israel: Gefen Publishing House LTD, 2007)

APPENDIX B

Conventional Oil Reserves by Country
June 2007

Rank	Country	Proved reserves (billion barrels) June 2007	Percentage world oil reserves
1	Saudi Arabia	264.3	21.9%
2	Iran	137.5	11.4%
3	Iraq	115.0	9.5%
4	Kuwait	101.5	8.4%
5	United Arab Emirates	97.8	8.1%
6	Venezuela	80.0	6.6%
6	Russia	79.5	6.6%

Rank	Country	Proved reserves (billion barrels) June 2007	Percentage world oil reserves
8	Libya	41.5	3.4%
9	Kazakhstan	39.8	3.3%
10	Nigeria	36.2	3.0%
11	United States	29.9	2.5%
12	Canada *	17.1	1.4%
13	China Qatar	16.3 15.2	1.3% 1.3%
	Total World Reserves	1,208,200,000,000	

* When oil sands are included, Canada ranks second with 178.8 billion barrels of proved reserve. Currently oil sands are excluded from classification as reserves by the US Securities and Exchange Commission and are not included in BP statistics.

NOTES

Introduction: Knowing the Signs

1. "Speech by Dmitri A. Medvedev," *The New York Times* online, 11 December 2007, www.nytimes.com/2007/12/11/world/europe/medvedev-speech.html (accessed 2 June 2008).

2. "UN warns of more unrest over food shortages," EuroNews, 23 April 2008, www.euronews.net/index.php?page=info&article=482404&lng=1 (accessed 2 June 2008).

3. Pascale Bonnefoy, "Evacuation Ordered as Chilean Volcano Begins to Spew Ash," 7 May 2008, http://www.nytimes.com/2008/05/07/world/americas/07chile.html?ref=world (accessed 7 May 2008).

4. Adam Entous, "Gaza headmaster was Islamic 'rocket maker,'" Reuters wire service, 5 May 2008; available at www.thestar.com.my/news/story.asp?file=/2008/5/5/worldupdates/2008-05-05T203555Z_01_NOOTR_RTRMDNC_0_-334136-1&sec=Worldupdates (accessed 2 June 2008).

5. Skip Heitzig, *How to Study the Bible and Enjoy It* (Carol Stream, IL: Tyndale House Publishers, 2002), 96.

6. Tim LaHaye, *The Rapture* (Eugene, OR: Harvest House Publishers, 2002), 88.

7. William Zinsser, *Writing About Your Life* (New York: Marlowe & Company, 2004), 155–156.

Chapter One: The Israel Connection

1. Romesg Ratnesae, "May 14, 1948," *Time*, http://www.time.com/time/magazine/article/0,9171,1004510,00.html (accessed 27 February 2008).

2. The Declaration of Independence (Israel), 14 May 1948, Israel Ministry of Foreign Affairs, "The Signatories of the Declaration of the Establishment of the State of Israel," http://www.mfa.gov.il/mfa/history/modern%20history/israel%20at%2050/the%20signatories%20of%20the%20declaration%20of%20the%20establis (accessed 25 February 2008).

3. Rabbi Binyamin Elon, *God's Covenant with Israel* (Green Forest, AR: Balfour Books, 2005), 12.

4. Mark Twain, "Concerning the Jews," *Harper's*, September 1899, 535.

5. "Jewish Nobel Prize Winners," Jewish Virtual Library, http://www.jewishvirtuallibrary.
org/jsource/Judaism/nobels.html (accessed 26 February 2008); "Nobel Laureate Facts,"
Nobelprize.org, http://nobelprize.org/nobel_prizes/nobelprize_facts.html (accessed 27
February 2008); and "Jewish Nobel Prize Winners," The Jewish Contribution to World
Civilization (JINFO), www.jinfo.org/Nobel_Prizes.html (accessed 27 February 2008).

6. Jewish People Policy Planning Institute, Annual Assessment 2007 (Jerusalem, Israel:
Gefen Publishing House LTD, 2007), 15.

7. David Jeremiah, Before It's Too Late (Nashville, TN: Thomas Nelson, Inc., 1982), 126.

8. Hal Lindsey, "I will bless them that bless thee," WorldNetDaily, 18 January 2008, www.
wnd.com/index.php?pageId=45604 (accessed 27 June 2008).

9. Elon, God's Covenant with Israel, 17.

10. Ibid.

11. Abraham Joshua Heschel, Israel: An Echo of Eternity (Woodstock, VT: Jewish Lights
Publishing, 1997), 57.

12. John Walvoord, "Will Israel Possess the Promised Land?" Jesus the King Is Coming,
Charles Lee Feinberg, ed. (Chicago: Moody Press, 1975), 128.

13. Quoted by Josephus, Antiquities xiv. 7.2, Leob edition, cited in A. F. Walls, "The
Dispersion," The New Bible Dictionary (Grand Rapids: Wm. B. Eerdmans Pub. Co.,
1962), 313–319.

14. Joseph Stein, Fiddler on the Roof screenplay, 1971.

15. Joel C. Rosenberg, from the audio track of the DVD Epicenter (Carol Stream, IL:
Tyndale House Publishers, Inc., 2007). Used with permission.

16. Rabbi Leo Baeck, "A Minority Religion," The Dynamics of Emancipation: The Jew in the
Modern Age, compiled by Nahum Norbert Glatzer (Boston: Beacon Press, 1965), 61.
Reprinted by permission of Beacon Press.

17. David McCullough, Truman (New York: Simon & Schuster, 1992), 619.

18. Gary Frazier, Signs of the Coming of Christ (Arlington, TX; Discovery Ministries, 1998),
67.

19. Chaim Weizmann, Trial and Error (New York: Harper & Brothers, 1949), 141–194.

20. Israel Ministry of Foreign Affairs, "The Balfour Declaration," http://www.mfa.gov.il/
MFA/Peace+Process/Guide+to+the+Peace+Process/The+Balfour+Declaration.htm
(accessed 27 February 2008); see also http://www.president.gov.il/chapters/chap_3/
file_3_3_1_en.asp.

21. Quoted in Gustav Niebuhr, "Religion Journal: Political Expressions of Personal Piety
Increase, as Bush and Gore Showed," The New York Times, 16 December 2000, http://
query.nytimes.com/gst/fullpage.html?res=990DEED61539F935A25751C1A9669C8B63
(accessed 27 February 2008).

22. Yossi Beilin, His Brother's Keeper: Israel and Diaspora Jews in the Twenty-first Century
(New York: Schocken Books, 2000), 99.

23. The Jewish People Policy Planning Institute: Annual Assessment 2007 (Jerusalem, Israel:
Gefen Publishing House LTD, 2007), 15.

24. Milton B. Lindberg, The Jew and Modern Israel (Chicago: Moody Press, 1969), 7.

25. Clark Clifford, *Counsel to the President* (New York: Random House, 1991), 3.

26. Ibid., 4.

27. Ibid., 7–8.

28. Ibid., 13.

29. Ibid., 22.

30. McCullough, *Truman*, 620.

Chapter Two: The Crude Awakening

1. "The Story of Oil in Pennsylvania," Paleontological Research Institution, www.priweb. org/ed/pgws/history/pennsylvania/pennsylvania.html (accessed 1 October 2007).

2. Fareed Zakaria,"Why We Can't Quit," *Newsweek*, http://www.newsweek.com/id/123482 (accessed 25 February 2008).

3. Ibid.

4. Ronald Bailey, "Oil Price Bubble?" Reason Online, 26 March 2008, www.reason.com/news/printer/125414.html (accessed 3 June 2008).

5. "This Week in Petroleum," Energy Information Administration, 19 March 2008, www. tonto.eia.gov/oog/info/twip.html (accessed 26 March 2008); and International Business Times: Commodities & Futures, "This Week in Petroleum", 19 March 2008, http://www. ibtimes.com/articles/20080319/this-week-in-petroleum-mar-19.htm (accessed 17 June 2008).

6. Dilip Hiro, "The Power of Oil," Yale Center for the Study of Globlization, 10 January 2006, http://yaleglobal.yale.edu/display.article?id=6761.

7. Oil-Proved Reserves, "BP Statistical Review of World Energy June 2007," BP Global, http://www.bp.com/liveassets/bp_internet/globalbp/globalbp_uk_english/reports_and_ publications/statistical_energy_review_2007/STAGING/local_assets/downloads/pdf/ statistical_review_of_world_energy_full_report_2007.pdf (accessed 4 March 2008). (Note: a complete chart with an explanation of Canadian reserves can be found in appendix B.)

8. Daniel P. Erikson, "Ahmadinejad finds it warmer in Latin America" (editorial), *Los Angeles Times*, 3 October 2007, www.latimes.com/news/opinion/sunday/commentary/la-oe-erikson3oct03,0,5434188.story (accessed 3 October 2007).

9. Robert J. Morgan, *My All in All* (Nashville, TN: B&H Publishing, 2008), entry for April 22.

10. "Country Energy Profiles," Energy Information Administration, http://tonto.eia.doe. gov/country/index.cfm (accessed 26 March 2008). (Note: this information is accessible under the "Consumption" tab in the "Top World Oil Consumers, 2006" table.)

11. Zakaria, "Why We Can't Quit."

12. Sara Nunnally and Bryan Bottarelli, "Oil Consumption Statistics: the European Union's Oil Consumption Growth," *Wavestrength Options Weekly*, 3 March 2007, www. wavestrength.com/wavestrength/marketreport/20070307_Oil_Consumption_Statistics_ and_Global_Markets_Market_Report.html (accessed 3 June 2008).

13. Michael Grunwald, "The Clean Energy Scam," *Time*, 7 April 2008, 40–45.

14. "Jimmy Carter State of the Union Address 1980," 23 January 1980, Jimmy Carter Library & Museum, www.jimmycarterlibrary.org/documents/speeches/su80jec.phtml (accessed 3 June 2008).

15. "Confrontation in the Gulf: Excerpts from Bush's Statement on the U.S. Defense of Saudis," *The New York Times*, 9 August 1990, http://query.nytimes.com/gst/fullpage.htm l?res=9C0CE0DC1F3FF93AA3575BC0A966958260&sec=&spon=&pagewanted=all (accessed 26 March 2008).

16. Ann Davis, "Where Has All the Oil Gone?" *Wall Street Journal*, 6 October 2007, http://www.energyinvestmentstrategies.com/infoFiles/articlePDFs/100607SpeculatorsOilPrice s.pdf (accessed 17 June 2008).

17. Remarks by Abdallah S. Jum'ah, "The Impact of Upstream Technological Advances on Future Oil Supply," speech transcript, Third OPEC International Seminar, 12–13 September 2006, http://www.opec.org/opecna/Speeches/2006/OPEC_Seminar/PDF/Abdallah%20Jumah.pdf (accessed 21 August 2007).

18. "Oil War," Global Policy Forum, Security Council, 26 March 2003, http://www.globalpolicy.org/security/oil/2003/0326oilwar.htm (accessed 26 June 2008).

19. Paul Roberts, *The End of Oil: On the Edge of a Perilous New World* (Boston: Mariner Books, 2005), 337. Reprinted by permission of Houghton Mifflin Harcourt Publishing Company. All rights reserved.

20. Ibid.

21. "Mrs. Meir Says Moses Made Israel Oil-Poor," *The New York Times*, 11 June 1973.

22. Tim LaHaye, *The Coming Peace in the Middle East* (Grand Rapids, MI: Zondervan, 1984), 105.

23. Aaron Klein, "Is Israel sitting on enormous oil reserve?" WorldNetDaily, 21 September 2005, www.worldnetdaily.com/news/article.asp?ARTICLE_ID=46428 (accessed 27 August 2007).

24. Ibid.

25. Zion Facts, "What are the terms of the Joseph License?" and "What are the terms of the Asher-Menashe License?" http://www.zionoil.com/investor-center/zion-faqs.html (accessed 31 March 2008).

26. Dan Ephron, "Israel: A Vision of Oil in the Holy Land," *Newsweek*, 13 June 2007, http://www.newsweek.com/id/50060 (accessed 2 October 2007).

27. Paul Crespo, "Author: 'Something Is Going On Between Russia and Iran,'" Newsmax, 30 January 2007, http://archive.newsmax.com/archives/articles/2007/1/29/212432.shtml?s=1h (accessed 26 March 2008).

28. Joel C. Rosenberg, *Epicenter* (Carol Stream, IL: Tyndale House Publishers, 2006), 113.

29. Amir Mizroch, "Israel launches new push to reduce its oil dependency," *Jerusalem Post*, 27 September 2007, posted at Forecast Highs, http://forecasthighs.wordpress.com/2007/09/27/Israel-launches-new-push-to-reduce-its-oil-dependency (accessed 2 October 2007).

30. Steven R. Weisman, "Oil Producers See the World and Buy It Up," *The New York Times*, 28 November 2007.

31. Don Richardson, *The Secrets of the Koran* (Ventura, CA: Regal Books, 2003), 161.

32. Nazila Fathi, "Mideast Turmoil: Tehran; Iranian Urges Muslims to Use Oil as a Weapon," *The New York Times*, 6 April 2002, http://query.nytimes.com/gst/fullpage.htm l?res=9A05E5D6173DF935A35757C0A9649C8B63&scp=3&sq=Nazila+Fathi&st=nyt (accessed 25 June 2008).

33. Paraphrased by Timothy George, "Theology in an Age of Terror," *Christianity Today*, September 2006; from C. S. Lewis, "Learning in Wartime," *The Weight of Glory and Other Addresses* (New York: Macmillan, 1949), 41–52.

34. C. S. Lewis, "Learning in Wartime," *The Weight of Glory and Other Addresses* (New York: Macmillan, 1949), 26.

35. Vance Havner, *In Times Like These* (Old Tappan, NJ: Fleming H. Revell, 1969), 21.

Chapter Three: Modern Europe . . . Ancient Rome

1. Adapted from David Jeremiah, *The Handwriting on the Wall* (Nashville, TN: Thomas Nelson, Inc., 1992), 15–16.

2. "The Mists of Time," Amazing Discoveries, http://amazingdiscoveries.org/the-mists-of-time.html (accessed 21 March 2008).

3. Tim LaHaye, Ed Hindson, eds., *The Bible Prophecy Commentary* (Eugene, OR: Harvest House Publishers, 2006), 226.

4. "The European Union," *Time*, 26 May 1930, http://www.time.com/time/magazine/article/0,9171,739314,00.html (accessed 8 October 2007).

5. William R. Clark, *Petrodollar Warfare: Oil, Iraq and the Future of the Dollar* (New Society Publishers, 2005), 198; see also W. S. Churchill, *Collected Essays of Winston Churchill, Vol. II* (London: Library of Imperial History, 1976), 176–186.

6. "The History of the European Union," Europa, http://europa.eu./abc/history (accessed 8 October 2007).

7. Compiled from "The EU at a glance—Ten historic steps," Europa, http://europa.eu (accessed 8 October 2007).

8. Michael Shtender-Auherbach, "Israel and the EU: A Path to Peace," The Century Foundation, 3 November 2005, http://www.tcf.org/list.asp?type=NC&pubid=1129 (accessed 10 October 2007).

9. Council of the European Union Presidency Conclusions, http://www.consilium.europa.eu/ueDocs/cms_Data/docs/pressData/en/ec/94932.pdf (accessed 17 June 2008).

10. "How are we organized?" Europa, http://europa.eu/abc/panorama/howorganised/index_en.htm (accessed 5 March 2008).

11. Alex Duval Smith, "Blair kicks off campaign to become EU President," *The Guardian*, 13 January 2008, http://www.guardian.co.uk/uk/2008/jan/13/politics.world (accessed 5 March 2008); see also Dan Bilefsky, "2 Leaders Back Blair as European Union President," *The New York Times*, 20 October 2007, http://www.nytimes.com/2007/10/20/world/europe/20europe.html?_r=1&oref=slogin (accessed 5 March 2007).

12. Arno Froese, *How Democracy Will Elect the Antichrist* (Columbia, SC: Olive Press, 1997), 165.

13. Quoted in David L. Larsen, *Telling the Old, Old Story: The Art of Narrative Preaching* (Grand Rapids, MI: Kregel, 1995), 214.

14. Jim Madaffer, "The Firestorm—Two Weeks Later," City of San Diego, www.sandiego. gov/citycouncil/cd7/pdf/enews/2003/the_firestorm.pdf (accessed 5 March 2008).

15. "Burned Firefighter Describes Cheating Death," NBC San Diego, 14 November 2007, www.nbcsandiego.com/news/14598732/detail.html (accessed 15 November 2007); Tony Manolatos, "Cal fire report recounts tragic incident, rescue," *Union Tribune* (San Diego), 9 November 2007, http://www.signonsandiego.com/news/metro/20071109-9999-1n9report.htm (accessed 5 March 2008); Tony Manolatos, "Pilot who rescued fire crew didn't feel like a hero," *Union Tribune* (San Diego), 30 October 2007, http://www.signonsandiego.com/news/metro/20071030-1400-bn30pilot.html (accessed 31 October 2007); and Tony Manolatos, "During rescue effort that turned tragic, an act of heroism," *Union Tribune* (San Diego), 23 October 2007, http://www.signonsandiego.com/news/metro/20071023-9999-bn23firedead.html (accessed 26 October 2007).

Chapter Four: Islamic Terrorism

1. Georges Sada, *Saddam's Secrets: How an Iraqi General Defied and Survived Saddam Hussein* (Brentwood, TN: Integrity Publishers, 2006), 285–286.

2. Ibid., 289.

3. "Public Expresses Mixed Views of Islam, Mormonism," Pew Research Center Publications, 25 September 2007, http://pewresearch.org/pubs/602/public-expresses-mixed-views-of-islam-mormonism (accessed 1 October 2007).

4. Sada, *Saddam's Secrets*, 289–290.

5. Adapted from "New Poll Shows Worry over Islamic Terror Threat, to Be Detailed in Special Fox News Network Report," Fox News, 3 February 2007, www.foxnews.com/story/0,2933,249521,00.html (accessed 16 October 2007).

6. "Hamas TV puppet 'kills' Bush for helping Israel," Reuters wire service, 1 April 2008, http://www.reuters.com/article/worldNews/idUSL0146737420080401 (accessed 1 April 2008).

7. Reza F. Safa, Foreword to Don Richardson, *The Secrets of the Koran* (Ventura, CA: Regal Books, 2003), 10.

8. Will Durant, *The Age of Faith* (New York: Simon & Schuster, 1950), 155.

9. Statistics compiled from "Major Religions of the World Ranked by Adherents," Adherents.com. http://pewresearch.org/pubs/483/muslim-americans (accessed 17 October 2007); and "Muslim Americans: Middle Class and Mostly Mainstream," Pew Research Center, www.adherents.com/Religions_By_Adherents.html (accessed 17 October 2007).

10. Durant, *Age of Faith*, 163.

11. Robert A. Morey, *Islam Unveiled: The True Desert Storm* (Sherman's Dale, PA: The Scholar's Press, 1991), 49.

12. Abd El Schafi, *Behind the Veil* (Caney, KS: Pioneer Book Company, 1996), 32.

13. Winfried Corduan, *Pocket Guide to World Religions* (Downers Grove, IL: InterVarsity Press, 2006), 80–85.

14. Information on the five pillars adapted from Norman L. Geisler and Abdul Saleeb, *Answering Islam*, 2nd ed. (Grand Rapids, MI: Baker Books, 2006), 301.

15. Benazir Bhutto, *Reconciliation: Islam, Democracy, and the West* (New York: HarperCollins, 2008), 2–3, 20.

16. "Text of Ibrahim Mdaires's Sermon," *The Jerusalem Post*, 19 May 2005.

17. Richardson, *Secrets of the Koran*, 69–71.

18. Oren Dorell, "Some say schools giving Muslim special treatment," *USA Today*, 25 July 2007, http://www.usatoday.com/news/nation/2007-07-25-muslim-special-treatment-from-schools_N.htm (accessed 16 October 2007); see also Helen Gao, "Arabic program offered at school," (San Diego) *Union Tribune*, 12 April 2007, http://www.signonsandiego.com/news/education/20070412-9999-1m12carver.html (accessed 16 October 2007).

19. Tony Blankley, *The West's Last Chance* (Washington, DC: Regnery Publishing, Inc., 2005), 21–23, 39.

20. Sada, *Saddam's Secrets*, 287.

21. Philip Johnston, "Reid meets the furious face of Islam," (London) *Telegraph*, 21 September 2006, http://www.telegraph.co.uk/news/uknews/1529415/Reid-meets-the-furious-face-of-Islam.html (accessed 13 March 2008).

22. Nick Britten, "Religions collide under the dreaming spires," (London) *Telegraph*, 4 February 2008, http://www.telegraph.co.uk/news/uknews/1577340/Religions-collide-under-the-dreaming-spires.html (accessed 13 March 2008).

23. "Sharia law in UK is 'unavoidable'," BBC News, 7 February 2008, http://news.bbc.co.uk/2/hi/uk_news/7232661.stm (accessed 13 March 2008).

24. Jonathan Wynne-Jones, "Bishop warns of no-go zones for non-Muslims," (London) *Telegraph*, 5 January 2008, http://www.telegraph.co.uk/news/uknews/1574694/Bishop-warns-of-no-go-zones-for-non-Muslims.html (accessed 13 March 2008).

25. "Vatican: Muslims now outnumber Catholics," *USA Today*, 30 March 2008, http://www.usatoday.com/news/religion/2008-03-30-muslims-catholics_N.htm (accessed 2 April 2008).

26. "Ahmadinejad's 2005 address to the United Nations," Wikisource: United Nations, http://en.wikisource.org/wiki/Ahmadinejad's_2005_address_to_the_United-Nations.

27. "Ahmadinejad: Wipe Israel off map," Aljazeera News, 28 October 2005, http://english.aljazeera.net/English/archive/archive?ArchiveId=15816 (accessed 4 June 2008).

28. Stan Goodenough, "Ahmadinejad: Israel has reached its 'final' stage,'" *Jerusalem Newswire*, 30 January 2008, www.jnewswire.com/article/2314 (accessed 4 June 2008).

29. Mark Bentley and Ladane Nasseri, "Ahmadinejad's Nuclear Mandate Strengthened After Iran Election," Bloomberg News, 16 March 2008, www.bloomberg.com/apps/news?pid=20601087&sid=aGUPH1VLn.7c&refer=home (accessed 4 June 2008).

30. John F. Walvoord and Mark Hitchcock, *Armageddon, Oil and Terror* (Carol Stream, IL: Tyndale House Publishers, 2007), 44.

31. "Roman Catholic Bishop Wants Everyone to Call God 'Allah,'" Fox News, 16 August 2007, http://www.foxnews.com/story/0,2933,293394,00.html (accessed 14 March 2008).

32. Stan Goodenough, "Let's Call Him Allah," *Jerusalem Newswire*, 21 August 2007, http://www.foxnews.com/story/0,2933,293394,00.html (accessed 14 March 2008).

33. "Roman Catholic Bishop," Fox News.

34. Ibid.

35. Hal Lindsey, "Does God care what He's called?" WorldNetDaily, 17 August 2007, www.wnd.com/index.php?pageId=43089 (accessed 27 June 2008).

36. Adapted from Dr. Robert A. Morey, *Islam Unveiled,* (Shermandale, PA: The Scholar's Press, 1991), 60.

37. Edward Gibbon, *The Decline and Fall of the Roman Empire* (London: Milman Co., n.d.), 1:365.

38. "A Testimony from a Saudi Believer," Answering Islam: A Christian-Muslim Dialog and Apologetic, http://answering-islam.org./Testimonies/saudi.html (accessed 20 April 2006).

Chapter Five: Vanished Without a Trace

1. "Firefighters Gain Ground as Santa Ana Winds Decrease," KNBC Los Angeles, 24 October 2007, http://www.knbc.com/news/14401132/detail.html (accessed 26 October 2007).

2. Bruce Bickel and Stan Jantz, *Bible Prophecy 101* (Eugene, OR: Harvest House Publishers, 1999), 124.

3. *Merriam-Webster Online*, s. v. "rapture," www.merriam-webster.com/dictionary/rapture (accessed 5 June 2008).

4. Alfred Tennyson, "Break, Break, Break," *Poems, Vol. II* (Boston: Ticknor, Reed and Fields, 1851), 144.

5. Tim LaHaye, *The Rapture* (Eugene, OR: Harvest House Publishers, 2002), 69.

6. "100 Nations' Leaders Attend Churchill Funeral," Churchill Centre, www.winstonchurchill.org/i4a/pages/index.cfm?pageid=801 (accessed 4 March 2008).

7. Bickel and Jantz, *Bible Prophecy*, 123.

8. Arthur T. Pierson, *The Gospel, Vol. 3* (Grand Rapids, MI: Baker Book House, 1978), 136.

9. Wayne Grudem, *Systematic Theology* (Grand Rapids, MI: Zondervan, 1994), 1093.

10. Gig Conaughton, "County Buys Reverse 911 System," *North County Times,* 11 August 2005, http://www.nctimes.com/articles/2005/08/12/news/top_stories/21_13_388_11_05.txt (accessed 4 March 2008); see also "Mayor Sanders Unveils New Reverse 911 System," KGTV, 6 September 2007, http://www.10news.com/news/14061100/detail.html (accessed 4 March 2008); Gig Conaughton, "Officials Laud High-Speed Alert System," North County Times, 27 October 2007, http://www.nctimes.com/articles/2007/10/26/news/top_stories/21_36_2110_25_07.txt (accessed 18 March 2008); Scott Glover, Jack Leonard, and Matt Lait, "Two Homes, Two Couples, Two Fates," Los Angeles Times, 26 October 2007, http://www.latimes.com/news/local/la-me-pool26oct26,0,3755059.story (accessed 26 October 2007).

Chapter Six: Does America Have a Role in Prophecy?

1. Adapted from Newt Gingrich, *Rediscovering God in America* (Nashville, TN: Integrity, 2006), 130.

2. Peter Marshall and David Manuel, *The Light and the Glory* (Old Tappan, NJ: Revell, 1977), 17, 18.

3. "President's Proclamation," *The New York Times*, 21 November 1982, http://select. nytimes.com/search/restricted/article?res=F30611FB395DOC728EDDA80994 (accessed 15 April 2008).

4. "The Journal of Christopher Columbus (1492)," The History Guide: Lectures on Early Modern European History, www.historyguide.org/earlymod/columbus.html (accessed 2 November 2007).

5. "Washington's First Inauguration Address, April 30, 1789," Library of Congress, www. loc.gov/exhibits/treasures/trt051.html (accessed 5 June 2008).

6. John F. Walvoord, "America and the Cause of World Missions," *America in History and Bible Prophecy*, Thomas McCall, ed. (Chicago: Moody Press, 1976), 21.

7. Gordon Robertson, "Into All the World," Christian Broadcasting Network, http://www. cbn.com/spirituallife/churchandministry/churchhistory/Gordon_Into_World.aspx (accessed 1 November 2007).

8. Luis Bush, "Where Are We Now?" Mission Frontiers, 2003, http://www. missionfrontiers.org/2000/03/bts20003.htm (accessed 1 November 2007).

9. Abba Eban, *An Autobiography* (New York: Random House, 1977), 126.

10. Ibid., 134.

11. "The Worst of the Worst: The World's Most Repressive Societies," Freedom House, April 2007, http://www.freedomhouse.org/template.cfm?page=383&report=58 (accessed 1 November 2007).

12. Ronald Reagan, "Inaugural Address, January 20, 1981," Ronald Reagan Presidential Library Archives, National Archives and Records Administration, www.reagan.utexas. edu/archives/speeches/1981/12081a.htm (accessed 5 June 2008).

13. Quoted in Newt Gingrich, *Winning the Future: A 21ˢᵗ Century Contract with America* (Washington, DC: Regnery Publishing, Inc., 2005), 200.

14. John Gilmary Shea, *The Lincoln Memorial: A Record of the Life, Assassination, and Obsequies of Abraham Lincoln* (New York: Bunce and Huntington Publishers, 1865), 237.

15. Benjamin Franklin, "Speech to the Constitutional Convention, June 28, 1787," Library of Congress, http://www.loc.gov/exhibits/religion/rel06.html (accessed 18 June 2008).

16. William J. Federer, ed., *America's God and Country—Encyclopedia of Quotations*, (St. Louis: Amerisearch, Inc., 2000), 696.

17. Ibid., 697–698.

18. Jared Sparks, ed., *The Writings of George Washington*, 12 vols. (Boston: Little, Brown and Company, 1837), vol. III, 449.

19. "The Gettysburg Address," http://www.loc.gov/exhibits/gadd/gadrft.html (accessed 18 June 2008).

20. Charles Fadiman, ed., *The American Treasury* (New York: Harper & Brothers, 1955), 127.

21. Jay Gormley, "LISD to Repaint 'In God We Trust' on Gym Wall," CBS11TV.com, 1 April 2008, http://cbs11tv.com/business/education/LISD.Repaints.motto.2.689875.html (accessed 7 April 2008).

22. "Laus Deo," Snopes Urban Legends Reference Pages, www.snopes.com/politics/religion/lausdeo.asp (accessed 7 April 2008); see also "Washington Monument," www.snopes.com/politics/religion/monument.asp (accessed 7 April 2008).

23. Tim LaHaye, as cited by Dr. Thomas Ice, "Is America in Bible Prophecy?" Pre-Trib Research Center, http://www.pre-trib.org/article-view.php?id=14 (accessed 18 June 2008).

24. Tim LaHaye, "The Role of the U.S.A. in End Times Prophecy," *Tim LaHaye's Perspective*, August 1999, http://209.85.173.104/search?q=cache:ZEQ46V4CQRYJ:www.yodelingfrog.com/Misc%2520Items/(doc)%2520-%2520Tim%2520LaHaye%2520-%2520The%2520Role%2520of%2520the%2520USA%2520in%2520End%2520Times%2520Prophecy.pdf+%22Does+the+United+States+have+a+place+in+end+time+prophecy%3F%22&hl=en&ct=clnk&cd=1&gl=us&lr=lang_en (accessed 18 June 2008).

25. John Walvoord and Mark Hitchcock, *Armageddon, Oil and Terror*, (Carol Stream, IL: Tyndale House Publishers, 2007), 67.

26. "President Bush Meets with EU Leaders, Chancellor Merkel of the Federal Republic of Germany and President Barroso of the European Council and President of the European Commission," press release dated 30 April 2007, The White House, http://www.whitehouse.gov/news/releases/2007/04/20070430-2.html (accessed 28 March 2008).

27. "Transatlantic Economic Council," European Commission, http://ec.europa.eu/enterprise/enterprise_policy/inter_rel/tec/index_en.htm (accessed 28 March 2008).

28. Jerome R. Cossi, "Premeditated Merger: Inside the hush-hush North American Union confab," WorldNetDaily, 13 March 2008, http://www.worldnetdaily.com/index.php?fa=PAGE.view&pageId=58788 (accessed 28 March 2008).

29. Ibid.

30. Walvoord and Hitchcock, *Armageddon*, 68.

31. Ed Timperlake, "Explosive missing debate item," *The Washington Times*, 5 March 2008, http://www.washingtontimes.com/news/2008/mar/05/explosive-missing-debate-item (accessed 28 March 2008).

32. Ed Timperlake, "Explosive missing debate item," *The Washington Times*, 5 March 2008, http://www.washingtontimes.com/news/2008/mar/05/explosive-missing-debate-item (accessed 28 March 2008).

33. Ed Timperlake, "Explosive missing debate item," *The Washington Times*, 5 March 2008, http://www.washingtontimes.com/news/2008/mar/05/explosive-missing-debate-item (accessed 28 March 2008).

34. "U.S. says N. Korea missile tests 'not constructive,'" Reuters, 28 March 2008, http://www.reuters.com/article/idUSWAT00920520080328 (accessed 28 March 2008).

35. Walvoord and Hitchcock, *Armageddon*, 65.

36. La Shawn Barber, "America on the Decline," La Shawn Barber's Corner, 25 February 2004, http://lashawnbarber.com/archives/2004/02/25/brstronglatest-column-america-on-the-declinestrong/ (accessed 28 March 2008).

37. Adapted from Carle C. Zimmerman, *Family and Civilization* (Wilmington, DE: ISI Books, 2008), 255.

38. Mike Evans, *The Final Move Beyond Iraq* (Lake Mary, FL: Front Line, 2007), 168.

39. Herbert C. Hoover, *Addresses upon the American Road 1950–1955* (Palo Alto, CA: Stanford University Press, 1955), 111–113,117.

40. Mark Hitchcock, *America in the End Times*, newsletter, The Left Behind Prophecy Club.

41. Herman A. Hoyt, *Is the United States in Prophecy?* (Winona Lake, ID: BMH Books, 1977), 16.

Chapter Seven: When One Man Rules the World

1. Erwin Lutzer, *Hitler's Cross* (Chicago: Moody Press, 1995), 62–63.

2. Tim LaHaye and Ed Hinson, *Global Warning* (Eugene, OR: Harvest House, 2007), 195.

3. Charles Colson, *Kingdoms in Conflict* (Grand Rapids, MI: Zondervan, 1987), 129–130.

4. Lutzer, *Hitler's Cross*, 73.

5. Arthur W. Pink, *The Antichrist* (Minneapolis: Klich & Klich, 1979), 77.

6. Marvin Kalb and Bernard Kalb, *Kissinger* (New York: Little, Brown and Company, 1974), 201–202.

7. Colson, *Kingdoms in Conflict*, 68.

8. Ibid.

9. Thomas Ice, "The Ethnicity of the Antichrist," Pre-Trib Research Center, www.pre-trib. org/article-view.php?id=230 (accessed 5 June 2008).

10. *Conservapedia*, French Revolution, http://www.conservapedia.com/French_Revolution (accessed 18 June 2008).

11. W. A. Criswell, *Expository Sermons on Revelation*, vol. IV (Dallas: Criswell Publishing, 1995), 109.

12. David E. Gumpert, "Animal Tags for People?" *Business Week*, 11 January 2007, www. businessweek.com/smallbiz/content/jan2007/sb20070111_186325.htm?chan=smallbiz_ smallbiz+index+page_today's+top+stories (accessed 11 April 2008).

13. Gary Frazier, *Signs of the Coming of Christ* (Arlington, TX: Discovery Ministries, 1998), 149.

Chapter Eight: The New Axis of Evil

1. "President Delivers State of the Union Address," press release dated 29 January 2002, The White House, http://www.whitehouse.gov/news/releases/2002/01/20020129-11. html (accessed 10 March 2008).

2. John F. Walvoord, *The Nations in Prophecy* (Grand Rapids, MI: Zondervan, 1978), 107.

3. Erik Hildinger, *Warriors of the Steppe: A Military History of Central Asia, 500 B.C. to 1700* (New York: DaCapo Press, 2001), 33.

4. Walvoord, *Nations in Prophecy*, 106.

5. Ibid.,101.

6. Edward Lucas, "The New Cold War," www.edwardlucas.com (accessed 6 June 2008).

7. Mike Celizic, "*Time*'s Person of the Year Is Vladimir Putin," *Today*: People-msnbc.com, 19 December 2007, http://www.msnbc.msn.com/id/22323855 (accessed 17 April 2008).

8. Nabi Abdullaev, "Speech Suggest Best Is Yet to Come," *Moscow Times*, 11 February 2008, http://www.moscowtimes.ru/article/1010/42/302320.htm (accessed 11 February 2008).

9. Oleg Shchedrov, "Putin in Jordan to demonstrate regional ambitions," Reuters AlertNet, 12 February 2007, www.alertnet.org/thenews/newsdesk/L12935084.htm (accessed 6 June 2008).

10. Ibid.

11. Hassan M. Fattah, "Putin Visits Qatar for Talks on Natural Gas and Trade," *The New York Times*, 13 February 2007, www.nytimes.com/2007/02/13/world/middleeast/13putin.html (accessed 17 April 2008).

12. Scott Peterson, "Russia, Iran Harden Against West," *Christian Science Monitor*, 18 October 2007, http://www.csmonitor.com/2007/1018/p06s02-woeu.html (accessed 18 June 2008).

13. "Russia scraps Libya's debts as Putin visits Tripoli," AFP (Agence France-Presse), April 2008, BNET Business Network, http://findarticles.com/p/articles/mi_kmafp/is_200804/ai_n25344293 (accessed 17 April 2008).

14. "EU should unite behind new Russia strategy: study," ViewNews.net, 7 November 2007, http://viewnews.net/news/world/eu-should-unite-behind-new-russia-strategy-study.html (accessed 18 June 2008).

15. Andris Piebalgs, "Gas warms EU-Russian ties," repost of *New Europe*, 7 April 2008, http://www.mgimo.ru/alleurope/2006/21/bez-perevoda1.html (accessed 21 July 2008).

16. "Iran," CIA-The World Factbook, https://www.cia.gov/library/publications/the-world-factbook/geos/ir.html (accessed 26 June 2008).

17. Borzou Daragahi, "Tehran sharing more nuclear data, agency says," *Los Angeles Times*, 31 August 2007, http://articles.latimes.com/2007/aug/31/world/fg-irannukes31 (accessed 31 August 2007).

18. "Ahmadinejad in new attack on 'savage animal,'" AFP news wire, 20 February 2008, http://afp.google.com/article/ALeqM5g_nrxYSrTbp_LIZcVU4VGCBpQ0hQ (accessed 6 June 2008).

19. Thom Shanker and Brandan Knowlton, "U.S. Describes Confrontation with Iranian Boats," *The New York Times*, 8 January 2008, http://www.nytimes.com/2008/01/08/washington/08military.html?scp=2&sq=U.S.+Describes+Confrontation+With+Iranian+Boats&st=nyt (accessed 26 June 2008).

20. Nazila Fathi, "Iran's President Says 'Israel Must Be Wiped Off the Map,'" *The New York Times*, 26 October 2007, http://www.nytimes.com/2005/10/26/international/middleeast/26cnd-iran.html (accessed 18 April 2008).

21. "UN boss alarmed by Hezbollah's threat against Israel,"Agence France-Presse, 3 March 2008, http://findarticles.com/p/articles/mi_kmafp/is_200803/ai_n24365391 (accessed 3 March 2008).

22. Aaron Klein, "Hezbollah: Rockets fired into Israel directed by Iran," WorldNetDaily, 7 May 2007, http://www.worldnetdaily.com/news/article.asp?ARTICLE_ID=55572 (accessed 5 September 2007).

23. Ibid.

24. "UN boss alarmed by Hezbollah's threat against Israel," Agence France-Presse, 3 March 2008.

25. Edward Gibbon, *The Decline and Fall of the Roman Empire* (London: Milman Co., London, n.d.), 1:204.

26. David L. Cooper, *When Gog's Armies Meet the Almighty* (Los Angeles: The Biblical Research Society, 1958), 17.

27. Theodore Epp, *Russia's Doom Prophesied* (Lincoln, NE: Good News Broadcasting, 1954), 40–42.

28. Barry L. Brumfield, "Israel; Politically and Geographically," Israel's Messiah.com, www.israelsmessiah.com/palestinian_refugees/israel_vs_arabs.htm (accessed 6 June 2008).

29. Matthew Kreiger, "7,200 Israeli millionaires today, up 13%," *Jerusalem Post,* 28 June 2007, http://www.jpost.com/servlet/Satellite?pagename=JPost%2FJPArticle%2FShowFull&cid=1182951032508 (accessed 17 April 2008).

30. Serge Schmemann, "Israel Redefines Its Dream, Finding Wealth in High Tech," *The New York Times,* 18 April 1998, http://query.nytimes.com/gst/fullpage.html?res=9502EED7123CF93BA25757C0A96E958260&sec=travel (accessed 6 June 2008).

31. "Land of milk and start-ups," *Economist,* 19 March 2008, www.economist.com/business/displaystory.cfm?story_id=10881264 (accessed 29 April 2008).

32. "Israel," Legatum Prosperity Index 2007, Legatum Institute, http://www.prosperity.org/profile.aspx?id=IS (accessed 29 April 2008).

33. "Israel," CIA-The World Factbook, https://www.cia.gov/library/publications/the-world-factbook/geos/is.html (accessed 26 June 2008).

34. Joel C. Rosenberg, *Epicenter* (Carol Stream, IL: Tyndale House Publishers 2006), 101.

35. H. D. M. Spence and Joseph Exell, eds., *The Pulpit Commentary,* vol. 28 (New York: Funk & Wagnalls, 1880–93), 298.

36. Robert J. Morgan, *From This Verse* (Nashville, TN: Thomas Nelson, Inc., 1998), entry for December 29.

Chapter Nine: Arming for Armageddon

1. Douglas MacArthur, "Farewell Address to Congress," delivered 19 April 1951, American Rhetoric, www.americanrhetoric.com/speeches/douglasmacarthurfarewelladdress.htm (accessed 6 June 2008).

2. Douglas Brinkley, ed., *The Reagan Diaries*, (New York: HarperCollins, 2007), 19, 24.

3. "American War Deaths Through History," Military Factory.com, www.militaryfactory.com/american_war_deaths.asp (accessed 6 June 2008).

4. Sylvie Barak, "Stephen Hawking says NASA should budget for interstellar travel: rising for the moon," The Inquirer (blog), 22 April 2008, www.theinquirer.net/gb/inquirer/news/2008/04/22/stephen-hawking-argues-nasa (accessed 6 June 2008).

5. Alan Johnson, The Expositor's Bible Commentary (Grand Rapids: Zondervan, 1981), 12:551.

6. Vernon J. McGee, Through the Bible, vol. 3 (Nashville, TN: Thomas Nelson, Inc., 1982), 513.

7. A. Sims, ed., The Coming Great War, (Toronto: A. Sims, Publisher, 1932), 7–8.

8. John Dryden, trans., Plutarch's Life of Sylla. Public domain.

9. Josephus, The Wars of the Jews, Book 6 from The Works of Josephus, translated by William Whiston (Peabody, MA: Hendrickson Publishers, 1987); available online: "Josephus Describes the Roman's Sack of Jerusalem," Frontline, http://www.pbs.org/wgbh/pages/frontline/shows/religion/maps/primary/josephussack.html (accessed 26 June 2008).

10. J. Dwight Pentecost, Things to Come—A Study in Biblical Eschatology (Findlay, OH: Dunham Publishing Company, 1958), 347–48.

11. "Hamas offers truce in return for 1967 borders," Associated Press, 21 April 2008, www.msnbc.msn.com/id/24235665/ (accessed 6 June 2008).

12. John Walvoord and Mark Hitchcock, Armageddon, Oil and Terror (Carol Stream, IL: Tyndale House Publishers, 2007), 174.

13. Alon Liel, Turkey in the Middle East: Oil, Islam, and Politics (Boulder, CO: Lynne Rienner Publishers, 2001), 20–21.

14. John F. Walvoord, "The Way of the Kings of the East," Light for the World's Darkness, John W. Bradbury, ed. (New York: Loizeaux Brothers, 1944), 164.

15. Larry M. Wortzel, "China's Military Potential," US Army Strategic Studies Institute, 2 October 1998, www.fas.org/nuke/guide/china/doctrine/chinamil.htm (accessed 6 June 2008).

16. Sims, The Coming Great War, 12–13.

17. Robert J. Morgan, My All in All (Nashville: B&H Publishers, 2008), entry for July 16.

18. Randall Price, Jerusalem in Prophecy (Eugene, OR: Harvest House Publishers, 1998), 1179–1180.

Chapter Ten: The Return of the King

1. Lehman Strauss, "Bible Prophecy" Bible.org, http://www.bible.org/page.php?page_id=412 (accessed 27 November 2007).

2. John F. Walvoord, End Times (Nashville, TN: Word Publishing, 1998), 143.

3. Tim LaHaye, The Rapture (Eugene, OR: Harvest House Publishers, 2002), 89.

4. Harry A. Ironside, Revelation (Grand Rapids, MI: Kregel, 2004), 187–188.

5. Charles Spurgeon, "The Saviour's Many Crowns," a sermon (no. 281) delivered 30 October 1859, The Spurgeon Archive, www.spurgeon.org/sermons/0281.htm (accessed 7 June 2008).

6. Ironside, *Revelation*, 189.

7. W. A. Criswell, *Expository Sermons on Revelation*, vol. 5 (Grand Rapids, MI: Zondervan, 1966), 31.

8. Ironside, *Revelation*; 189–190.

9. Kenneth Woodward, "Heaven," *Newsweek*, 27 March 1989, 54.

10. C. S. Lewis, *The Problem of Pain* (New York: Macmillan, 1940, 1973), 28.

11. Walvoord, *End Times*, 171.

12. Vance Havner, *In Times Like These* (Old Tappan, NJ: Fleming H. Revell Company, 1969), 29.

13. Based on Sir Ernest Henry Shackleton, *South! The Story of Shackleton's 1914–1917 Expedition*, public domain, available at Project Gutenberg, www.gutenberg.org/files/5199/5199-h/5199-h.htm (accessed 7 June 2008).

Appendix B: Conventional Oil Reserves by Country, June 2007

1. Oil-Proved Reserves, "BP Statistical Review of World Energy June 2007," BP Global, http://www.bp.com/liveassets/bp_internet/globalbp/globalbp_uk_english/reports_and_publications/statistical_energy_review_2007/STAGING/local_assets/downloads/pdf/statistical_review_of_world_energy_full_report_2007.pdf (accessed 4 March 2008).

About the Author

DR. DAVID JEREMIAH IS THE SENIOR PASTOR OF SHADOW Mountain Community Church in El Cajon, California. He is the author of several best-selling books, and his popular syndicated radio and television Bible-teaching program, *Turning Point*, is broadcast internationally. David and his wife, Donna, have four children and ten grandchildren.

Discover other

BIBLE PROPHECY SERIES

by Dr. David Jeremiah

The Handwriting on the Wall

The Handwriting on the Wall shows how an understanding of prophecy opens the pathway to dynamic living today. What you believe about the issues in this book can determine whose side you are on when God decides to draw the curtain on the drama of history. To know the book of Daniel is to learn how to live faithfully today, and to anticipate the future with confidence.

Resources Available:

    Book

    Study Guide (Volumes 1 - 3)

    CD Audio Albums (Volumes 1 - 3)

    31 messsages

For pricing information and to order
The Handwriting on the Wall, contact us at
www.DavidJeremiah.org or call (800) 947-1993.

Escape the Coming Night

No one can deny that the world is in trouble. Tragedy stalks our streets. Violence and bloodshed fill the news. Today's political debates spotlight the deep and bitter divisions in a society that often seem to be coming apart at the seams. How do we explain so much chaos? How do we live with such turmoil? Is there any hope for peace in our time?

Dr. David Jeremiah's dramatic narrative on the Book of Revelation answers these and many more challenging questions, guiding the reader on an electrifying tour of a world careening headlong into climactic times. His perceptive analysis of what many have called "the most ignored and most misunderstood book in the Bible" proves that we are living in the very times described by St. John the Apostle in his amazing prophecies.

Escape the Coming Night is a penetrating look at the prophetic time machine that is in the book of Revelation and a vivid reminder of how, in the face of coming darkness, we should live today.

Resources Available:

Book

Study Guide (Volumes 1 - 4)

CD Audio Albums (Volumes 1 - 4)
43 messsages

For pricing information and to order
Escape the Coming Night, **contact us at**
www.DavidJeremiah.org or call (800) 947-1993.

Until Christ Returns

Drawing from the Olivet Discourse in the book of Matthew, *Until Christ Returns* outlines priorities for believers in an era of heightened stress and confusion. The Shepherd has spoken! Some of His words comfort; others rebuke. Though heaven and earth pass away, not one of His words ever will. This is no time for the church to panic, to become distracted, to be confused by prophetic rabbit trails, or to miss priceless opportunities. In fact, these may be the best days to proclaim Christ since the first century. Learn more about the opportunities we have as Christians in this series by Dr. Jeremiah, *Until Christ Returns.*

Resources Available:

Book

Study Guide

CD Audio Album
25 messsages

OTHER BOOKS
by Dr. David Jeremiah

CBGHBK

Captured by Grace
By following the dramatic story of the "Amazing Grace" hymnwriter John Newton and the apostle Paul's own encounter with the God of grace, David Jeremiah helps readers understand the freeing power of permanent forgiveness and mercy.

LWOHBK

Life Wide Open
In this energizing book, Dr. David Jeremiah opens our eyes to how we can live a life that exudes an attitude of hope and enthusiasm . . . a life of passion . . . a LIFE WIDE OPEN! *Life Wide Open* offers a vision, both spiritual and practical, of what our life can be when we allow the power of passion to permeate our souls.

SLFHBK

Signs of Life
How does the world recognize us as God's ambassadors? In *Signs of Life* you will take a journey that will lead you to a fuller understanding of the marks that identify you as a Christian, signs that will advertise your faith. Personal imprints that can impact souls for eternity.

MHDHBK

My Heart's Desire
How would you answer a pollster who appeared at your church asking for a definition of worship? Is it really a sin to worship without sacrifice? When you finish studying *My Heart's Desire*, you'll have not just an answer, but the biblical answer to that all-important question.

Searching for Heaven on Earth

SFHBK

Join Dr. Jeremiah as he traces Solomon's path through the futility of:

- The search for wisdom and knowledge
- Wild living and the pursuit of pleasure
- Burying oneself in work
- Acquiring as much wealth as possible

Dr. Jeremiah takes readers on a discovery to find out what really matters in life, the secret to enjoying "heaven on earth."

When Your World Falls Apart

WFABK

When Your World Falls Apart recounts Dr. Jeremiah's battle against cancer and the real-life stories of others who have struggled with tragedy. Highlighting ten Psalms of encouragement, each chapter is a beacon of light in those moments when life seems hopeless.

Slaying the Giants in Your Life

STGBK

Loneliness. Discouragement. Worry. Anger. Procrastination. Doubt. Fear. Guilt. Temptation. Resentment. Failure. Jealousy. Have these giants infiltrated your life? Do you need the tools to slay these daunting foes? With practical appeal and personal warmth, Dr. Jeremiah's book, *Slaying the Giants in Your Life*, will become your very own giant-slaying manual.

Turning Points & Sanctuary

TPDHBK
SANHBK

These 365-day devotionals by Dr. Jeremiah will equip you to live with God's perspective. These topically arranged devotionals enable you to relate biblical truths to the reality of everyday living—every day of the year. Perfect for yourself or your next gift-giving occasion, *Turning Points* and *Sanctuary* are beautifully packaged with a padded cover, original artwork throughout, and a ribbon page marker.

These resources from Dr. David Jeremiah can be ordered at www.DavidJeremiah.org

⬆ MAXIMUM CHURCH

READY! SET! GROWTH!

LET DR. JEREMIAH'S MAXIMUM CHURCH TAKE YOUR CHURCH THERE.

With a united vision to strengthen the Body of Christ and reach the community, your church can experience spiritual and fiscal growth through creative and compelling campaigns.

With over 40 years of ministry experience, founder Dr. David Jeremiah now shares his passion for pulpit teaching and church leadership by offering solid Bible teaching campaigns designed to stimulate the spiritual and fiscal growth of local churches. Maximum Church campaigns are created for full-spectrum ministry, including preaching, teaching, drama, small group Bible curriculum, and suggested Sunday school material— all supported by electronic, print, and audio visual files.

Signs of Life

Lead your church to become one of Christ-like influence in your community as you take the five Life Signs discussed in this book and apply them to the lives of your congregation.

This campaign is based on Dr. David Jeremiah's best-selling book *Signs of Life*.

Captured by Grace

Based on the best-selling book *Captured by Grace* by David Jeremiah, this ministry growth campaign will help your church and community discover the depths of God's unrelenting love and grace.

**For more information on Maximum Church,
visit www.MaximumChurch.com**